'Drawing on decades of meticulous research on racial extremist movements and far-right terrorist groups, Blee, Futrell, and Simi document the continuity, the growing influence, and the extreme threat to democracy posed by violent white supremacist movements that have moved from the margins to the mainstream in the Trump era. Accessibly written and filled with new insights about the longstanding role of white supremacy in the United States, *Out of Hiding* is one of the most important books of our time!'

Verta Taylor, *Distinguished Professor of Sociology, University of California Santa Barbara, Santa Barbara, California, United States*

'From three of the foremost experts on white supremacist extremism, *Out of Hiding* is the definitive tome for understanding how the fringes moved so quickly into the mainstream. Its cultural lens is original, timely, and essential for understanding domestic extremist growth – making this book an instant classic.'

Cynthia Miller-Idriss, *Professor and Founding Director of Polarization & Extremism Research & Innovation Lab (PERIL), American University, Washington, DC, United States*

'*Out of Hiding* provides a crucial framework for understanding how American white supremacy has, once again, emerged from the fringes to influence mainstream politics and fuel a surge in discriminatory policies. The authors show us how racial extremists draw on broader societal features, driven by America's long history of racial hatred, to opportunistically fuel their movements, which have waxed and waned throughout American history. Today, they wax, along with rising hate violence and domestic terrorism. It is not a pretty picture, but thankfully the authors provide a roadmap to address this multifaceted problem, giving us a difficult, but possible path, out of these punishing historical cycles.'

Heidi Beirich, *Co-Founder, Global Project Against Hate and Extremism*

'*Out of Hiding* is a bracing, well researched screed on the United States' founding principle and most enduring evil: white supremacy. And when I say "well-researched," I'm using the academic definition of research. Not the all too common social media definition, that just means, "I googled stuff." This book is like a stiff shot of homemade whisky that you knock back to steel yourself for the upcoming battle. And yes, it is a battle. This book shows that we all have to be prepared to out-think, out-hustle, out-strategize, and outwork white supremacy and the people in this country who want it to remain the law of the land. Like garlic on a vampire, this is the antidote to Tucker Carlson.'

W. Kamau Bell, *NYT* Bestselling author of *Do The Work! An Antiracist Activity Book*, Director and Executive Producer

OUT OF HIDING

Out of Hiding: Extremist White Supremacy and How It Can Be Stopped explains how white supremacist extremism endures, the varied forms it takes, its relationship with systemic racism, and what to do about it.

The book draws on more than 30 years of extensive data and direct experiences with extremists to describe how white supremacy moved into the spotlight during the first two decades of the 21st century. The argument focuses on three moments between 2008 and today during which white supremacists took opportunities to move from pockets of underground activism to violent protests across the United States. The authors offer a corrective to observers who mischaracterize today's racial extremism as a new form of 'alt-right' conservatism or 'white nationalism' emanating from an isolated, poorly educated, and economically disenfranchised online fringe. These misunderstandings reflect the limited attention given to the varied and persistent forms of racial extremism that have long simmered in America and an inability to acknowledge the appeal white supremacist messages can hold for a broad swath of the U.S. population. This volume contributes a longer view than other books to demonstrate that today's white supremacy is less a unique eruption than a continuation – and an acceleration – of longstanding U.S. white supremacy.

This is essential reading for scholars and activists interested in racism, white supremacy, and far-right extremism.

Kathleen M. Blee is Distinguished Professor of Sociology at the University of Pittsburgh, Pennsylvania, United States, and a member of the Scientific Advisory Board of C-REX, the Center for Research on Extremism in Oslo, Norway.

Robert Futrell is Professor of Sociology at the University of Nevada, Las Vegas, United States, and longtime expert on right-wing extremism.

Pete Simi is Professor of Sociology at Chapman University, Orange, California, United States, and Executive Committee member for the National Counterterrorism, Innovation, Technology, and Education (NCITE) Center at the University of Nebraska, Omaha, Nebraska, United States.

Routledge Studies in Extremism and Democracy

Series Editors: Caterina Froio, *Sciences Po, Paris, France*, Andrea L. P. Pirro, *Università di Bologna, Italy* and Stijn van Kessel, *Queen Mary University of London, UK*
Founding Series Editors: Roger Eatwell, *University of Bath, UK* and Cas Mudde, *University of Georgia, USA*

This series covers academic studies within the broad fields of 'extremism' and 'democracy', with volumes focusing on adjacent concepts such as populism, radicalism, and ideological/religious fundamentalism. These topics have been considered largely in isolation by scholars interested in the study of political parties, elections, social movements, activism, and radicalisation in democratic settings. A key focus of the series, therefore, is the (inter-)relation between extremism, radicalism, populism, fundamentalism, and democracy. Since its establishment in 1999, the series has encompassed both influential contributions to the discipline and informative accounts for public debate. Works will seek to problematise the role of extremism, broadly defined, within an ever-globalising world, and/or the way social and political actors can respond to these challenges without undermining democratic credentials.

The books encompass two strands:

Routledge Studies in Extremism and Democracy includes books with an introductory and broad focus which are aimed at students and teachers. These books will be available in hardback and paperback.

Pathways to Violence Against Migrants
Space, Time and Far Right Violence in Sweden 2012–2017
Måns Lundstedt

Out of Hiding
Extremist White Supremacy and How It Can Be Stopped
Kathleen M. Blee, Robert Futrell and Pete Simi

For more information about this series, please visit: www.routledge.com/Extremism-and-Democracy/book-series/ED

OUT OF HIDING

Extremist White Supremacy
and How It Can Be Stopped

Kathleen M. Blee, Robert Futrell and Pete Simi

Routledge
Taylor & Francis Group

LONDON AND NEW YORK

Designed cover image: TBC

First published 2024
by Routledge
4 Park Square, Milton Park, Abingdon, Oxon OX14 4RN

and by Routledge
605 Third Avenue, New York, NY 10158

Routledge is an imprint of the Taylor & Francis Group, an informa business

© 2024 Kathleen M. Blee, Robert Futrell and Pete Simi

British Library Cataloguing-in-Publication Data
A catalogue record for this book is available from the British Library

Library of Congress Cataloging-in-Publication Data
Names: Blee, Kathleen M., author. | Futrell, Robert, author. |
    Simi, Pete, author.
Title: Out of hiding : extremist white supremacy and how it can be
    stopped / Kathleen M. Blee, Robert Futrell, and Pete Simi.
Description: Abingdon, Oxon ; New York, NY : Routledge, 2024. |
    Series: Routledge studies in extremism and democracy | Includes
    bibliographical references and index.
Identifiers: LCCN 2023030728 (print) | LCCN 2023030729 (ebook) |
    ISBN 9781032344768 (hardback) | ISBN 9781032333892 (paperback) |
    ISBN 9781003322337 (ebook)
Subjects: LCSH: White supremacy movements—United States. | White
    nationalism—United States. | Radicalism—United States. | Racism—
    United States. | United States—Race relations.
Classification: LCC E184.A1 B55825 2024 (print) | LCC E184.A1 (ebook) |
    DDC 320.56/909073—dc23/eng/20230822
LC record available at https://lccn.loc.gov/2023030728
LC ebook record available at https://lccn.loc.gov/2023030729

ISBN: 978-1-032-34476-8 (hbk)
ISBN: 978-1-032-33389-2 (pbk)
ISBN: 978-1-003-32233-7 (ebk)

DOI: 10.4324/9781003322337

Typeset in Sabon
by Apex CoVantage, LLC

We dedicate this book to our families for their unconditional love and support, to all individuals and organizations committed to social justice who are brave enough to believe in the impossible, and to those victimized by the very extremism Out of Hiding *details. We hope this work can play a small role toward preventing future violence and realizing democracy's true potential.*

CONTENTS

ACKNOWLEDGMENTS

We are deeply indebted to the researchers and activists who have successfully exposed the hidden workings of white supremacist extremism, bringing its destructive force out of hiding. Many of their works are included in our bibliography.

We thank the series editors for very helpful advice on the direction of the book. In writing and rewriting the manuscript, we were aided enormously by the assistance of Shayna Alexander, Simon Aizenstein, and Jackie Maloy. We also benefitted from the far-sighted effort of Amy Spitalnick, former Executive Director of Integrity First for America, to create a publicly accessible repository of documents from the *Sines v Kessler* legal case, which we used as the basis for some of the analysis in Chapter 4.

Our thinking about white supremacist extremism has been enriched, and sometimes challenged, by many colleagues, including panelists and audiences at the 2022 American Sociological Association annual meeting (Simi); the University of Central Florida and National Counterterrorism Innovation, Technology, and Education Center (Simi); the 2018 Annual Mobilization Conference (Futrell and Simi); the 2023 Annual Mobilization Conference (Futrell); Cambridge University (Blee); the Nordic Conference on Violent Extremism (Blee); Scuola Normale Superiore (Blee); and the 2021 American Sociological Association Annual Meeting (Blee).

Lastly, we thank the funding agencies and organizations listed in the Data appendix for supporting the research and data collection that underlie the arguments of this book.

1
OUT OF HIDING

White supremacist extremism has come out of hiding in the United States. The Republican Party is more deeply connected to racial extremism than any major party since the Ku Klux Klan and other segregationists infected the 1948 'Dixiecrat' Democratic Party. Racist ideas and symbols, once tucked away in society's corners, are now widely circulated across digital landscapes and political discourse and in the graffiti and hate messages that scar neighborhoods, military bases, and college campuses. Millions subscribe to racist, antisemitic, and Islamophobic conspiracies. Domestic terrorism is on the upswing. Even democracy itself is under attack, as voting becomes more racially restricted, and a terrifying proportion of people in this country regard violence as a viable political strategy.[1] How did this happen?

Many factors contributed to the extremism that powered into the heart of 21st-century U.S. society. But the overall story is relatively simple. Over the past two decades, there were multiple moments at which the nation had the chance either to move more definitely toward racial equality and a multiracial democracy or to allow white supremacism to expand. We identify three moments as critical junctures[2] when political and cultural leaders and ordinary citizens could have altered the resurgence of extremist white supremacy by broadly rejecting it, but instead allowed and enabled white supremacists to advance toward tightening their current grip on the nation's politics and society. This book delves into the ascendancy of extremist white supremacism during each moment, tracing both dramatic events and the less-noticed trends that shaped and followed from these events.

We begin our explanation by tracking changes in extremist white supremacist practices in the decades prior to Barack Obama's election. Responding to various societal pressures flowing from the post-civil rights

DOI: 10.4324/9781003322337-1

victories for racial equity and inclusion, extremist white supremacist factions mostly withdrew from public protest to avoid social controls, nourish their fragmented networks, and bide their time for new opportunities. But they continued to draw from and intensify a well of racism, resentment, and anger throughout the 1980s and early 1990s. They allied with militia networks around conspiratorial suspicions about a government that they cast as increasingly interventionist and globalist. Militia networks grew rapidly as they sowed deep mistrust and encouraged a righteous struggle to protect America from shadowy interests they imagined were organized to destroy constitutional freedoms. Extremists stoked fears and indignation over government policies about immigration, abortion, and gun control. And they drew inspiration from government operations turned spectacle in Ruby Ridge, Idaho, and Waco, Texas. Militia networks also brought many people with no prior association with extremism into an activism that celebrated racist and anti-government sentiments as true patriotism. Those networks eventually splintered after the 1995 Oklahoma City bombing as their members withdrew from overt activism, but they had laid the groundwork for future eruptions.

We then turn to Barack Obama's 2008 presidential election as our first moment, which some heralded as the beginning of a 'post-racial' era, even as white supremacists erupted online, and pockets of extremists called for violence to combat what they claimed was genocide against the white race. Extremist white supremacists faced limited opportunities to press their goals. Yet, they successfully persisted in hidden cultural spaces and gradually grew their numbers. As Obama's election stoked fears among committed racists, they strategically altered their rhetoric and style to disguise their allegiances and create more palatable ways to express their racism, antisemitism, and misogyny to outsiders. Their efforts kept them largely under the radar of policy makers, journalists, and most citizens. Even across most of Obama's two presidential terms, his administration dismissed white supremacy as an annoyance at best with no real political or cultural viability. Yet, worrisome signs were everywhere. Growing populist anger coalesced in electoral politics through insurgent Tea Party factions who railed against the Republican establishment and drew on dangerous wells of conservative commitment, including Christian zealotry, racial resentment, and status insecurity. They drew in old-school anti-government, segregationist adherents, as well as previously unaffiliated and newly enraged whites who perceived they were losing their country. A second wave of paramilitary militias, including Three Percenters and Oath Keepers, formed to press even more hardline positions, buoyed by a righteous, racialized 'patriotism.' Extremist white supremacy pushed onto the national stage in 2014 during confrontations over the police killing of an unarmed Black teen in Ferguson, Missouri. Oath Keepers appeared in Ferguson as paramilitary mercenaries to confront Black Lives Matter-led protests.

Missouri Klan members threatened violence. Overt public racism escalated after the Ferguson conflict as extremists were primed to act.

Extremist white supremacists also took advantage of the expanding social media landscape to grow their networks, intensify their messages, and radicalize ordinary racists. They exploited a combination of mainstream mega platforms like Facebook and Twitter and more fringe platforms, such as 4chan and Telegram, to connect and spread their virulent racist, antisemitic, and misogynist ideas and emotions that pushed extremist white supremacy to new levels. Extremists also found 'niche markets' to exploit, drawing both followers and money to the cause. Using digital media was nothing new for extremist white supremacists, and they quickly adapted the new tools for their purpose. As they deepened their digital reach, they created rabbit holes filled with extremist content to connect and confirm hardcore beliefs or introduce racist, antisemitic conspiracies to curious newcomers who they sought to draw into extremism. In the end, rather than quelling racial conflict, Obama's ascendance into the White House, along with newly powerful digital communication tools, helped catalyze extremist white supremacist networks and their corrosive effect on our democracy and civic life.

Our second moment centers on the highly visible 2017 'Unite the Right' (UTR) rally in Charlottesville, Virginia, when white supremacists armed with weapons and Nazi chants surprised many by descending on a small college town to attack anti-racist protestors and bystanders. By this point, few could deny that extremist white supremacy was on the rise and emboldened to step back into the public eye. Donald Trump's presidential campaign and election had invigorated extremist white supremacists who were already agitated and eager for action. His Make America Great Again (MAGA) vision, based on racist and xenophobic rants about immigration and fear mongering about demographic change, stoked existing racial resentment among many White people and garnered higher than expected levels of support from Asians and Latina/os.[3] Extremist white supremacist activists tried to capitalize on what they perceived as an opportunity to come fully out of hiding, to brazenly and brutally promote racial extremism and 'Unite the Right.' The violent rally failed to produce broad public approval for racial extremism, although it did not face strong government suppression either. In fact, Trump's claim that there were 'very fine people on both sides' legitimated and emboldened white supremacists. The UTR aftermath revealed organized and widespread white supremacist networks, even if the fallout momentarily undermined their public momentum.

Extremism's acceleration brought on the third moment only four years later, with the January 6, 2021 (J6) insurrectionary attack on the U.S. Capitol. J6 reflected how far intense and overt racism, misogyny, and antidemocratic forces animating extremism had pushed into the mainstream. The GOP's embrace of extremists in the party introduced a volatile additive into white supremacy. Trump, in his belligerent strongman style,[4] broadcast fantastical conspiracies about white genocide and plans for migrant attacks on the United States to stoke fears precisely aligned with extremist white supremacy ideas and emotions.[5] His rhetoric energized those who were increasingly receptive to extremist and conspiratorial beliefs which were amplified across the digital landscape. The symbiotic relationship between Republicans and extremists spawned more virtual communities on mainstream and niche platforms, diversifying extremism across Christian Nationalist networks, misogynist groups in the 'manosphere,' and resurfacing paramilitary-styled extremist white supremacy groups, such as Patriot Front, Proud Boys, and Oath Keepers. Unsurprisingly, racial violence and antisemitism increased. Then, COVID-19 offered new, unanticipated opportunities for extremist white supremacists as they entered battles over masking and vaccine mandates to sow conspiracies about Jewish elites and a tyrannical federal government. QAnon conspirators also embraced Trump as a savior against demonic forces and the 'deep state' controlled by a pedophilic cult of powerful Democrats.

As the 2020 election loomed, Trump increasingly nodded to Proud Boys and Oath Keeper networks in speeches and debates to 'stand back and stand by' as he set the stage for his stolen election conspiracy. By J6, Trump had lost the election, but he intensified his claims that it was 'rigged,' mobilizing both extremist white supremacist networks and radicalized 'ordinary' folks across fervent networks of MAGA Trump supporters, Christian Nationalists, and QAnon conspiracists. J6 demonstrated how the gap between extremist and ordinary white supremacy had drastically narrowed since Obama's presidency. Extremist white supremacists moved strategically into the mainstream as they normalized racism and spread their ideas about dispossession, victimization, and resentment. But, those who embraced Trump's angry and bigoted politics also marched toward the extreme, creating what political scientist Cas Mudde calls a 'pathological normalcy'[6] that roiled civic life and produced insurrection. We remain in the J6 moment with open questions about where the nation will land in its struggle against racist, antidemocratic forces. We conclude with a sober assessment of what works and what does not work to dismantle extremist white supremacy.

Extremist white supremacist persistence

To understand how extremist white supremacy persists, we contribute a novel interpretation of it as a dynamic constellation of practices, ideas, and emotions that supports white, male, and Western supremacy. This is a more complex and more useful interpretation of white supremacist extremism than standard views that address racist extremism as a collection of fragmented and sporadically organized people, groups, networks, and organizations. We use the idea of a constellation to explain the persistent and destructive effects of white supremacy extremism in U.S. society both when it is hidden and when it is out of hiding.[7] Emphasizing extremist white supremacy's core characteristics, rather than a fluctuating set of people and organizational forms, highlights a unity of purpose that extends from neo-Confederates to neo-Nazis, from loosely organized white power skinheads to highly coordinated militias, and from online communities defending white racial domination to small groups intent on launching a violent race war. Extremist white supremacy's core characteristics spill over into other networks in the broader field of far-right culture warriors and religious extremists, including manosphere communities, Christian nationalists, anti-abortion and anti-transgender activists, and conspiracy networks like QAnon. They share anti-government sentiments, general opposition toward racial and gender equality, and conservative social values. Thinking of extremist white supremacy as a constellation of practices, ideas, and emotions also offers us a way to explain how it subtly – and often covertly – burrows into spaces of public and private life, including political parties, media ecosystems, music scenes, online communities, and families.

We emphasize how people, groups, and networks embrace and deploy the practices, ideas, and emotions of extreme white supremacy in ways that enable its persistence, despite changing names, labels, and structures. Admittedly, what we consider extremist white supremacy is capacious. It stretches across the political field that scholars label as right-wing extremism, right-wing populism, and the far-right and across positions researchers describe as white nationalist, racist extremism, and white power.[8] Extremist white supremacy includes groups that its participants describe as alt-right, white nationalist, white pride, patriot, and other terms intended to shield the core focus on maintaining white, male, and Western domination. We balance our focus on both specific manifestations of extremist white supremacy and the practices, ideas, and emotions that have sustained its persistent eruptions throughout modern U.S. history.

In the extreme white supremacist constellation, core practices are actions strategically directed to capture and support white racist and misogynist domination. Acts of violence and terrorism against perceived enemies are central, always regarded as a feasible option and frequently employed. Other practices are expressed differently in various contexts. In some eras, extremist white supremacist practices have included running candidates for electoral office to embed white superiority in government; in other eras, extremist white supremacists work to undermine elections to collapse institutions of democratic governance and usher in a race war. In some eras, they work at both simultaneously. How do racial extremists communicate their ideas and express their style shifts across different moments? They are opportunists who hide their commitments in periods when they perceive the public as less accepting of overt racism, and come out of hiding when they think the waters are safer to test. They also shift their rhetoric and outward appearance to help make their ideas and emotions more palatable to people who might balk at more overt, stigmatized extremist forms. They strategically utilize new tools, especially in the digital sphere, to circulate their ideas and emotions to broader networks. These tactics are about playing the long game as they navigate the cultural waters, seeking acceptance for their ideas and emotions.

While practices can change over time, extremist white supremacy's core ideas stay consistently centered on the biological and cultural superiority of the white race and the inferiority of persons they define as 'non-white.' Moreover, they generally define 'nonwhites,' including Jews, as evil, non-human, animalistic, infectious, and even as descendants of Satan.[9] Extreme white supremacists also traffic in social hatred toward those they regard as antagonists of the white race, such as the federal government, women, and LGBTQ+ persons, antipathies often rooted in racist and antisemitic beliefs. For example, extremist white supremacists commonly characterize the federal government as 'ZOG' (Zionist Occupied Government) or rely on more subtle references to 'globalists,' a type of shorthand or code for 'the international Jew,' and describe white women as feminist race traitors[10] if they resist their racial obligation to bear and raise white children.

That said, many ideas embraced by extremist white supremacists are cloudy and, often, contradictory. Consider their claims about whiteness and racial hierarchy. White is a surprisingly flexible racial category that has evolved over time, expanding to accommodate shifting social, political, and economic contexts. In the United States, groups that were once not considered fully white, such as Irish, Italian, and Jewish people, are now accepted by most in that category.[11] Extremist white supremacists almost always regard Jews and Muslims as 'non-white,' as well as most persons with African, Asian, or Latin American ancestry. But, to complicate matters even more, not all white supremacists appear to be White. Take for instance, Daniel Burros, the 1960s Jewish American neo-Nazi and Klansman, or Leo Felton, the mixed race, white supremacist with a Black father and White mother (both civil rights activists) who was eventually arrested on federal charges related to domestic terrorism. Or consider two of the most prominent white supremacists today: Nick Fuentes, who traffics in racism and antisemitism, is Hispanic, and Proud Boys leader Enrico Tarrio, who spins white supremacist racism as 'western chauvinism,' is the son of Cuban immigrants. Tarrio uses his Latino background to claim that he cannot be a white supremacist, while aggressively pushing white supremacist ideas and instigating violence.[12] So, loyalty to extremist white supremacist practices, ideas, and emotions can override geographical ancestry and physical appearance.[13]

Finally, extreme white supremacy operates through a core set of emotions that support its agenda of white domination, most commonly the negatively expressed emotions of rage, fear, anger, sadness, resentment, and indignation about perceived threats and impediments to securing white racial superiority and the positively expressed emotion of white racial pride.[14] These emotions permeate white supremacists' messages to followers, potential recruits, and racial targets and are strategically deployed in offline gatherings and in online communities. Extreme white supremacist emotion is often displayed through expressions of hypermasculine thuggery that make aggressive action, even violence, appear to be a necessary response to perceived threats. White supremacists' emotional repertoire, grounded in anger and fear, also serves the many swindlers and grifters who gravitate to extremist politics as a source for private gain.

Some people worry that the term *white supremacy* is overused, poorly defined, and applied too frequently. Certainly, those critiques hold a degree of merit and should remind us about the danger of categorizing too broadly with a construct like white supremacy. But often, the opposite happens. Tepid, overly cautious characterizations describe nearly every facet of white supremacy without ever uttering those words. People talk around white supremacy, diverting attention from its pernicious effects. They use terms such as xenophobia, antisemitism, and racism but too often stop short of calling out the common well of white supremacy from which these ideas are drawn. We focus on this common well of practices, ideas, and emotions to mark extremist white supremacy's primary characteristics and trace their changes and consistencies over time.

A cultural approach

Extremist white supremacy's history of internal conflict, battles among leaders, and tendency to break into competing factions raise an important question. How has it endured across decades through varied forms, in myriad offline and online networks, drawing in different participants and leaders, but seldom demonstrating any effective centralized command structure?[15] Our answer highlights a *common extremist white supremacist culture* built on practices, ideas, and emotions that adherents embrace and share through their networks. Simply tracking groups and leaders who come and go is a fool's game that has led some to conclude that extremist white supremacy is simply too fractured and weak to pose much threat to democratic society. But as history shows, extreme white supremacist culture resonates over time as people seek scapegoats to explain threats they perceive to their power and privileges, or to explain their failings. While extremist white supremacy sometimes fades from public view, it also endures and, at times, erupts. Even as its followers shift and outward expressions change, extremist white supremacy's core cultural practices, ideas, and emotions offer lasting anchor points that attract new adherents and sustain old ones over time.

Scholars often use metaphors such as 'toolkit,' 'repertoire,' and 'library' to describe the dynamic qualities of a culture. These metaphors highlight how social groups create products, signs, and symbols and strategically select, combine, and use them in different time periods and circumstances. The metaphors emphasize agency, choice, and creativity as adherents generate meanings and materials, choose how to use and apply them, and pass them on over time. People transmit cultural meanings and materials across generations through songs, stories, rituals, language, and symbols[16] that encourage certain practices, ideas, and emotional expressions and discourage others. And, as participants align themselves with others in their culture, their commitment to its shared interpretations intensifies.[17]

A common extremist white supremacist culture is key to the simultaneous stability and flexibility of its violent, racist, antisemitic, and misogynistic constellation since the first Ku Klux Klan a century and a half ago. Core extremist white supremacist ideas embrace a clear inviolable racial, ethnic, and gendered hierarchy and a commitment to violence and intimidation to secure power. But the ways that different people and groups express and enact these core ideas vary widely in intensity, content, and style. As we show throughout this book, different currents in extremist white supremacy culture ascend as others recede over time. Some extreme white supremacist currents that seemed long defunct returned to prominence later.

Extremist white supremacists seek power. They desire to control culture, politics, and the economy, which means ultimately being embraced as normal, safe, and mainstream, rather than unusual, dangerous, and deviant. Extremist white supremacist culture morphs as social conditions change and advocates try to align with popularly resonant ideas and practices. As we explain throughout the book, racial extremists shift how they portray threats to white power and how they consolidate their networks. They also modify their outward appearance and language and even adjust how they define their successes. Extreme white supremacists opportunistically probe with ideas, arguments, and visions as they try to resonate with a broader public, especially people they want to attract to the fold. They sometimes mask their true intentions to seem innocuous and avoid unwanted attention and attacks. But the core practices, ideas, and emotions in the extremist white supremacy constellation remain virtually constant, reflecting long-term ambitions for white, Western, and male domination. Many observers mistake changes in appearance with changes in the central aims of extremist white supremacy, a misperception that has helped it avoid much systematic scrutiny and persist, even thrive, over time.

Cultures exhibit 'marked' and 'unmarked' qualities that influence how they are seen by those inside and outside the culture.[18] For example, the longstanding tendency for outsiders to associate extremist white supremacy exclusively with groups like the KKK and neo-Nazis means that when they do not see cultural markers of those groups, such as white hoods and swastikas, they assume extremist white supremacy is absent. However, narrowly marking white supremacy only by these obvious signs both distorts it and leaves many facets of its culture underacknowledged. As we discuss later, many observers expressed shock and surprise that the mostly young 'clean-cut' men in khakis and polo shirts marching across the University of Virginia campus in 2017 during the Unite the Right rally represented the faces of extremist white supremacy. We were told time and again some version of 'They just didn't look like white supremacists'[19] because they did not outwardly display the stereotypical cultural markings. But that was exactly the point. The rally organizers sought new 'optics' to soften extremist white supremacy and make its face more inviting and relatable to other White people who might hesitate to embrace older extremist styles. What people see as extremist white supremacy not only shapes their cognitive assessments about what is and what is not extremism, but also may influence the likelihood that they will embrace its practices, ideas, and emotions. In the years following Charlottesville, many new people did embrace extremist white supremacy.

The widespread surprise and confusion about Charlottesville highlight a critical, but too often overlooked, principle about how social movements form (and re-form) over time. Movements typically enter popular consciousness through public rallies and demonstrations, so observers tend to look for identifiable groups and leaders to assess the strength of a movement. But public actions, including 'fighting in the streets,'[20] often come late in the process of movement formation. Focusing on extremist white supremacy movements only when their groups operate in public misses the critical cultural and networked processes involved as people identify their commonalities and who they oppose, form a shared sense of purpose and belonging, and translate their cohesiveness into action.[21] Rather than a protest movement's starting point, public protest actions are a vapor trail flowing from longer, prior efforts to build and integrate individuals and networks into a relatively cohesive block and to coordinate their willingness to act. Throughout the book, we draw out numerous threads that illustrate how extremist white supremacy persisted under-the-radar, then morphed and moved out of hiding and into more public actions.

Our cultural focus helps us explain how extremist white supremacy can integrate people and coordinate their actions. Cultures integrate people by creating social occasions and networks where participants share interpretations about the world and behaviors that reflect these interpretations. In settings that range from small intimate connections to larger, more public events, people build a sense of cultural belonging through ritual practices that evoke strong ideas and emotions and may include a feeling of transcending the ordinary.[22] Such rituals, which range from retelling family stories to joining in massive celebrations of solidarity among those embracing identities such as white nationalist or white power, shape participants' practices, ideas, and emotions in the ritual setting as well as other situations.[23] Social scientists regard 'collective identity' as a key outcome in a network's cultural integration efforts that creates a 'we' feeling, an *esprit de corps*, an emotional, cognitive, and behavioral camaraderie or solidarity that binds people together in cultures that range in size from a family to a nation.[24] Cultures that seem reasonable, rational, and legitimate to outsiders and unlikely to be stigmatizing face fewer obstacles to drawing in new participants. As we show later, extremist white supremacist culture often de-emphasizes its extremism in public to appear normal and swell its size, even while shaping an extremist culture internally that mobilizes adherents to fight the racial enemies they imagine are arrayed against them.

It is important to understand that extremist white supremacist culture does not require people to fully embrace its collective ideology. As cognitive sociologists show, motivations for actions may, in some cases, follow, rather than precede, behavior, contrary to the common assumption that what people do typically reflects their preexisting beliefs.[25] Our studies find that many people took actions on behalf of extremist white supremacy goals, such as participating in rallies or street fighting, even before fully embracing its belief system. They found comfort in the relationships they built before fully comprehending or deeply adopting extremist white supremacy as their worldview. Only after bonding with other extremists and participating in extreme white supremacist activities did the vague, partial, or implicit beliefs about 'racial differences' that they held before being exposed to extremist white supremacy start to consolidate into an extremist worldview.[26] Indeed, extremist white supremacy recruitment efforts often rely on drawing people into practices and ideas that may not initially appear extreme, such as attending music shows or questioning government corruption, economic globalization, or immigration patterns. But as those people ramp up their involvement, they are taught the intricacies of extremist white supremacy, such as its conspiratorial ideas about Jewish elites, the new world order, anti-immigrant hatred, and the necessity for using violence to achieve political goals. Over time, new adherents gain exposure to the organized system of extremist racism with its menu of motivations, justifications, and rationalizations for why adopting its outlandish practices, ideas, and emotions 'makes sense.'[27]

For decades, critics argued with us that extremist white supremacy is so rife with organizational fractures and incompetent leaders that it is relatively powerless, innocuous, and nothing much to worry about. But the fact is that extremist white supremacy has survived and reemerged over and over even as its leaders and groups change. It comes into public view when it has sufficient mainstream appeal and seeks to demonstrate its power. But often it is veiled to avoid exposure by authorities and watchdog groups. During these hidden or 'abeyance,'[28] periods, extremist white supremacists cultivate an underground hate culture. They forge secretive networks while avoiding formal member-ship groups that authorities could surveil and harass. They nourish collec-tive sentiments and identities based on racial hatred and violent fantasies in settings that range from mundane family and friendship networks to racist concerts, intentional communities, and extremist Internet spaces. They trans-mit and sustain extremist white supremacy practices, ideas, and emotions through narratives, bonding rituals, images, and messages they invest with vitriolic racism. They shift their external style to blend with mainstream cul-ture, distancing themselves from deeply stigmatized belligerent, combative, deviant, in-your-face styles in favor of more respectable presentations in pub-lic, while retaining extremism inside their culture.

Extremist white supremacy's submerged networks and hidden social spaces are the product of collective efforts, but they can appear fragmented and transitory, bolstering the conclusion that extremist white supremacy, with its ideological divisions and organizational schisms, can be written off as relatively innocuous and unimportant.[29] But this obscures the structured and strategic dimensions that persist among racial extremist networks even when they are hidden. The fluid and informal networks that periodically coalesce in extremist spaces flow from deliberate, calculated, and organized efforts to sustain and spread racist culture by creating occasions in which people can congregate with like-minded others, experiment with and rein-force their dedication to extremist white supremacy, and draw others into their ranks. In prior work, we described these spaces and occasions as an infrastructure of hate.[30]

Our book reveals both the individuals and organizations that carry extremist white supremacy, and how extremist white supremacy persists out-side and beyond those actors. Against the common overemphasis on specific people and groups – which diverts attention from the underlying uniform-ity of extremist white supremacy – we focus on how core extreme white supremacist practices, ideas, and emotions endure over time.[31] We show how individuals and groups access, circulate, and promote white supremacist cul-ture, latching onto facets that appeal to them. And we show how, despite a constant churn of people and groups, white supremacist culture continues on as a set of practices, ideas, and emotions that people continually draw from and deploy.

Ordinary white supremacy

Extremist white supremacy is not the sole carrier of white supremacism.[32] What we refer to as ordinary white supremacism also supports white domi-nance and perpetuates racial disparities, often in invisible and unacknowl-edged ways. We use the term ordinary to emphasize common, regular, and everyday aspects of race and racism in U.S. society. Ordinary white supremacy is so deeply ingrained in U.S. culture and institutions that its discriminatory aspects all too often go underacknowledged or explained away as 'just the way things are'. As critical race theorists Richard Delgado and Jean Stefancic explain, 'racism is ordinary, not aberrational – 'normal science,' the usual way society does business, the common, everyday experience of most people of color in this country.'[33] Ordinary white supremacy is ordinary in the sense that it is normalized, subtle, covert, and embedded in institutions such as banks and courts, and in practices such as mortgage redlining and racially disparate sentences for drug offenses.[34] It is ordinary in the sense that it is part of the 'everyday racism' made up of racial assumptions, conventions, figures of speech, and ways of acting that make whiteness the standard.[35] Ordinary white supremacy includes informal cultural practices that occur within families and peer groups, such as racist humor and expressions of racist stereotypes, and in the popular culture when movies and television shows explicitly or implicitly endorse white supremacy. It is not ordinary in the sense of being nonthreatening, as ordinary white supremacy supports radically inequitable racial power structures and outcomes. It is ordinary, and powerful, because it is systemic and legitimated.

The historian Robin D.G. Kelley talks about how White people's indifference ensures that 'spectacular and mundane acts of everyday racism are normalized or simply not seen.'[36] Indeed, White people's collective indifference to racial inequality represents a long-term blemish on the country's professed ideals. Indifference, like other forms of 'everyday racism,' although not outwardly hostile, refuses to acknowledge what is patently obvious: the nation's grotesque history and the continuing presence of racial oppression. Maybe even worse, indifference can manifest in acknowledging the obvious but still refusing to act, as when a racist joke is told or a hateful meme reposted and is met with silence rather than condemnation. Or when White people find excuses for failing to support social movements for racial justice. As the sociologist Joe Feagin eloquently, but sadly, states,

> The majority of whites are willfully ignorant or misinformed when it comes to understanding the difficult life conditions that African Americans and other Americans of color face today. Interestingly in another survey, white respondents were asked if they 'often have sympathy for blacks' and again if they 'often feel admiration for blacks.' Only 5% of whites said yes to both questions.[37]

We cannot explain white supremacism without keeping an eye on both extremist white supremacy and ordinary white supremacy. From the earliest days of brutal European settlement of North America, an intricate web of laws, policies, institutions, and practices has provided a foundation for white domination of social, political, and economic life.[38] But, while white supremacism has been a core logic within U.S. society, it is not the only core logic, and it has been challenged in many ways. Anti-racism also stands as a core logic, expressed in a long and deep history of progressive, inclusionary, and anti-fascist practices, ideas, and emotions. Marginalized and minoritized persons and communities and many white allies have fought against discrimination, inequality, and exclusion, and their activism has chipped away at white hegemony. Yet, because those who are determined to maintain existing structures of white racial power fiercely resist change and because it is difficult to reshape entrenched institutions and cultures, the white racial power structure remains largely intact.

Part of the problem is that racism is typically conceptualized as individual acts, ignoring its collective and systemic features. Our dominant racial ideology[39] and language tend to reduce racism to a person's psychological dispositions. As sociologist Eduardo Bonilla-Silva explains, we hunt for individual racists to distinguish among the 'good and bad, tolerant and intolerant.'[40] This bad apple approach imagines that if we just root out the racist individuals, we will root out racism itself, giving little regard to how racism also operates as collective, systemic power that structures U.S. society around white privilege.[41] Even after Donald Trump's explicitly racist and nativist presidency drove racial resentment, discrimination, hate crimes, and extremism,[42] individual explanations for racism persist. The bad apples framing appears in the occasional media-driven hand-wringing over a politician or celebrity caught using offensive racist language or when racial extremists lash out publicly. As linguist Jane Hill notes, 'the offensive remark [or action] is repeated again and again, over days and even weeks, both by those who wish to defend the speaker and by those who are on the attack.'[43] But, when the focus highlights individuals, attention moves away from structured, systemic ordinary white supremacy.

Extremist and ordinary white supremacy are too often treated as distinct and sometimes even unrelated. Such distinctions ignore the highly integrated and reinforcing nature of white supremacism. Extremists seek race war to assure white power. But ordinary white supremacy, rooted in the U.S. racial value system, preserves entrenched racist practices in areas such as wealth and income, employment, schools, policing, healthcare, housing, and politics.[44] These systematic practices consistently shape social advantages and disadvantages and perpetuate the very divisions that give life to extreme racist ideas. As Black Feminist scholar Barbara Smith writes,

[The problem] is that this country has never done anything to eradicate the root cause of [racism]. America abolished chattel slavery, but quickly instituted peonage, Jim Crow, and mass incarceration; it extended civil rights then proceeded to erode them, especially voting rights; it ended legal segregation but preserved widespread de facto segregation in schools, housing, and jobs; and despite initiating affirmative action, allowed employment discrimination and vast economic inequality to persist.[45]

And as long as ordinary white supremacy is intact, extremist white supremacy will survive and, at times, thrive.

We do not see sharp distinctions between ordinary and extremist white supremacy since the white supremacist logic that drives racial extremism informs the practices, ideas, and emotions of institutional and everyday racism, from white-centered children's books to racially biased digital algorithms.[46] The complementarity is evident when White people exchange racist jokes,[47] or when racist extremists borrow and adjust multiculturalism and anti-racist slogans to frame themselves as favoring civil rights and opposing discrimination toward whites.[48] Although our book focuses on extremist white supremacy, as the most virulent, concentrated, and recognizable form of white supremacy, we understand that white supremacist logic circulates through virtually all sectors of U.S. society and reinforces extremist white supremacy.

We also realize that ordinary and extremist white supremacy represent only a part of society's full complexity. There are many political, economic, and cultural currents, past and present, that encourage anti-racism and push forward practices, ideas, and emotions that advance multicultural democracy, inclusion, and equality. Anti-racists stand against white domination, authoritarianism, and social inequality. Some aspects of U.S. society push back on extremist and ordinary white supremacy, even as other aspects support or ignore white supremacism. Various practices and beliefs both reinforce and undermine the white supremacism carried by extremist and ordinary white supremacy across many facets of social organization, including electoral politics, social movements, schools, religion, families, and popular culture.

Extremist and ordinary white supremacy vie for more cultural space, legitimacy, and power to, ultimately, position their practices, ideas, and emotions as dominant in the wider society. Rather than persisting as a violent, deviant subculture, extremist white supremacists seek to normalize extremist 'white power' as the acceptable and proper way to organize society. Extremist white supremacy seeks to reshape society by colonizing institutions and influencing cultural norms to include more overt forms of white power. Ordinary white supremacy provides established anchor points that extremist white supremacy uses to build their claims, while denigrating opposing views. In sociologist Cynthia Miller-Idriss' terms, white supremacists want to see the 'extreme gone mainstream,' permeating and defining the broadest contours in political, economic, and cultural life.[49]

Our approach highlights a tension in how we understand ordinary and extremist white supremacy's power. Some analysts argue that white supremacy is most powerful when it goes unnoticed and unacknowledged.

It is largely unnoticeable to many people because it is societally ingrained in cultural, economic, and political systems, while simultaneously cloaked in a neutral or colorblind veneer.[50] Ordinary white supremacy succeeds in this covert form by shaping and perpetuating racial disparities in education, employment opportunities, housing, and criminal justice. It does not require individual intent or explicit acts of racism to persist. When white supremacy remains invisible, people struggle to recognize and challenge its impact. The absence of explicit racial bias or discrimination on the surface can lead people to believe that racism is no longer a significant issue, while overlooking the underlying systemic structures that perpetuate racial disparities. In this way, ordinary white supremacy defines a deeply ingrained system that upholds white dominance and advantages through implicit biases, systemic policies, and unspoken cultural norms. Recognizing and confronting ordinary white supremacy require actively examining and dismantling the hidden structures that perpetuate racial inequities. They involve acknowledging historical and ongoing injustices, amplifying marginalized voices, advocating for inclusive policies, and actively working toward creating a more equitable society.

If ordinary white supremacy's power is rooted in its covert character, does it mean that its most formidable ways for maintaining racial dominance are waning when extremist white supremacy comes out of hiding? We do not think so. Ordinary white supremacy defines the kind of racism that structures daily life and offers a grounding for more extreme forms. When extremist white supremacy moves into the open, it reinforces social hierarchy by explicitly promoting white dominance and superiority. Openly expressing white supremacy creates a climate of fear and intimidation among marginalized communities and many others. Fear can suppress dissent and resistance, further consolidating power in the hands of white supremacists. More open white supremacy leads to discriminatory laws and regulations that disproportionately benefit White people and marginalize those labeled as minorities. Open expressions of white supremacy also attract new followers as visibility can rally others to join their networks. And more visibility for white supremacist ideas and emotions means that they can gradually be normalized and accepted by broader audiences, which can further entrench white supremacy and make it difficult to challenge or dismantle systemic racism.

Debating about whether white supremacy is more powerful when it is visible or invisible distracts from the reality that how much mainstream social influence extremist and ordinary white supremacy carry at any moment varies over time. Ordinary and extremist white supremacy intertwine as two parts in the same insidious threat to manipulate and control cultural space and political power. In certain times, places, and events, both ordinary and extremist white supremacy lose currency, as during the brief period of racial reckoning after the 2020 videotaped Minneapolis police murder of George Floyd, when a broad segment of the public expressed concern about racially targeted violence by law enforcement.[51] At other points, extremist white supremacy movements and ordinary white supremacy expand throughout mainstream society, as when Republican politicians, major media outlets, and religious leaders coordinate and spread racist conspiracies, such as the 'great replacement' theory about white genocide that was generated in the vilest corners of white supremacist extremism.[52]

Who we are and how we did this

Before we move on, we want to introduce ourselves and briefly explain how we developed our arguments in this book. We are sociologists who have worked on extremist white supremacism for decades.[53] This book is the product of an equal co-authorship in which we each brought our experiences and ideas into the collaboration, then learned immensely from each other. It was formed through myriad phone calls, text exchanges, and emails during which we honed our ideas and helped each other through the emotional rollercoaster that comes with studying the racial extremism that threatens to dismantle our country. When the text refers to what 'we' think or recommend, it reflects a genuinely collaborative process, not scholarly arm wrestling.

We conceived this book as a distinctive contribution to a research area that has turned into something of a cottage industry filled with efforts to understand far-right extremism after Trump's election and the 2017 Unite the Right rally. These efforts contribute important facets to understanding our complex, changing political landscape. We contribute a longer, more detailed view than most other efforts to explain how today's white supremacy is less a unique eruption than a continuation and an acceleration of U.S. white supremacy. Our view reveals connections between extremist white supremacy animated in activist networks and expressed in racial intimidation and violence and systemic racism endemic to U.S. culture and institutions. Specifically, we trace how the most virulent and concentrated forms of white supremacy ebb and flow in public life along with shifts in white supremacists' strategies, front and backstage tactics, and coded messaging as they spread their racist ideas and draw others toward extremism. We link these changes to the white supremacist logic that permeates and defines almost all parts of our society.

Our focus departs from previous work that tends to overlook crucial interconnections between different forms of white supremacy. Some argue that focusing on extremists diverts attention from more important systemic features linked to institutionalized racism. Others prioritize racial extremism and its connection to violence while ignoring how ordinary white supremacy reflects institutional practices tucked deep into cultural assumptions that mark whiteness as the standard. But, elevating systemic issues or discussing extremist white supremacy as divorced from broader institutional and cultural forces ignores the ways that white supremacists derive power and resonance from a sociocultural system grounded on policies and practices that have long stacked the deck for white power. In contrast, we offer a contextually rich, historically centered interpretation that establishes important relational connections between racial extremists and the broader societal features they draw from and that explicitly and tacitly buttress white supremacy.

We feel that our extended view gives us a clear-eyed vantage point for realistic suggestions on how to contest and curb white supremacy. We explore ways to combat or outcompete white supremacy with alternatives to cultural hatred and political division. But we do not offer a rosy outlook. White supremacy maintains a strong position in the U.S. political landscape. And, that in itself offers the main lesson we must come to terms with.

We wrote this book thinking about ourselves as guides who will help walk you through the story of how extremist white supremacism regained prominence and influence in the United States over the past several decades. We want to take you beyond treatments of the present moment, which give too little attention to processes rooted in the past. Instead, we focus on the past processes that built toward the present moment and trace them as they unfolded over time. We use an approach that, in the words of the social movement scholars Lorenzo Bosi and Stefan Malthaner, pays attention to 'temporal sequence, interpretative frameworks, and political contexts' and that can address 'conjunction and contingency, as well as the impact of transformative events.'[54] Put another way, we show how the past weighs on the present, and how people and groups push historical trajectories and culture in certain directions using persistent practices, ideas, and emotions. We ask readers to look backward in time as we trace the threads that were most important in each step toward the growth and acceleration of extremist white supremacy in the mainstream. Our goal is to help clarify these processes as we bring the past into the present. Admittedly, we find it difficult to pinpoint the next consequential moment beyond our stopping point in this book. But, we do know that the dangers inherent in extremist white supremacy will not fade anytime soon and will likely intensify in very worrisome and risky ways.

We conclude with recommendations for short-term 'fixes' and longer-term strategies to address the deep-rooted maladies on which white supremacist extremism thrives. We also recognize the complications inherent in attacking a problem that has been dismissed and ignored for decades. Our immediate fixes include efforts to counter the resurgence of white supremacist extremism, such as deradicalization programs; additional emphasis on hate crime prosecutions; and the development of models for anti-racism in classrooms, workplaces, and parenting. To quote a parent whose child was convicted of a hate crime: 'We didn't teach our child to hate but we also didn't teach him not to hate.' Our longer-term strategies focus on undermining the racial divisions and inequalities that white supremacism reproduces and depends on. White supremacist groups thrive on resisting moments for progressive change. They assume that their extreme ideas and violence will terrorize and intimidate their opponents so that social justice is abandoned in favor of retaining a more familiar racialized, gendered, and cultural hierarchy. Too often, their bet on the cowardice or timidity among the broader population of White people has been correct, as when large numbers recoil at desperately needed major transformations in the criminal justice system. Although we are not unduly optimistic about the likelihood of success, we chart how it is possible to seize on this moment to create a different, more equitable, and just racial future.

Notes

1 Brownstein, 2021; Southern Poverty Law Center, 2008; German, 2020; Ralston, Motta, and Spindel, 2022; Daniels, 2009; Fielitz and Thurston, 2019; Mitchell, Jurkowitz, Oliphant, and Shearer, 2020; Cox, 2021; Anti-Defamation League, 2021c; Zuboff, 2021.
2 The idea of critical moments builds on social science efforts to identify times in which significant changes to social structures are possible, particularly the work of William Sewell (1996) on 'events' and of Donatella della Porta (2020) on 'momentous times.'
3 Wang, 2017.
4 Ben-Ghiat, 2020.
5 Greef and Karasz, 2018; Nakamura, Hudson, and Stanley-Becker, 2018; Fritze, 2019; Romero, 2018.
6 Mudde, 2010, p. 1168.
7 In his February 2021 remarks to the U.S. Senate Committee considering his nomination as U.S. Attorney General, Merrick Garland (2021) asserts the continuity of white supremacism, from the first Klan to the insurrection of January 6, 2021.
8 Thomas and Osborne, 2022; Pirro, 2021; Mudde and Kaltwasser, 2017.
9 At the same time, extremist white supremacists may also adopt rhetoric that suggests that the hatred of 'nonwhites' is not part of their ideas and emotions or at least not any more than is common among all people across the globe.
10 'Race traitor' is a term used in extremist white supremacy for whites who oppose, betray, or fail to join the cause of white supremacy and have fallen victim to anti-white brainwashing. Racist extremists assert that a 'mass cleansing' may be necessary at some point, a scenario widely termed the 'Day of the Rope' after a passage in *The Turner Diaries*, one of the most cited works among extremist white supremacists, in which a large number of white race traitors are murdered to establish a society in which the majority of whites adhere to the movement's beliefs and goals.
11 Jacobson, 1999.
12 Orecchio-Egresitz, 2020; Rhodes, 2023.
13 See also Blee (2002) on how loyalty can convey whiteness in racist groups. Additionally, consider that a relatively large segment of Latino/as now identify as white or select 'other' and/or 'two or more races' when self-reporting race. See Noe-Bustamante, Gonzalez-Barrera, Edwards, Mora, and Lopez, 2021.
14 Knops and Petit, 2022.
15 Episodic efforts to promote unity, such as the World Congress of the Aryan Nations (AN), have not been sustained for long (Barkun, 1994; Aho, 1990; Blee, 2002; Simi and Futrell, 2010; Dobratz and Shanks-Meile, 2000; Ezekiel, 1996).

16 Snow, Owens, and Tan, 2014.
17 We refer to both individual and collective memory, following Olick (1999, p. 346) who notes that '"memory' occurs in public and in private, at the tops of societies and at the bottoms, as reminiscence and as commemoration, as personal testimonial and as national narrative, and that each of these forms is important.'
18 Brekhus, 1998; Zerubavel, 1999.
19 Data collected August 2, 2022.
20 McAdam, Sampson, Weffer, and MacIndoe, 2005.
21 Melucci, 2009; Eyerman and Jamison, 1991; Flesher Fominiya, 2010.
22 Durkheim, 1912.
23 Cultural practices of food, music, religion, and stories such as those found in Greek food festivals, Italian feast day processions, and St. Patrick's Day events not only celebrate the ethnic roots of people in the United States, but also create shared interpretations about what it means to be Greek-American, Italian-American, or Irish-American. On the behavioral level, cultural norms press toward behaviors that distinguish a group – for example, as respectable fans of a sports team or those who practice a particular religion – and that create a sense of solidarity and collective identity. Behaviors like wearing modest clothing, tailgating at a team's game, and displaying religious items bind individuals together (Blee and Simi, 2020, p. 9).
24 Lizardo et al., 2016; Lizardo, 2004; Goffman, 1974; Swidler, 1986; Blee, 2012; Latif, Blee, DeMichele, and Simi, 2018.
25 Berger and Luckmann, 1966; Lizardo et al., 2016; Vaisey, 2009.
26 Latif, Blee, DeMichele, and Simi, 2018; Blee, 2002; Simi, Sporer, and Bubolz, 2016.
27 See Berger and Luckmann's (1966) discussion of sense making. At the macro level, numerous studies highlight this historical fact as it relates to the development of modern racism and its relationship with the African slave trade. Rather than racism acting as a causal agent that motivated the practice of slavery, the historical record suggests the opposite. The practice of slavery was first executed which then led to the development of an organized although dynamic system of thought, necessary for moralizing and justifying the brutal economic labor practice already in place. Certainly, there were ideas that helped facilitate the slave trade from its inception, but their concretization into a fully developed system of thought followed slavery rather than preceding it (Kendi, 2016).
28 Taylor, 1989; Taylor and Crossley, 2013; Simi and Futrell, 2020.
29 For instance, Mattias Gardell (2003, p. 71) says, 'The level of discord, mutual enmity, organizational fragmentation, and ideological division characterizing the world of white racism [is] far too high to be able to speak of a white racist movement in any meaningful way.'
30 Simi and Futrell, 2010.
31 For instance, if we compare a David Duke political rally from the late-1980s during his bid for Louisiana governor and one of Donald Trump's 2015 speeches during his presidential campaign bid, we see that the PIE they both express is virtually indistinguishable. Duke's prominent connections to the KKK identified him as an extreme white supremacist at the time, while Trump's less obvious extremist connections did not stigmatize him in the same ways, even though he often advocated violence toward racial others, sometimes with more inflammatory language than Duke's. See Saric (2022).
32 Carrigan and Webb, 2003; Burris, Smith, and Strahm, 2000.
33 Delgado and Stefancic, 2001, p. 7.
34 What we call ordinary white supremacy is sometimes referred to as systemic white supremacy or institutional white supremacy.
35 Essed, 1991.

36 Yancey, 2022.
37 Feagin, 2009, p. 3.
38 Whites own a disproportionate share of the country's wealth. Even in 2020, white males represented nearly 90% of the Fortune 500 CEOs (Zweigenhaft, 2020).
39 Hill (2008) calls this the 'folk theory of race and racism' that defines racism solely in individualist terms while ignoring how racism operates as a collective system of power to organize U.S. society around white privilege.
40 Bonilla-Silva, 2013, p. 15.
41 Hodges, 2016; Bonilla-Silva, 2013; Feagin, 2009.
42 Researchers link Trump's inflammatory rhetoric to encouraging people with racist and nativist attitudes to openly express and act on their prejudices, which some call the *Trump effect* (Newman et al., 2021; Crandall, Miller, and White, 2018; Edwards and Rushin, 2018; Schaffner, 2018).
43 Hill, 2008, p. 43.
44 To take an historical example, Indigenous people were slaughtered in mass killing raids that sought to advance extremist white supremacy's agendas of 'civilization' and Christianity across the continent. They also died in large numbers in the course of white westward settlement, under a legal system rooted in ordinary white supremacy that allowed whites to employ private violence to seize their lands. Explicit calls to exterminate peoples whom European settlers regarded as 'savages' may look different from legally sanctioned evictions. But both fueled racial genocide.
45 Smith, 2020.
46 Feagin, 2009; Ture, Carmichael, and Hamilton, 1967.
47 Pérez, 2017.
48 Berbrier, 1999, 2000.
49 Miller-Idriss, 2018.
50 Bonilla-Silva, 2013; Ray, 2019; Feagin, 2009.
51 Reny and Newman, 2021.
52 Confessore and Yourish, 2022; Goodwin, 2022.
53 The arguments in this book are based on our wide-ranging and unique empirical data, much of it collected directly by the authors. See Data appendix.
54 Bosi and Maalthaner, 2022. See also, Bosi, 2021; Abbott, 1997.

2

BEFORE OBAMA

Extremist white supremacy, animated in activist networks that express racial intimidation and violence, has at times commanded widespread political attention and power. The Ku Klux Klan (KKK) is the most notable example in U.S. history.[1] Founded in the aftermath of the Civil War, the Confederate vigilante group defined its purpose as 'to maintain the supremacy of the White race in the republic' during Reconstruction.[2] Joined by other White Southerners, Klan-led guerilla war campaigns killed thousands of Black people and others who challenged White political control.[3] As Jim Crow laws secured White power, this first-era Klan disbanded. A second-era Klan reemerged in 1915 in reaction to fears about communism and immigration, drawing in millions across all regions of the United States. By the 1920s, between 2.5 and 5 million white, native-born Protestants claimed membership in the Ku Klux Klan, marking it as one of the more powerful political forces in U.S. history.[4] In the 1960s, the KKK and White Citizens Councils overtly challenged civil rights to preserve segregation and white power across the South.[5]

At other times, racial extremists have faced hostile cultural and political climates during which they pulled back from their more overt political efforts. The civil rights era of the 1960s and 1970s shifted political culture toward progressive inclusionary goals. As federal authorities and counter-movements pressured racial extremists,[6] their networks splintered. But they did not vanish. Neo-Nazis and racist skinheads emerged in the 1980s and 1990s to instigate a new phase in white supremacy's persistent and evolving threat. Their militant displays brought intense, albeit episodic, media attention and renewed confrontations with authorities and anti-racist groups. In response, extremist leaders advocated for a strategic withdrawal from traditional public approaches to activism and recruitment, in favor of more

DOI: 10.4324/9781003322337-2

informal, private, and individualistic tactics. They embraced new practices, such as 'lone-wolf' terrorism, to avoid repression directed at white power leaders, organizations, and networks while still lashing out at their enemies. By the early 1990s, racial extremists also infiltrated and aligned with militia groups that had moved into public prominence. These militia networks expanded rapidly, spreading mistrust of the government and a righteous struggle to protect citizens from shadowy interests seeking to destroy their freedoms. But the militias, although they foundered after the 1995 Oklahoma City bombing, left a deep well of extremist practices, ideas, and emotions for white supremacists to draw on. At the turn of century, extremist white supremacy was persisting mostly in underground social networks and on Internet forums where participants advocated varied combinations of white supremacist, anti-government, and religio-racist beliefs.[7]

Extreme white supremacy moves into abeyance

Activism often waxes and wanes as political climates change. Researchers use the terms 'abeyance'[8] and 'dormancy'[9] to describe periods when activists draw back from more public protest efforts because the political climate no longer appears as receptive to their ideas. Typically, movement participants decide to draw back on their public activism as they face organizational challenges, declining resources, and changing opportunities to effectively press their claims. Relatedly, cultural changes and state repression can drive up risks associated with activism, reducing movement involvement. When a political movement loses support, as sociologist Verta Taylor writes, 'activists who had been most intensely committed to its aims become increasingly marginal and socially isolated,'[10] creating activist cadres who must find a niche for themselves. When movements lose status and move into relative hiatus, activists must alter their goals and tactics. To persist, they often create 'pockets of movement activity, or free spaces'[11] where they continue to cultivate and sustain their connections with one another and stay ready to rally committed members when the political climate changes and they see new openings for their ideas to (re)gain traction.

From the civil rights era until very recently, extremist white supremacists have not seen signals that they have powerful allies to ease repressions and advocate for their goals. To the contrary, they perceived high consequences for being fully 'out' about their aims. They were challenged by anti-racist counter-movements that typically mobilized much larger numbers[12] to publicly challenge them. As individuals, they faced serious and persistent stigmatization, social scrutiny, violent repression, job loss, blacklisting, and the disruption of personal relationships.[13] Their abeyance efforts aimed, in part, to shield members from stigma, marginalization, and repression, while they nourished collective connections and transferred movement culture from seasoned members to new recruits to keep the cause alive.

Drawing back from public efforts does not mean that activism stops, that change efforts fail, or that their core practices, ideas, and emotions fade. Rather, the activists move their focus from frontstage politics to more covert backstage actions until times appear more conducive to their cause. They shelve or repurpose practices that bring unwanted attention and repression and adopt new ones that help them to sustain their commitments to the cause.

We can see the power of social movement abeyance by tracing how extremist white supremacist networks responded to increasing marginalization and repression in the post-civil rights era. They were able to endure fading political and cultural power, while keeping key extremist white supremacist practices, ideas, and emotions active and energized. They persevered in small, fragmented pockets, many that were not entirely insular or exclusively white supremacist, while imagining that opportunities to revitalize and grow their networks would emerge. And, we know now that through a combination of broader political shifts and extremist's strategic efforts, those opportunities did emerge decades later.

After the Klan's resurgence during the Civil Rights era, white supremacy morphed as KKK support waned and networks splintered in the 1970s. Neo-Nazi networks, rooted in Hitler's Third Reich racial purity fascism, and the American Nazi Party, founded in 1958 by George Lincoln Rockwell, grew during the 1980s. Sociologists Val Burris, Emery Smith, and Ann Strahm explain that 'umbrella groups such as the Aryan Nations led Klan members, racist skinheads, and others toward Nazi symbolism and ideology, along with racist Christian Identity theology, to create a broader white supremacist worldview.'[14] By the late 1980s, racist skinheads emerged as the youthful face of American neo-Nazis and coalesced into loosely-organized gang networks.

For many extremist youth, Tom Metzger acted as a key bridge between KKK networks and neo-Nazism. Metzger floated through right-wing groups including the John Birch Society, tax protesters, and Christian Identity networks before joining David Duke's Knights of the Ku Klux Klan, where he reached Grand Dragon status. He led the Klan Border Watch that patrolled for Mexican immigrants in Southern California and violently harassed Asian and Latino Americans. During the 1980s, Metzger organized White Aryan Resistance (WAR) and the Aryan Youth Movements as notorious neo-Nazi groups who sought to 'cleanse [the U.S.] of all nonwhite mud-races.'[15] WAR and WAR-affiliated skinhead groups known as 'WAR Skins' along with other neo-Nazis combined white power rhetoric and ideology with a youthful aesthetic expressed through music and Nazi symbolism. The media started paying attention to their public displays, which helped form a new white supremacist stereotype – the young, wild-eyed, tattoo-laden, belligerent, in-your-face skinhead.

Unlike many white supremacists, Metzger and his followers embraced all the media attention they could grab. Metzger hosted a public-access cable television show, *Race and Reason,* that he used to push his racist and antisemitic views into public view. In 1988, his son, John Metzger, and several neo-Nazi skinheads appeared on the nationally syndicated *Geraldo* talk show where they brawled with audience members and security. The show's host Geraldo Rivera ended up with a broken nose after a neo-Nazi threw a chair during the melee. This notoriety served Metzger's goal of spreading terroristic hate into mainstream consciousness. But the attention also brought unwanted suppression efforts from government and watchdog groups. WAR and Metzger were eventually bankrupted from a lawsuit filed by the Southern Poverty Law Center (SPLC). The Center sued Metzger and his son for civil liability related to the murder of Mulugeta Seraw by racist skinheads affiliated with WAR. The trial ended with a $12.5 million judgment against the Metzgers for inciting the skinheads to commit violence against minorities.

Between 1979 and 2000, the SPLC won several other impactful legal cases, using innovative civil litigation strategies to hold organizations responsible for their individual member's crimes. Their success undercut organized, overt white supremacist efforts. They charged notorious KKK leader Louis Beam and his followers in the Texas Emergency Reserve with harassing and intimidating Vietnamese shrimpers near Galveston, Texas.[16] The Carolina Knights of the KKK and the White Patriot Party disbanded after courts found the groups guilty of operating a paramilitary organization and threatening and harming people in Black neighborhoods.[17] The SPLC forced the United Klans of America into bankruptcy for lynching Black teen Michael Donald in Mobile, Alabama, and took down the Christian Knights of the KKK for their members' arson of a 100-year-old Black church in South Carolina.[18] Arguably the most significant judgment the SPLC won came against the Aryan Nations in Hayden Lake, Idaho, after its guards attacked a mother and her son who had mistakenly driven near the compound. Aryan Nations stood as a powerful symbol for many white supremacists. AN youth assemblies and Congresses drew white supremacist extremists from across the movement and provided opportunities for adherents to share inspirational stories through movement networks. AN's demise helped to solidify strategic shifts among white supremacists away from high-attention public displays toward more covert actions.[19]

Militia formation and extremist white supremacy

As extremist white supremacists struggled to gain a political foothold in the post-civil rights movement era, they helped organize militia networks around conspiratorial worries about a government that appeared to them increasingly interventionist and globalist. During the 1980s, survivalists and white supremacists formed paramilitary networks that included the Christian Patriot Defense League; the Covenant, Sword, and Arm of the Lord; the Texas Emergency Reserve; and the White Patriot Party. These networks drew, in part, from anti-government ideology formulated by 1960s' tax protesters and 1970s' sovereign citizen and Posse Comitatus movements, which combined racism, antisemitism and deep mistrust toward state and federal government.[20] They imagined a conspiracy enacted by global financial elites and bureaucrats to capture the federal government and destroy U.S. sovereignty. For many militia adherents, the solution was to protect or restore the 'legitimate government' by paramilitary force. They viewed the federal government as increasingly interventionist as it also took positions on gun control, abortion, and the Federal Reserve's power over currency regulation, which right-wing extremists deeply opposed. Although the KKK had considered government an ally in the 1920s, by the 1970s and 1980s, extreme white supremacists aligned with other far-right conservatives to redefine government as the enemy. Ironically, even the Chief Executive of the government, Ronald Reagan, defined government as the problem not the solution during the 1980s.[21] The growing ideological alignment between white supremacists and anti-government militia members drew them closer to one another and propelled their growth.[22]

Anti-abortion extremists also joined the volatile extremist mix in the 1980s and ramped up its violence in the 1990s. Embracing violence as a reasoned and righteous solution to stop state-sanctioned abortions, extremist anti-abortion advocates moved toward increasingly militant and revolutionary positions. During the 1980s and into 1990s, anti-abortion extremists, led by loose networks calling themselves the Army of God and Pro-Life Action Network, committed murders, attacks, bombings, arson, stalking, and vandalism and threatened and intimidated abortion doctors, clinics, and judges.[23] During the 1990s, any distinct lines among anti-abortion activists, militia groups, and extremist white supremacists started to blur, and Christian Identity activists, most notably Phineas Priests, driven by intense antisemitic theology, carried out anti-abortion bombings and other attacks.[24] The cross-fertilization extended into propaganda strategies. For instance, the fantasy mini-novel *Rescue Platoon* detailed a future of righteous insurrectionary anti-abortion violence against providers and the federal government, offering a blueprint to extremists in the same way as *The Turner Diaries* laid out a vision for white supremacist revolution and inspired the Oklahoma City bombing.

While newly engaged, white supremacist-influenced militia drew from enduring practices, ideas, and emotions with a long history in U.S. politics. As sociologist Lane Crothers observes, 'the contemporary militia is not "alien' or "exceptional," [but] invokes core principles . . . commonly recognized as central to American political life.'[25] They embraced what they feel is a righteous struggle to protect America from shadow interests they imagine are organized to destroy American freedoms. They claimed to protect their rights to bear arms, free assembly, and to organize a militia to combat a corrupted government.

Militia and extremist white supremacists perceived a common threat by the state. During the 1990s, so-called Patriots and gun rights groups decried federal gun control efforts as a sign of a police state seeking to disarm citizens. At the same time, a powerful national gun lobby pushed legislation to limit controls on gun owners and gun shows. The result was a flourishing gun show circuit that offered easy gun access and 'a town square where extremists can gather information, make contacts, and mingle with the likeminded.'[26] As sociologist Stuart Wright notes, militia and patriot groups used gun shows as 'key dissemination points for weapons, paramilitary paraphernalia, anti-government invectives . . . and a gateway into the militia subculture.'[27] Moreover, Lane Crothers explains that many 'militia groups and sympathizers reopened an ideological and political dialogue with the racist right . . . transforming into a more explicitly racist movement.'[28]

Militia and extremist white supremacy networks fueled their resistance with rage and indignation to fight disarmament and other limits on their ability to purchase and use guns. They advocated for violence if they were pushed too far and planned for it through training, stockpiling weapons, and strategizing scenarios against their enemies. Understanding these affinities, extremist white supremacy leader and *The Turner Diaries* author, William Pierce, called gun shows 'a natural recruiting environment' for white supremacists.[29]

From Ruby Ridge and Waco to Oklahoma City

Two pivotal incidents involving federal raids for weapon violations fueled rage on the right in the 1990s.[30] In August 1992, federal agents initiated a tactical strike in Ruby Ridge, Idaho, on white supremacist Randy Weaver, who refused to appear in federal court to face a weapon charge. In a bungled attempt to lure Weaver from his isolated cabin to arrest him, agents shot and killed Weaver's 14-year-old son and the family dog.[31] A U.S. marshal was also killed in the shootout. During the subsequent 11-day standoff, FBI snipers wounded Weaver and a family friend and killed Weaver's wife. More than 100 protesters, mostly extremist white supremacy Christian Identity and patriot adherents, gathered at the gates to support the Weavers, and national media began broadcasting the standoff. Gun owners of American activists Bo Gritz and Jack McLamb arrived to act as intermediaries and eventually negotiated an end to the siege.

Only six months later, federal authorities targeted the Branch Davidian compound in Waco, Texas. Led by David Koresh, the Davidians were a small, isolated, and apocalyptic religious sect heavily armed and with a history of violence.[32] Federal agents saw the Davidians as an extremist group planning violence against the government, though Koresh appeared willing to cooperate with the ATF's investigation about his wholesale weapon purchases that he intended to resell for profit at gun shows. They also justified their attention on the Davidians based on child abuse and sexual molestation allegations.[33] The ATF declined Koresh's initial offer to inspect the Davidians' compound for firearms and missed multiple chances to avoid the deadly raid on the group's compound that killed more than 80 Branch Davidians by asphyxiation, fire, and gunshot wounds.[34] Millions watched the federal authority's stake out and assault on national television and read about it in national newspapers.[35] While some surviving Davidians were convicted on weapons charges, Congressional investigations also exposed mismanagement and overreach by the ATF and FBI.

The raid amplified tensions about federal overreach among far-right extremists. As Crother's explains, the far-right embraced 'the myth of Waco' that cast the Davidians as 'innocent, God-fearing, ordinary citizens victimized by the evil forces of an oppressive, corrupted government . . . [making] Waco the symbol of everything dangerous about government.'[36] Long before Trump's Big Lie myth about a stolen election, the myth of Waco, pushed in part by two videotapes – *Waco: The Big Lie* and *Waco: The Big Lie Continues* – circulated widely in extremist white supremacist and militia networks. The videos cast the federal government as cold-blooded killers who indiscriminately attacked innocent citizens including children. To right-wing extremists, Ruby Ridge and Waco offered ample evidence that the government was willing to murder anybody who dared to stand in its way. They also demonstrated how extremist white supremacists created propaganda. Decades later, white supremacists extended their practices, ideas, and emotions across extremist networks by pushing conspiracies on Twitter, Facebook, and more surreptitious virtual platforms to help spread another 'Big Lie' fantasy about corrupt Democrats and their allies who illegally seized power in the 2020 election from Trump and his 'true patriot' followers.

To be fair, extremists' suspicions about federal culpability in Ruby Ridge and Waco had some merit. Randy Weaver and his associate Kevin Harris were charged with murder, conspiracy, and assault in Idaho state court. Jury selection started just days before the Waco siege and continued throughout the standoff. The trial began five days before the ATF assaulted the Davidian compound. Sociologist Stuart Wright explains that seeing parallels between Ruby Ridge and Waco,

> Judge Edward Lodge . . . instructed the jury not to watch, listen to, or read news coverage about the burning of the Davidian complex. But the incidents involved significant comparisons and overlapping that could not be ignored. A parade of FBI, ATF, and Justice Department officials ferried

between the [siege and the trial]. Moreover, media coverage . . . cast a more intense light on Ruby Ridge and the Weaver trial, drawing comparisons for a wider audience.[37]

When the trial ended in July, the jury acquitted Weaver of all major charges[38] and determined that the ATF had entrapped him. The federal government then settled subsequent civil suits that Weaver and his daughters filed, as well as one filed by Kevin Harris. Although the feds did not admit wrongdoing in the settlements, many observers felt the Weavers would have won had their trial gone to court. Subsequent federal investigations by the DOJ, the Senate, and the U.S. Government Accounting Office found major problems with the rules of engagement used by authorities in both Ruby Ridge and Waco. The Senate determined that those used at Ruby Ridge were unconstitutional. These findings bolstered far-right conspiracies about federal overreach and corruption.

During October 1992, just between Ruby Ridge and Waco, Christian Identity leader Pete Peters convened the Estes Park conference in Colorado that drew, according to Wright, 'a wide cross section of far-right leaders to unify against an emergent police state.'[39] Prominent white supremacists and militia leaders, including KKK leader Louis Beam, Militia of Montana founder John Trochmann, and Aryan Nations' founder Richard Butler, spoke about Ruby Ridge as a spark to awaken 'Christian soldiers' to carry out God's judgment. They downplayed white supremacist beliefs to focus on the Weavers as 'good Christians' who were victims of the New World Order. Louis Beam intoned that far-right factions

> are all viewed as the same, the enemies of the state. When they come for you, the federals will not ask if you are a Constitutionalist, a Baptist, Church of Christ, Identity Covenant believer, Klansman, Nazi, homeschooler, Freeman, New Testament believer, [or] fundamentalist. . . . Those who wear badges, black boots, and carry automatic weapons, and kick in your doors already know all they need to know about you. You are enemies of the state.[40]

Wright explains that Beam and others saw Ruby Ridge as an opportunity to unite disparate and fragmented far-right militia and white supremacist factions against a common enemy.[41] Guns Owners of America founder Larry Pratt voiced the need for armed citizen militias to engage in spiritual battles against the state's attack on liberty. Beam advocated for a new incarnation of leaderless insurgency using decentralized terrorist cells to fight federal surveillance and tyranny. Together, Ruby Ridge and the Estes Park convening laid the grounds for more tightly interweaving militia and white supremacist networks and aligning adherents along key ideological lines. The Waco massacre provided the glue to seal the connections between the groups and their anger at the government provided a theme to mask their white supremacist foundation. Though strong white supremacist currents have always flowed through militia networks, security analyst Catrina Doxsee notes that Waco's anti-government emphasis 'gave the nascent movement some cover against allegations of racism after Ruby Ridge primarily mobilized white separatists.'[42]

By late-1993, numerous far-right leaders, including militia conspiracists John Trochmann and Linda Thompson,[43] urged forming new militia groups to limit federal power and avoid another Ruby Ridge or Waco. The 'militia' title carried particular meaning for their goals. 'Militia' falsely conveys that they were legitimate groups derived from the so-called 'Unorganized Militia' referenced in federal and state laws. Trochmann's Militia of Montana (MoM) and the Michigan Militia were among the first of scores of paramilitary groups formed in 1994 that called themselves names such as unorganized militias, citizens' militias, and constitutional militias.[44] Militia leaders continued to spread movement propaganda through a wide array of right-wing countercultural Christian Patriot media,[45] including shortwave radio programs, VHS tapes, survivalist expos and gun shows, fax chains, right-wing newsletters and pamphlets, and, by 1995, Usenet and the nascent World Wide Web. In a remarkably short period of time, several hundred militia groups had emerged across 36 states.[46] By 1996, the Southern Poverty Law Center had identified more than 400 militia networks in all 50 states, with a total membership between 20,000 and 60,000.[47] This growth brought many people with no prior association with right-wing extremism into militia activism.

In April 1995, Timothy McVeigh and Terry Nichols bombed the Murrah Federal Building in Oklahoma City, killing 168 people, including 19 children, and injuring several hundred more. According to the FBI, 'it was the worst act of homegrown terrorism in the nation's history.'[48] Neither McVeigh nor Nichols were card-carrying militia members, but, as Doxsee explains,

> McVeigh was inspired by pro-militia and other conspiracy theory literature and had traveled to witness the Waco siege. He conceived the attack on the Alfred P. Murrah Federal Building as a response to the government's actions at both Waco and Ruby Ridge.[49]

He briefly participated in the KKK, sold copies of *The Turner Diaries* and other paraphernalia at gun shows, and had ties with the white supremacist community Elohim City outside Muldrow, Oklahoma. Criminologist Mark Hamm also suspects that members from the Aryan Republican Army actively helped McVeigh plot and carry out the bombing.[50] According to the SPLC, McVeigh's 'anti-government co-conspirator Terry Nichols had connections with the extremist militia group called the Wolverine Watchmen – the very same organization whose members were arrested for plotting to kill Michigan Gov. Gretchen Whitmer' in 2020.[51]

The Oklahoma City attack brought tremendous negative attention for the militia movement as media reports linked the bombing to militia ideology. Armed militias began to scatter, and for a decade or so, their numbers declined. In 2005, the SPLC estimated that there were 152 anti-government groups in approximately 30 states.[52] But the publicity around the Oklahoma City bombing also created opportunities for many others who were previously unaware of the movement's existence to learn about, and eventually join, militia groups.

After the 9/11 terror attacks, the country focused on foreign threats and the wars that followed. With militias out of the spotlight, and many regarding the G.W. Bush presidential administration as less threatening than previous ones, militia membership plummeted. But anti-government networks did not vanish. They devolved into smaller, lower profile networks aligned over conspiratorial anxieties about impending Y2K catastrophes, that the U.S. government orchestrated 9/11, and that a secretive totalitarian New World Order government was conspiring to rule the world.[53] Their persistence in the early 2000s attracted little attention.

Masking extremist white supremacy

During the 1990s, many extremist white supremacists reluctantly drew back from traditional protest modes as they found their older tactics outmoded and ineffective for retaining members and recruiting new ones. Their adaptations and adjustments responded to the decreasing public support for, and increasing repression of, the movement. Their strategic shift into abeyance was more than simple experimentation; it was a concerted effort to avoid repression and take advantage of new means for networking and more surreptitiously extend their influence.

Various white supremacist pockets consciously advocated tactical shifts to sustain existing networks and to eventually expand the movement by providing routes into activism, which were less likely to garner attention and pushback. Leaders increasingly called for 'lone wolf' tactics and 'leaderless resistance' to disconnect adherents' actions from movement networks and to avoid government infiltration and the legal challenges that the SPLC had so effectively wielded. Louis Beam, an infamous and influential KKK leader who helped create Liberty Net, the first white supremacist online bulletin board, was also editor for *The Seditionist*. Beam used the racist zine to distribute an essay on 'leaderless resistance,' which rippled through white supremacist networks. He encouraged white supremacists to avoid broad organizational efforts and to instead form small cells to act out decentralized terror plots 'when they feel the time is ripe, or will take their cues from others

who precede them.'[54] Beam and others argued that openly white supremacist organizations were too vulnerable to disruption and prosecution, but
that individuals or small cells who took self-directed action and were loosely
coordinated through movement-distributed information would be harder
to connect to formal movement organizations. So, while lone actors draw
inspiration from the ideological writings, videos, and propaganda circulating though the movement, they would act independently to avoid the far-
reaching losses likely when law enforcement or watchdog groups infiltrate or
file charges against white supremacist targets. The lone actor tactic to avoid
membership lists, withdraw from public rallies or meetings, and otherwise
act in secrecy resonated with some extremists who took up the call to do it
alone for the cause.[55]

Like so many parts of U.S. white supremacy, lone actor violence was not
a new practice. It was just reemphasized and labelled as a tactic for the most
committed. For example, between 1977 and 1980, Joseph Paul Franklin
traveled around the country killing at least 15 people he believed to be 'race
traitors' and 'racial enemies.'[56] He first bombed a Jewish lobbyist's home in
suburban Washington DC, then a synagogue in Chattanooga, Tennessee. He
moved to a series of sniper attacks, beginning with a synagogue in St. Louis,
MO, followed by an attempt to assassinate the civil rights leader, Vernon
Jordan.[57]

Franklin is typically described as an 'American serial killer,' which techni-
cally speaking is correct, but this designation ignores his deep commitments
to extremist white supremacy and ideologically motivated terror tactics.[58]
In the years leading up to his attacks, Franklin had been a member of the
American Nazi Party (ANP) before joining the States Rights Party and an
Atlanta-based Ku Klux Klan group, where he mixed with the likes of ANP
founder George Lincoln Rockwell, William Pierce, J.B. Stoner,[59] and James
Mason. Years later, Mason would become one of the inspirations for the
contemporary terrorist cell – the Atomwaffen Division (AWD). Franklin saw
himself as a white supremacist warrior executing a longstanding American
insurgency against minorities and Jews. His violence impressed National
Alliance founder and *The Turner Diaries* author William Pierce so much that
he dedicated his second white supremacist fantasy novel, *Hunter*, to the real-
life terrorist.[60] But Franklin was neither the first white supremacist to rely on
this tactic, nor tragically the last.[61]

More broadly, the leaderless resistance strategy informed a general move
among white supremacists to withdraw into hiding, avoid repression, and
sustain extremist networks and culture. Marginalization meant that white
supremacists faced difficult choices about publicly communicating their
beliefs.[62] They saw some whites as simply unenlightened about the true nature
of white superiority and who, with effective recruitment efforts to spread
white supremacist ideas, could be converted to the white racist 'truth.' Yet,

many extremists also saw great risks in publicly expressing white supremacist ideas. Being out as a white supremacist could disrupt their personal relationships with neighbors, employers, and others. Stories abounded in movement networks of neighbors picketing the residences of white supremacists and extremists being fired from their jobs after co-workers and bosses found out about their extremist beliefs.[63] More than half of the extremist white supremacist participants we interviewed in 1990s and 2000s attributed their loss of a job to an employer's opposition to their extremist beliefs.[64] They felt severely repressed and worried about losing their jobs, being shunned, or even surveilled and arrested if their activism became known.[65]

Respectability rhetoric, infiltration, and under-the-radar style

During the 1990s and early 2000s, white supremacists moved underground, in part, using subterfuge about their identities and beliefs. Tom Metzger, once among the movement's most openly militant attention-seeking racists, joined other leaders in encouraging activists to strategically hide their extremism in public to better blend into the mainstream. They stressed clandestine white supremacy to avoid repression by limiting overt displays that might tip off others about their allegiances. Many racial extremists began living double lives. They covered their racist tattoos, grew out their hair, hid extremist insignia, and outwardly projected an image that concealed their beliefs. Leaders also encouraged them to infiltrate institutions to secure political, economic, and cultural influence. They talked about moving through society undetected; rising to positions of wealth, power, and respectability; giving resources back to the movement; and becoming role models for future generations.

In 1990, after losing his civil trial for the Mulugeta Seraw's beating death, Metzger proclaimed:

> The movement will not be stopped. . . . We're too deep. We're embedded now. Don't you understand? We're in your colleges. We're in your armies. We're in your police forces. We're in your technical areas. Where do you think a lot of the skinheads disappeared to? They grew their hair out, went to college. They've got the program. We planted the seeds.[66]

He and other extremist white supremacy leaders had specifically encouraged racist skinheads to change their look, stay out of trouble, earn college degrees, find good jobs, and raise children in a stable environment filled with potent movement idealism. Before long, white supremacists were working to suppress their racist leanings in public, and soon, Kathleen M. Blee writes, 'those who use[d] overtly racist symbols in public or who adopt an exaggerated racist style [were seen as] movement novices.'[67]

As part of their push toward 'respectability,' savvy racial extremists worked to reframe their rhetoric to appeal to mainstream conservative whites. Their goal was to normalize and, eventually, mainstream extremist white supremacy by neutralizing its public stigma. They recast racial and antisemitic hatred as 'White heritage preservation,' 'White nationalism,' and, eventually, 'the alt-right.' They experimented with various strategies to legitimize their claims, including efforts to reframe racism as 'White civil rights' and 'cultural heritage,' to frame 'hatred' as in-group love, and to associate whiteness with victimhood.[68] Today's hashtags and other propaganda slogans such as '#whitegenocide,' 'It's Ok To Be White,' and 'Anti-racist is Code Word for Anti-White' follow from this long-term strategy to find cultural and political themes that resonate among a broader swath of the white population. While many commentators reacted to the recent generation of 'khaki and polo-wearing' white supremacists and online racist trolls as if they were surprisingly new, their practices, ideas, emotions, and the networks that sustain them stretch much farther back into our history.

Taking cues from veteran white supremacists, racial extremists during the 1990s pushed to frame a pseudointellectual approach laden with more digestible rhetoric to improve the movement's image. Drawing from strategies sketched by white supremacist leaders Wilmot Robertson, Thom Robb, David Duke, Jared Taylor, and others, this 'new racist rhetoric,' as sociologist Mitch Berbrier called it, presented an image that suppressed outward expressions of hatred, irrationality, and violence.[69] They pursued a two-part goal to simultaneously attract and mobilize new members, especially moderate and conservative whites, to the cause, while softening their image among non-White, non-racist, and liberal opponents. This new effort to repackage white supremacist extremism for the masses created early successes for David Duke and others, but the broader and longer-term cultural successes flowing from this 'new racism' came more gradually. As the new racial rhetoric penetrated white supremacist networks, extremists became adept at managing outward impressions. They grew their influence, while authorities, policy makers, and the public ignored ominous signs.[70]

In another attempt to move toward 'respectability,' extremists sought to 'intellectualize' racism and white supremacy by legitimizing 'whites' to be equivalent to racial and ethnic minority groups. At the same time, they worked to make white supremacists less identified with their actual core beliefs, such as the idea that whites are inherently superior in terms of moral, intellectual, and cultural pursuits. For instance, in the words of sociologists Betty Dobratz and Stephanie Shanks-Meile, they worked to reframe traditional racism's 'crude bigotry centered around a belief system that maintained the racial superiority of Whites,' toward new racist claims that rest 'more upon the idea of recognizing differences between peoples and wanting to maintain the difference.'[71]

Extremists also adopted more gimmicks and rationalizations, including a cultural pluralistic position usually associated with inclusionary progressives, which portrays racial and ethnic diversity and tolerance toward differences as a societal good.[72] They tried to align their ideas with values for a diverse democracy by arguing that individuals can maintain a pride in and love for their ethnic or racial heritage, while also maintaining allegiance to a broader, multicultural state. They framed these in-group affections as scientifically based and universally valid, deceptively claiming, as Berbrier writes, 'that their only interest is in everybody's positive and culturally-valued love of their own people.'[73] New racist rhetoric presented white supremacists as cultural pluralists who merely wanted to represent White ethnics in an increasingly diverse cultural landscape.[74] The claims that follow from this pluralistic logic set up equivalences related to access to political, economic, and cultural resources between 'Whites' and other racial or ethnic groups, primarily Blacks or African-Americans, Jews, and Hispanics, and other groups defined as 'ethnic.'

White supremacists perceived a government subservient to ethnic minority interests, so they sought to position themselves to be worthy of recognition and power, a claim they imagined would resonate among moderate and conservative Whites. Duke was among the first to put this into action when he broke from the KKK in the 1980s and formed the National Association of the Advancement of White People (NAAWP) as the 'White answer to the NAACP' (National Association for the Advancement of Colored People).[75] He talked about creating the NAAWP as a way to 'expose the hypocrisy of minority racists dominating America'[76] and described it as a pro-White organization for white civil rights. Duke claimed that the group was 'not about oppressing Blacks or other minorities, but simply the advancement of our own race.' He went beyond just claiming to represent Whites by portraying 'minority racists' as the oppressors.

Claims of reverse discrimination and white victimization amplify perceptions about unequal treatment toward Whites.[77] According to this logic, if 'Black Pride' carries non-racist meaning, then so should 'White Pride.' White supremacists latched onto these equivalences, reversal, and victim strategies to help justify their positions and to appeal to moderate conservatives' sense of equity and justice in ways that might attract them to the fold.

In this period, the practices, ideas, and emotions that previously distinguished extremist and ordinary white supremacy started to align more closely. Architects of Ronald Reagan's presidential ascendency helped intensify White people's anger with race-baiting about brazen Blacks and other minorities living regally off the dole, while Whites worked hard, played by the rules, and still fell behind.[78] David Duke rode this new racist language to the Louisiana statehouse as an elected Republican representative in 1989, unsuccessfully ran for Governor in 1991 although he won the majority of

White voters in Louisiana, and briefly tried to secure the Republican presidential nomination in 1992.[79] He wasn't elected to the legislature solely by white supremacist extremists but by many more moderate sympathizers, or 'Middle American Radicals,' as Donald Warren[80] calls them. Duke's 'White interest group politics' imagined racial injustice as giving new rights, privileges, and preferential treatment to racial minorities including Blacks, Jews, and Latino/as.[81] Duke gave permission to many people to express racism and spread fear about 'racial threats' cast in more palatable language that many White voters endorsed.[82] This same fear, and the language driving it, indelibly shaped the 2016 election that put Trump into the White House.[83]

White supremacists worked to transform the meaning of racism into an idea that better serves their interests. They pushed the notion that everyone's interests lay in simply recognizing fundamental biological and cultural differences among racial groups and then realizing 'value' in keeping them separated physically, socially, and biologically. They claimed that their position was not deviant but rather normal, natural, and common to all racial and ethnic groups. They might be 'racist,' but they argued that this did not differentiate them from any other racial or ethnic group. They tried to side-step hate and bigotry with their repackaged racism, while promoting an image of people just attempting to maintain the integrity of their group like other minorities do.

These rhetorical moves set in motion a gradual but effective shift in white supremacy's tone and style to appeal to people who might normally disagree with extreme racist views. They set the stage for more moderate sympathizers to view such politics as merely expressing white interest group politics, thereby making the viewpoint more appealing to a broader swath of the white population. As Berbrier[84] noticed in the late 1990s and early 2000s, U.S. political culture turned increasingly receptive to this kind of 'digestible' racist rhetoric. The effect was not so much to amplify blatant support for white supremacy as to help move political debate sharply rightward, creating what he called the 'terrifying possibility' that an impression-managed extremist white supremacy might deeply reshape mainstream conservative politics toward extremists' aims.[85] And, by framing their claims in the cloak of reasoned debate and multicultural values, extremist white supremacists simultaneously undermined some attacks by anti-racists and other opponents.

This sanitized 'white-collar supremacy,' as Historian Kelly J. Baker calls it, helped to rebrand white supremacy and align it with broader populist conspiratorial anxieties about demographic change, immigration, and governmental overreach that were pushed by far-right pundits, networks of militia, sovereign citizens, nativists, and Tea Partiers. As we explain in the next chapter, these ideas also tied into Oath Keepers' and Birther ideologies. But, none of this reframing altered core white supremacist attitudes. They just sought a softer veneer for their virulent racist and antisemitic practices, ideas, and emotions to avoid repression and to draw extremist white supremacists and ordinary white supremacists closer.

Nourishing extremist white supremacy behind closed doors

As white supremacists tried to soften their outward guise, they also sustained their true extremist vitriol, anger, and hatred in hidden activist pockets or free spaces.[86] Some pockets were mostly private, hyper-local settings where small, tight-knit extremist networks assembled to reinforce their relationships, and racist practices, ideas, and emotions. These settings represented their imagined 'Whites-only' future and offered extremist white supremacists real-life experiences that 'prefigured' total white power. In family homes, Bible study groups, house parties, and other guarded gatherings, white supremacists built powerful temporary spaces in which they could openly express their ideals in relative safety from authorities and other outsiders. Simultaneously, they drew local extremist networks into broader white supremacist culture through a music scene and, especially, through Internet platforms in ways that reinforced their solidarity and commitment to the cause. They used what Robert Futrell and Pete Simi term a 'bi-leveled infrastructure of spaces' to support network ties and practices that sustain collective emotions, ideas, and commitments in a hostile socio-political context.[87]

Families and small gatherings

Extremist white supremacists give particular importance to families as the core site for resistance where they can foster extremist fantasies and live them out on a small scale. Families provide the earliest opportunities for shaping young children's identities, and parents can feel powerful activist emotions as they attempt to indoctrinate their kids into the cause. Inside their homes, they can more overtly express their commitments than they can in other social spaces. They use cultural materials such as names, stories, symbols, paraphernalia, verbal styles, rituals, and clothing. For instance, some adherents display pictures of Adolf Hitler alongside other family photos as if he were a grandparent. Some decorate their homes with racist and antisemitic posters, cards, newsletters, comic, and coloring books. Some parents give children 'movement uniforms' such as miniature Klan robes or more common items like T-shirts and fatigues which are less clearly connected to the movement but can still provide meaningful ways for parents to shape their children.

Other private practices reinforce a white supremacist identity and explicit connections to the movement, such as the daily rituals of prayers, dinners, and bedtime routines that instill white power viewpoints. Likewise, parents often label children, and even pets, with surnames or nicknames tied to extremist ideas to link their children's sense of self with extremist white supremacism. They also use homeschooling as a systematic approach to politically socialize their children. Homeschooling allows families to control over the dissemination of extreme white supremacist ideas while masking and delegitimating 'mainstream' worldviews.

Families are not just havens to raise committed white supremacist children. Within these spaces, parent-activists experience their role as an opportunity to reinforce their own political commitments.[88] By expressing their politics through family rituals, rules, stories, and symbolism, extremist white supremacist parents establish their activist identity as relevant and pervasive across myriad daily experiences. Parents see their efforts to infuse extremism in the home as an important, strategic socialization process for their children that also reinforces and sustains their own political commitments.

As other movement strategies seemed less viable because of mainstream hostilities in the 1990s and 2000s, the family became more important than ever among white supremacists for fostering racist practices, ideas, and emotions that could sustain their commitment to the cause. Political scientist Richard Couto explains, 'when the conditions of repression are paramount and the possibility of overt resistance is small, narratives are preserved in the most private of free spaces, the family.'[89] We do not mean that extremist white supremacists' efforts to use families as a vehicle for resistance was anything new, but that they embraced it more than ever because other outlets for their activism appeared limited.

Extremist white supremacists also used informal gatherings to continuously engage members. They held and participated in smaller, more casual, and much more confidential meet ups, often disguised as routine social functions such as parties or Bible study groups to conceal their extremist features to outsiders. These gatherings mainly kept existing members engaged in extremist white supremacist practices, ideas, and emotions to sustain their commitments to the cause. Their private character meant they were less about recruiting new members, though at times, extremists might use them to draw curious, but uncommitted, acquaintances into the fold. Their strategic hiding worked well enough that authorities seemed unconcerned about the threats extremist white supremacy posed.

Some followers gathered in small independent churches, Bible study meetings, and Pagan gatherings in extremist's homes. Christian white supremacists searched for 'true' biblical insight instead of watered-down '*Jew*deo-Christian' rhetoric, as they called it. Pagan extremists resurrected Nordic mythology as a tribalist warrior religion for White Europeans. Participants felt immense autonomy to elaborate and refine white supremacist ideologies with the support of like-minded activists, under the guise of ordinary theological or spiritual study. Some factions combined Bible study with retreats to places the movement identified as spiritually sacred and racially pure, such as northern Idaho. White supremacists imbued these spaces with racialized and religious meanings and used their excursions as bonding rituals among true believers.

Racists used small parties, ranging from backyard patio get-togethers to field parties, to bond with one another and explore their ideology, experimenting with various white supremacist sentiments. They regaled one another with morality tales that justify white power and detailed ways to live committed 'white lifestyles' and supported one another's efforts to get by in an 'anti-white' world. They often repeated their origin stories about their 'political enlightenment' or detailed their individual resistance efforts that might include late-night leafleting in neighborhoods or on college campuses, harassing 'non-White' neighbors, and physical violence directed against their 'racial enemies.'[90] Their stories provided others with ideas and encouragement to remain committed until new opportunities emerged.

Some gatherings included only close friends with staunch extremist beliefs, while at other gatherings non-adherents and, at times, even people of color attended. The white supremacists tried to assess the makeup at each gathering, and their assessments might affect how they expressed their racial sentiments. At the most private gatherings, open extremist expression was the norm. Activists showed off movement affiliation with jackets emblazoned with white power patches, military-style boots, Confederate flags, Nazi-salutes, and tattoos. But at gatherings that included some outsiders, the same activists consciously dressed down to conceal their white power sentiments. They were more hesitant to use racialized rhetoric and images because they wanted to avoid confrontations. Some activists engaged the non-extremists in political conversations to gauge their receptiveness to racist ideas. When they sensed that someone might be a good recruit, they focused on building a friendship and, ultimately, drawing the person into the fold.[91]

Sociologist Eric Hirsch notes 'successful recruitment to a revolutionary movement is more likely if there are social structural-cultural havens available where radical ideas and tactics can be more easily germinated.'[92] Extremists used these seemingly innocuous contexts to enact resistance away from public scrutiny, retain existing members, and recruit new ones. Parties, Bible study meetings, and various outings helped them anchor white power ideals, induce and maintain solidarity, and talk about ways to further the cause. Activists found comfort and security in these low-key gatherings when they faced hostility in other spheres of their lives.

Semi-public gatherings

While extremist white supremacists used their very private activist spaces to anchor them to other activists, they also embraced some relatively controlled semi-public gatherings to draw larger networks together, build alliances, and communicate movement identity. They used music events and the Internet to bring together a wider range of people and networks and create a sense of vibrancy and continuity for a somewhat fragmented movement.

White power music gained momentum in the 1970s and grew into a prominent feature of white supremacist culture. By the mid-1980s, movement leaders and activists were organizing impromptu home concerts and bar shows that drew members together in powerful contexts for transmitting movement identity and supporting movement networks.[93] By the late 1980s, they held semi-private festivals. And, by 2000, white supremacist music had evolved into one of the most pervasive means of racist expression among both veteran and newly recruited activists. Many gatherings included music produced by more than 100 U.S. white supremacist bands and more than 200 bands in 22 countries.[94] At that time, two of the most notorious white supremacist organizations – the National Alliance and Hammerskin Nation – were closely tied to the two most prominent white supremacist recording companies, Resistance Records and Panzerfaust Records.[95]

Music events, from bar concerts to multi-day festivals, offered activists emotionally-loaded experiences that nurtured commonality and connection to one another. Participants could tap into extremist emotions such as dignity, pride, pleasure, love, kinship, and fellowship in these settings that inspired, vitalized, and sustained their commitments to the cause.[96] The events ranged from medium-sized shows held at bars, restaurants, and other public halls to large multi-day festivals held on private property. By bringing together a much wider range of people and networks together in semi-public settings, they created a sense of vibrancy and continuity for a still fragmented movement. In fact, these semi-public performances symbolized a continuous and viable cause to both the participants and those hearing about them from afar. The events also served as much more planned and controlled public presentations than marches and rallies that were more prone to disorganization and counter-movement attacks.

Even more than music, the Internet offered extremist white supremacists their most critical tool for connecting individuals to extremist networks worldwide. As we mentioned earlier, white supremacists were among the earliest Internet adopters, developing the Liberty Net in 1983,[97] and they embraced cyberspace to facilitate communication, organization, and recruitment, which were all pivotal to sustaining activist connections. Many researchers and watchdog groups have noted white supremacists' early savvy at linking members and organizations through list-servers, chat rooms, and bulletin boards that provided space for real-time communication to create virtual communities.[98] Their early adoption enabled extremist activists to create dense inter-organizational connections and spaces for 'virtual organization.'[99] Early links were especially common between Klan and neo-Nazi skinhead sites, and between Christian and non-Christian white supremacist sites, both nationally and internationally.[100] These sites provided information about the movement and incentives to get involved. Extremists also used these virtual networks to market and distribute white power music, books, and movement paraphernalia and to advertise and coordinate bar shows and music festivals.

The Internet offered extremist white supremacists critical opportunities for planning and networking that simply did not exist before, and they took full advantage.[101] As white power websites grew in number and diversity, potential adherents could find their way into the movement with discretion and anonymity through a group they felt most suitable for them.[102] As Todd Schroer explained, these forums help 'reduce the perceived risk of contacting these groups. If you have to go to a Klan rally or actually write to [groups] to get involved in hate, that's a big barrier to overcome [in an extremely oppositional climate].'[103] Virtual spaces offer degrees of both intimacy and safety not found in other extremist white supremacy settings. Consequently, they played a crucial role in attracting new activists, drawing peripheral members closer to the movement, and maintaining the commitment among those already active.

Extremist white supremacists used under-the-radar spaces to enact their culture and identity largely out of view of the public eye. They embedded their extremist practices, ideas, and emotions in many routine, everyday activities that did not typically draw much attention. In these 'free spaces,'[104] followers felt removed from physical and ideological controls of opponents; members could nourish solidarity and commitment to their cause. These networks of recognition[105] continually validated adherents' commitments and provided covert routes to participate in the movement, helping members better avoid the stigma that comes by participating in more public activism. In short, the extremist white supremacy practices, ideas, and emotions enacted in these gatherings help forge and sustain a shared racist agenda, internal solidarity, and a sense of efficacy amid public hostility toward the movement.

Extremist white supremacy persistence

Extremist white supremacy has long ebbed and flowed in size and across different activist networks, including various permutations such as anti-government and anti-immigration groups.[106] In the decades following the civil rights conflicts in the 1950s and 1960s to Barack Obama's election, extremist white supremacists struggled to find ways to cultivate and spread their virulent racism and antisemitism. Popular media and government authorities vilified extremist white supremacists, portraying them as a motley crew of belligerent racist skinheads or fringe wackos in robes and hoods. Public opinion weighed strongly against extremist white supremacy.[107] During the 1990s, many white supremacists were tied to militia networks, but those networks splintered in the years following the 1995 Oklahoma City bombing.[108]

In the early 2000s, as key national leaders died or were indicted and sent to jail, extremist white supremacists found it even more difficult to achieve any political or cultural traction.

Ordinary white supremacy in the United States shares important assumptions with extremist white supremacy ideology, but there were also important differences that distinguished ordinary from extremist white supremacy. As Blee explained in 2002,

> [T]he ideas that racist activists share about whiteness are more conscious, elaborated, and tightly connected to political action than those of mainstream Whites. . . . The difference between everyday racism [among ordinary white supremacists] and extraordinary racism [among extremist white supremacists]] is the difference between being prejudiced against Jews and believing that there is a Jewish conspiracy that determines the fate of individual Aryans, or between thinking that African Americans are inferior to whites and seeing African Americans as an imminent threat to the white race.[109]

Moreover, notions of an impending 'race war,' a 'Zionist Occupied Government,' and the then current 'genocide of the white race,' now called the 'great replacement,' were core ideas widely shared by extremist white supremacists. But in the early 2000s, they did not resonate with most people. Perhaps the most telling indication of the extremist white supremacy's marginalization from the mainstream was the tendency among those immersed in ordinary white supremacism to disavow and disassociate themselves from the Klan, skinheads, neo-Nazis, and other openly racist groups.

While extremist white supremacy networks faced limited opportunities, they still found ways to persist, and, by some estimates, to gradually grow their numbers in spaces where they hid from public view. By nourishing their networks outside the public eye, extremist white supremacy groups such as the National Alliance, World Church of the Creator, and Hammerskin Nation slowly increased their membership during the 1990s and early 2000s.[110] They also worked to shift perceptions about extremist white supremacy by gradually altering their rhetoric and changing their style to neutralize extremist stigma. They sanitized their language, limited overt displays of their allegiance, and lived double lives. They strategized about moving through society undetected; rising to positions of wealth, power, and respectability; giving resources back to the movement; and becoming role models for future generations.

Extremist white supremacists altered some practices to suppress their racist leanings in public, but their dangerous ideas and emotions remained. They hoped to create a softer veneer for their virulent racism and antisemitism, their conspiratorial fears about a new world order, and their hatred toward those who challenge their righteousness. They sought a cosmetic overhaul intended to rebrand their look and bide them time to draw in a broader segment of white Americans and secure political power. These efforts were nothing more than a ploy to disguise the worst form of racial extremism. And, it worked, at least to an extent. By the 2008 election, most policy makers, journalists, and citizens seemed to consider organized extremist white supremacy as a past relic or, at best, a nagging annoyance on the right that would never really amount to any viable political force. We now know how wrong they were.

Notes

1 McVeigh, 2009.
2 Simi and Futrell, 2015, p. 2.
3 Trelease, 1971.
4 In *Birchers: How the John Birch Society Radicalized the American Right,* historian Matthew Dallek argues that the John Birch society did more than any other conservative group in the United States to propel anti-civil rights racism, antisemitism, conspiracy theories, and intimidation and harassment tactics embraced by contemporary extremism. At its peak, the Birchers had between 60,000 and 100,000 members, including wealthy white business elites, with upwardly mobile suburbanites who viewed themselves as a vanguard trying to educate the public about the alleged communist conspiracy that was destroying the United States. Dallek suggests that the Birchers helped to forge an alternative political tradition on the far right based on a core anti-establishment, apocalyptic, conspiratorial, anti-globalist, explicitly racist, and violent mode of politics. They confronted questions about public morality from an evangelical Christian position to advocate for banning abortion, as well as sex education in schools, and trying to insert what they called 'patriotic texts' into libraries and classrooms. Women played particularly influential roles in the Birchers' cultural wars as 'teachers' to instruct the public about the threats from liberalizing culture. Among the most powerful was conservative anti-equal rights amendment (ERA) movement leader, Phyllis Schlafly, who successfully fought ERA ratification in the 1970s. She stood against feminism, abortion, and gay rights and effectively tapped into conservative religious sentiment over what she termed 'family values.' For more on Birchers, see McGirr (2015).
5 Cunningham, 2012.
6 McAdam, 1999; Morris, 1984.
7 Simi and Futrell, 2015.
8 Taylor, 1989; Taylor and Rupp, 1987; Taylor and Crossley, 2013.
9 Johnston, 1991.
10 Taylor, 1989, p. 762.
11 Taylor and Crossley, 2013, p. 64.
12 Dobratz and Shanks-Meile, 2000; Daniels, 2009.
13 Simi and Futrell, 2009.
14 Burris, Smith, and Strahm, 2000, p. 218.
15 Atkins, 2011, p. 55.
16 Belew, 2018.
17 Yost, 1987; Southern Poverty Law Center, n.d. 'Person v. Carolina Knights of the Ku Klux Klan.'
18 Dees and Fiffer, 1993; Southern Poverty Law Center, n.d. 'Donald v. United Klans of America.'
19 Other nongovernmental organizations, including the Simon Wiesenthal Center and Anti-Defamation League, also pressured white supremacists through infiltration operations and lawsuits.

20 In the early 1970s, former John Birch Society member William Potter Gale first drew some anti-government Christian Identity believers together as 'sovereign citizens' who claimed that

> [n]on-white people were not human, and that Jews possessed a satanic plot to take over the world. They identified themselves as Posse Comitatus, which is Latin for 'power of the county' and centers on the idea that county sheriffs are the highest governmental authority.
> (Southern Poverty Law Center, n.d. 'Sovereign Citizens Movement')

Today, sovereign citizens consist of loose networks of tax protesters and conspiracists who believe they are immune from all federal, state, and local laws and courts (Sarteschi, 2021). The FBI designates them as domestic terrorists.

21 Reagan, 1981.
22 Stern, 1997; Pitcavage, 2001.
23 According to Pitcavage (2015), from the early 1993 to 2013, only white supremacist attacks exceeded violence by anti-abortion extremists. He also notes that several of the most notorious anti-abortion terrorists demonstrated commitment to white supremacy and anti-government beliefs, including Olympic Park bomber Eric Rudolph, Larry Peck, Richard Poplawski, Scott Roeder, and Daniel Wacht.
24 Clarkson, 1998b.
25 Crothers, 2003, p. 2.
26 Rand, 1996.
27 Wright, 2007, pp. 116–117.
28 Crothers, 2003, p. 7.
29 Wright, 2007, p. 116.
30 Crothers, 2003.
31 Wright, 2007.
32 Newport, 2006; Villiers, 2018.
33 Rimer and Verhovek, 1993.
34 U.S. House of Representatives, 1996.
35 Churchill, 2009.
36 Crothers, 2003, p. 115.
37 Wright, 2007, p. 148.
38 Jurors only convicted Weaver for failing to appear voluntarily in court. Weaver's failure to appear for a 1991 court hearing on the gun charges led to the 11-day confrontation: Jackson (1995).
39 Wright, 2007, p. 149.
40 Dees and Corcoran, 1996, p. 51.
41 Wright, 2007.
42 Doxsee, 2021.
43 Vest, 1995; Kovaleski, 1995.
44 Pitcavage, 2001.
45 Churchill, 2009.
46 Crothers, 2003, p. 119.
47 Wright, 2007, p. 174.
48 Federal Bureau of Investigation, n.d.
49 Doxsee, 2021.
50 Hamm, 2002.
51 Southern Poverty Law Center, 2021.
52 Chermak and Freilich, 2008.
53 Anti-Defamation League, 2004.
54 Kaplan, 1997, p. 88.
55 Hamm and Spaaij, 2017.
56 Even earlier, in 1963, Byron de la Beckwith relied on the single-actor attack strategy to assassinate civil rights activist Medgar Evers. De la Beckwith had been

a long time Klan and White Citizens Council supporter and eventually became an ordained Christian Identity minister. In the years following Evers' murder, de la Beckwith dubbed himself a 'Phineas Priest' – a reference to a Biblical story in the Book of Numbers – a title white supremacists employ to denote violence committed for the larger cause (Mitchell, 2020). White supremacists believe that in this story, a Hebrew named Phineas killed an interracial couple and was subsequently rewarded by God for his actions. Richard Hoskins's 1990 book, *Vigilantes of Christendom: The Story of the Phineas Priesthood,* further popularized the story among extremist white supremacists. As further illustration of the back and forth between extremist white supremacist propaganda and concrete acts of violence inspired, in part, by that same propaganda, several years after Hoskins' book appeared, a small network of individuals associated with various groups, such as the Aryan Nations and Army of Israel, formed a Phineas Priesthood cell around the Spokane, Washington, area. The terror cell executed two bombings: one targeted an abortion clinic, and another targeted the *Spoken Review* newspaper office. The terror cell planned both bombings in coordination with bank robberies to help fund their efforts (Hill, 2020). de la Beckwith faced two trials for Evers' murder and they both ended in hung juries. He walked free until he was retried and convicted 30 years later. During his two original trials, a tax-funded state agency, the Mississippi Sovereignty Commission, provided financial support for the de la Beckwith defense team to identify sympathetic jurors. And while de la Beckwith was awaiting trial during his incarceration, Mississippi officials provided him with special privileges not granted to other inmates. Institutional white supremacy embraced de la Beckwith's extremism (Mitchell, 2011).

57 Ayton, n.d.

58 Federal Bureau of Investigation, 2014.

59 J.B. Stoner, who was a serial bomber and terrorist in his own right, targeted African American churches, elementary schools, and synagogues as part of the shadowy Confederate Underground, a network of extremist white supremacists who initiated a terror campaign to oppose integration during the 1950s. In 1980, Stoner was convicted of one church bombing and sentenced to 10 years in prison but would return from prison after serving three and a half years to his role as a racist leader until his death in 2005 (Martin, 2005).

60 *Hunter* tells the story of Oscar Yeager, a Washington DC Department of Defense consultant who moonlights as an assassin targeting interracial couples and civil rights leaders. In the novel, Yeager's actions lead to copycat attacks and eventually help foment an underground revolutionary resistance movement (Terry, 2014.)

61 In 1996, Eric Rudolf bombed Centennial Olympic Park in Atlanta, Georgia, as a blow to 'global socialism' and protest over government-sanctioned abortion (Schuster and Stone, 2005). Six months later, he also bombed an abortion clinic and a lesbian bar in Atlanta, and then an abortion clinic in Birmingham, AL, a year later. Rudolph reportedly drew upon extremist white supremacy Christian Identity ideas in some letters and claimed to act on behalf of the extremist white supremacy terror group Army of God (Seegmiller, 2007). He also claimed adherence to strict Catholic principles against abortion and LGBTQ+ people. Whatever 'true' beliefs drove his attacks, extremist white supremacists embraced him as a hero, and more '"patriots' and racists join[ed extreme anti-abortionists] with explosive results' (Clarkson, 1998a). There is an extensive history of anti-abortion violence. See Mason (2002).

62 Dobratz and Shanks-Meile, 2000.

63 Bjørgo, 1998; Blee, 1996; Kaplan, 1995.

64 Futrell and Simi, 2004.

65 For similar findings, see Blee (2002) and Dobratz and Shanks-Meile (2000), p. 23.

66 Perry, 2020.

67 Blee, 2002, p. 167. Also see, Cooter (2006).
68 Berbrier, 1998, p. 440, 1999, 2000, p. 180; Vysotsky and McCarthy, 2017.
69 Berbrier, 1999.
70 As Berbrier (1998, p. 432) noted more than two decades ago:

> In some ways this strategy is not so 'new.' For example, in its waning years, the Second Ku Klux Klan (which lasted from about 1915 to 1925) made some efforts that were extremely similar in form to . . . NRWS rhetoric . . . and apparently for similar reasons. That is, as the Klan lost its popular base among the mainstream and middle-classes, there developed a destigmatizing rhetoric denying supremacist attitudes and decrying violence. . . . [For example,] one representative of the Klan . . . emphasiz[ed].

71 Dobratz and Shanks-Meile, 1994, as quoted in Berbrier (1998, p. 432).
72 Berbrier, 1998.
73 Berbrier, 1998, p. 442.
74 Berbrier, 1998.
75 As quoted in Berbrier (1998, p. 439).
76 Berbrier, 1998, p. 439.
77 Berbrier, 1998; Van Dijk, 1992. Ideas about white victimization have permeated U.S. racism. It was the central theme in the 1915 motion picture *The Birth of a Nation*, which portrayed a factually inaccurate, but wildly influential, version of the Reconstruction Era, where White Southerners faced persecution at the hands of freed slaves whose incompetence and criminal nature led to social collapse and lawlessness. This sense of victimization continued to surface during the civil rights era and beyond. By the late 1970s, white victimization was commonly termed 'reverse discrimination,' evoking language from the Supreme Court case that struck down racial quotes in college admission in *Regents of the University of California v. Bakke*, 1978. It advanced the right-wing effort to dismantle affirmative action programs by indicating that these were a reverse discrimination that victimized Whites. By the 1990s, reverse discrimination complaints to the federal Equal Employment Opportunity Commission (EEOC) doubled (Evans, 2004).
78 López, 2014; Lucks, 2020.
79 In the years that followed, he attempted other unsuccessful election bids. He also continued to promote strategies to help effectively mainstream the movement (and line his own pocketbook, which was always a top priority for Duke). By 2000, he founded EURO (European-American Unity and Rights Organization) and continued relying on talking points like 'pro-White civil rights.' During this same time, Duke's close friend and colleague Donald Black promoted a similar vision through his Stormfront web forum. He used the term 'White Nationalist' to shape the narrative away from Nazism, hate, and violence. Stormfront was launched in 1995 as the first major white supremacist website in the world and eventually became one of the most influential web forums.

  Duke and Blacks' efforts also included the 2004 New Orleans Protocol, signed during a EURO-hosted event over the Memorial Day weekend. The authors designed the protocol to increase unity among extremist white supremacists following the death of National Alliance founder, William Pierce. The protocol also recommended that extremists continue forging ahead with mainstreaming efforts. Along with Black and Duke, signers of the protocol represented a 'who's who' of elder leaders within the extremist white supremacy world including Liberty Lobby and Populist Party founder, Willis Carto; longtime Klan attorney and anti-communist cold warrior Sam Dickson; and National States Rights Party founder Ed Fields. The protocol advocated further sanitization strategies such that extremist white supremacy could continue to infiltrate society as part of a larger effort to rebrand white supremacy.

80 Warren, 1976.
81 Omi and Winant, 1986; Berbrier, 1998, p. 114.
82 Barrouquere, 2019.
83 Mutz, 2018.
84 Berbrier, 1998, 2000.
85 Berbrier, 1999, p. 428.
86 Simi and Futrell, 2015; Futrell and Simi, 2004.
87 Futrell and Simi, 2004.
88 Simi, Futrell, and Bubolz, 2016.
89 Couto, 1993, p. 77.
90 Extremist white supremacists often define adversaries in broad terms including whites whom they believe are race traitors. As Blee and Simi (2020, p. 14)
   explain,

> Race traitor is a term generally used for whites who oppose, betray, or
> fail to join the cause of white supremacy, and who, in the perspective of
> white supremacists, have fallen victim to anti-white brainwashing. . . . In
> addition, the strikingly amorphous definition of the core antagonists of the
> white race – 'Jews,' 'communists,' 'mud people,' 'leftists,' 'race traitors,' and
> 'antifa' – means that individuals from these groups are not easily identifiable.
> To be clear, it is difficult, if not impossible, to determine whether a person is
> a Jew, a communist, a 'mud' person, a leftist, a race traitor, or a member of
> antifa simply by looking at them. Lumping people together in such figurative
> categories prevents knowing if any given person might be part of the plot to
> destroy the white race. Even the idea that the destruction of the white race
> is imminent is vaguely inexact. In our research, we have found adherents to
> white supremacism who believed that the race war is currently underway,
> those who believed that it is just around the corner, and those who believed
> that it is coming in some indefinite future time.

91 Simi and Futrell, 2015.
92 Hirsch, 1990, p. 2016.
93 Futrell, Simi, and Gottschalk, 2006.
94 Southern Poverty Law Center, 2002.
95 Dyck, 2016.
96 Futrell, Simi, and Gottschalk, 2006.
97 Back, Keith, and Solomos, 1998; Belew, 2018; Daniels, 2009.
98 Burris, Smith, and Strahm, 2000; Burghart, 1996; Hoffman, 1996; Back, Keith,
   and Solomos, 1998.
99 Burris, Smith, and Strahm, 2000.
100 Burris, Smith, and Strahm, 2000.
101 Hoffman, 1996.
102 Burris, Smith, and Strahm, 2000.
103 Schroer, 2001.
104 See Evans and Boyte, 1992; and Futrell and Simi, 2004. Evans and Boyte intend
   the notion of 'free spaces' to apply to the creation of progressive, democratic
   communities. But as Polletta (1999, p. 7) has asked, 'is there any reason why free
   spaces do not play a role in right-wing movements' as well? Obviously not, as
   the concept is just as useful when applied to radical, regressive, right-wing white-
   power movement communities. Just as communal associations can become free
   spaces and breeding grounds for democratic change, they also can be breeding
   grounds for radical, right-wing, racist activism. The importance and role of 'free
   spaces' should not be assessed on the basis of a movement's political orientations
   and aims but rather on the radical reach of their goals. The more a movement's

goals diverge from mainstream ideologies, the more crucial free spaces become to enable members to develop collective identity and attract participants.

105 Pizzorno, 1986; Emirbayer, 1997.
106 Zeskind, 2009.
107 Lewis and Serbu, 1999.
108 Crothers, 2003.
109 Blee, 2002, p. 76; See also Feagin and Vera (2001).
110 Anti-Defamation League, 1998; Dobratz and Shanks-Meile, 2000, p. 25.

3

WHITELASH

Barack Obama's election to the U.S. Presidency in 2008 offered new optimism to those who embraced a progressive vision for a democratic multiracial society. A nation founded on white supremacist principles now supported a biracial political leader who rose to power promoting 'hope and change.' At the very least, this, our first moment, signaled to many Americans that the country had reached a decisive turning point in the long fight for civil rights. But we remained a deeply racialized society. Extreme white supremacists expressed their outrage in online chats and gatherings denouncing racial inclusion and calling for violence to combat what they described as white genocide. Though exasperated that they seemed further than ever from meeting their racist goals, they continued to support a robust white supremacist culture that thrived in what we have called a hidden and not so hidden 'infrastructure of hate.'[1] In these spaces, white supremacists experimented with and refined efforts to sustain their networks until opportunities emerged that allowed them to enact their desire to reshape the United States.

This chapter explains the multiple factors that fueled the whitelash or what African American Studies professor Carol Anderson describes as 'white rage' in the period between Obama's election and the 2017 assault on Charlottesville, from an empowered militia movement to the strategic use of 'lone actor' violence, the rising social media culture, and Trump's incendiary presidential bid.[2] We also analyze how the Ferguson, Missouri, protests during Obama's second term launched Black Lives Matter (BLM) into the national spotlight, energized a broad movement for racial justice, and simultaneously drew far-right extremism more squarely into the public eye.

Across these changes, we reveal the practices, ideas, and emotions that underlay what otherwise might appear disjointed, local, and historically

DOI: 10.4324/9781003322337-3

specific outbursts of white racial extremism. As we pointed out in Chapter 1, certain issues and events function as points of attraction and acceleration that different factions draw from to reduce the distance between ordinary and extreme white supremacy.[3] The Ferguson protests and riots over the police shooting of an unarmed Black man served as one of those events. The ideas and emotions that circulated through mainstream and alternative social media platforms helped galvanize the white supremacist response to BLM protests in Ferguson and beyond. A similar convergence of ideas and emotions circulated via social media which facilitated the organization of the other two moments as we will explore in Chapters 4 and 5: the two-day Unite the Right event in Charlottesville, Virginia, and the January 6th insurrection in our nation's capital. In each moment, extreme white supremacists revitalized their networks and tried to win back political power they felt was rightfully theirs.

Chapter 2 described a strategy of withdrawal among extremist white supremacists during the 1980s, which relied on different types of cultural practices to sustain their core ideas and emotions. But extremist white supremacists also grew their networks by helping organize anti-government, paramilitary militias across the United States during the 1990s while also relying on early versions of the Internet to organize offline and online spaces. In the chapter, we show how age-old offline, in-person practices, like storytelling and the spread of disinformation, became the drivers for extremist white supremacy going viral in the 21st century. Social media allowed extremists to reach broader audiences and intermingle with 'normies' to radicalize some in the mainstream. Racial extremists relied on a virtual buffet of platforms, from video hosting sites to peer-to-peer messaging. But extremism's surge into the broader culture involved more than social media. Major media conglomerates like Fox News played an outsized role as a conveyor belt serving up a consistent stream of white grievance and resentment. For years, the Fox strategy paid off in ratings and, in 2016, helped elect the most openly racist presidential candidate since Alabama segregationist George Wallace's 1968 bid for the White House.

Post-racial?

Barack Obama's election in 2008 appeared to mark a fundamental turning point in U.S. race relations. Decades after the Civil Rights Movement, the Black Power Movement, and new policies aimed at racial inclusion, a Black person stepped into the White House proclaiming hope for a more equitable society. The election result galvanized emotions for those who imagined that it marked a move into a post-racial world in which racial tensions would simply fade as a societal problem. But reality did not live up to fantasy. Race remained a potent and divisive force. The election also galvanized racist ideas and emotions, leading more people toward an expanding far-right constellation. The nation's politics became more polarized over racial issues than they had been in several decades, even while the President tried to neutralize race as a political factor. As political scientist Michael Tesler points out, an era imagined as post-racial turned into the 'most-racial,' as racial tensions intensified and infected U.S. politics and culture more deeply.[4]

Like other observers tracking domestic terrorism, we were deeply worried about the hopeful post-racial narrative because it seemed to distract attention from the long-term pattern of far-right extremism. The ground-level reality of white supremacy's persistence, combined with growing economic tensions from the Great Recession, and indicators of rising fascism, nativism, and authoritarianism worldwide clearly demonstrated that the post-racial hope was an illusion. The Birther Movement that emerged during Obama's campaign provided an opportunity for an amalgam of U.S. far-right extremists to rally around a racist cause that was cloaked under thinly veiled questions about Obama's citizenship and legitimacy to serve as president. Inflamed by rumors floating around since 2004 about Obama's birthplace, Donald Trump and other Birthers claimed the President's birth certificate was a forgery and his actual birthplace was Kenya.[5] And the vitriol stirred up among white supremacists led the U.S. Secret Service to provide Obama a security detail earlier than any other presidential candidate in history due to crowd sizes and because, as they said, 'Mr. Obama's African-American heritage is a cause for very violent . . . hated reactions among some people.'[6]

White supremacist extremists were both angry and fearful about Obama's ascendance to the White House, and his election ignited familiar extremist practices, ideas, and emotions. Fury, violence, and interest in racist ideology ramped up in the hours and days after the election. On the election night in 2008, the world's largest (at the time) white supremacist web forum Stormfront lit up with posts that expressed fantastical visions of violence to combat 'white racial genocide' and 'negro rule.'[7] The Stormfront platform crashed from the surge of users who rushed to vent their rage, resentment, and disbelief.[8] Scholars of the far-right, Anton Tőrnberg and Petter Tőrnberg, found that 'Many users [took] this one step further, framing the election as the end of the White race – either through 'race mixing' or through replacement and suppression/subjugation.'[9] Stormfront users also imagined Obama as an economic threat, variously portraying him

> as a 'Jewish socialist,' a 'liberal socialist Muslim,' and perhaps most commonly, a 'cultural Marxist.' Along these lines, users describe how Obama's 'Semitic communism' with 'socialized medicine,' 'redistributed wealth,' 'taxation of the rich,' and increased governmental regulation will lead to economic stagnation.[10]

Despite these frustrations, white supremacists also saw opportunity following Obama's election. They imagined that as society descended into chaos, a growing number of whites would experience a racial awareness 'wakeup call.' White supremacists believed this newfound consciousness would catalyze action, draw even more people to embrace extremist white supremacy, and, ultimately, provide the means to successfully fight a race war. Some advocated to expand their free spaces where growing numbers could migrate and gather in communities to model white supremacist rule. During Obama's first term, white supremacists in Kalispell, Montana, created a racist enclave they dubbed 'Pioneer Little Europe.'[11] More commonly, white supremacists embraced ideas about mobilizing and fighting within the system by infiltrating the Republican Party or starting a new white nationalist party that would promote racist extremism from below. White supremacists also continued to push infiltration strategies to secure themselves respectable positions in schools, finance, business, electoral politics, military, and law enforcement. The infiltration approach extended long-established mainstreaming efforts to normalize racist and antisemitic attitudes and appeal to more moderate conservative White people.

Populist fury targets the federal government

A growing populist fury sparked by Obama's election extended directly into electoral politics through the insurgent Tea Party factions that emerged to the right of the GOP over their dissatisfaction with Republican conservatism. Early national Tea Party leaders railed against deficit spending and the national debt, but local Tea Party groups drew on traditional sources of conservative commitment, including religious faith, racial resentment, and status insecurity.[12] Following a vast Tax Day protest in 2009, more than 1,000 grassroots groups mobilized, and the 2010 mid-term elections swung hard to the right. The Tea Party's demographics were predominantly White, and their power was anchored in the combination of a grassroots base and national network.[13] Local Tea Party activism was amplified by far-right monied interests, especially the billionaire Koch brothers and Fox News and elected officials, such as the founder of the U.S. House of Representative's Tea Party Caucus Michele Bachmann.[14] Although Sarah Palin's ascendance to the national stage happened when John McCain selected her as his 2008 running mate, she became a Tea Party favorite giving the keynote speech at the 2010 Tea Party National Convention. In many respects, Palin was 'Trump' before Trump, helped to popularize a post-truth approach to politics and stoking racial fears and resentment.[15] During her time as Alaska Governor, she proudly and defiantly stated that she had no intention of hiring any minority staffers.[16] Though there were early indications of turbulence on the right before 2008, few imagined the scale of the 2010 electoral victories, how this moment would catalyze a decade-long conservative battle against Democrats, and the opportunities created for Donald Trump to eventually take the presidency without winning the popular vote.[17]

The Tea Party's anti-government rage followed a long-established script based on New World Order conspiracies that animated right-wing fringes since the John Birchers emerged in the late-1950s. Far-right media pundits like Glenn Beck and Alex Jones and figures associated with the Christian Right like Pat Robertson painted a dark vision that Obama's election signaled a catastrophic shift for the country that would upend U.S. sovereignty, leading to a godless, one-world dictatorship dominated by the U.N. and its secret global cabal. The psychoanalyst David Lotto locates Tea Party indignation in the common 'paranoid style of American politics' that directs animus, fear, and bizarre beliefs at enemies that they blame for the dire threats they perceive.[18]

President Obama was a primary target for Tea Party members' conspiratorial anxieties, and racial resentment was a prime motivation. While Tea Party members typically disavowed charges that their activism was grounded in racial prejudice, their actions tell a different story. At Tea Party events across the country, attendees displayed signs with racial caricatures of President Obama and racist slogans such as: *Obama-nomics – Monkey See, Monkey Spend*; *A Village in Kenya is Missing its Idiot: Deport Obama!*; along with Confederate battle flags and other racist symbols.[19] They also paraded reverse-racism slogans on signs such as *Obama's Plan, White Slavery* that evoked Reconstruction-Era fears related to white victimization. Other signs associated Obama with fascism (e.g., *Obamacare and Obama Fascism* along with a swastika). Far-right scholars Devin Burghart and Leonard Zeskind note that some Tea Party organizers sponsored people of color 'as speakers or entertainers at Tea Party rallies as if to say: look, this is a racially diverse movement that wants to add more color to its ranks.'[20] But in reality, Tea Party leaders provided a platform for racists and antisemites to mask their bigotry in anti-government rhetoric.

Tea Party leaders also framed Obama's election as a terrifying symbol marking White voters' waning political dominance in the United States. Demographic changes catalyzed rhetoric that is now widely known as the 'great replacement.' Tea Party leaders particularly focused on the projections that in 2011, for the first time, non-Hispanic White people would total less than half of all births, and that by 2043 non-Hispanic White people would fall below 50% of the population. Tea Partiers asserted that their political control was slipping away, and they needed to 'take back' their country. Tea Party supporters carried strong out-group anxiety and a concern over the social and demographic changes in America.[21] As journalist Rick Perlstein observes, anti-government rage in the United States carries a racial component, because it imagines liberalism as an 'ideology that steals from hard-working, taxpaying Whites and gives the spoils to indolent, grasping blacks.'[22] Surveys uncovered both specific anti-Black racism among Tea Party supporters and more general hostility about status loss and policies perceived as helping the 'undeserving.'[23]

Tea Partiers embraced traditional sources of conservative commitment, including a combination of religious faith, racial resentment, and status insecurity, which drew in old-school anti-government, segregationist adherents, as well as previously unaffiliated and newly enraged White voters who perceived they were losing their country. As the political scientist Sidney Tarrow explains, 'Along with their conspiratorial views, Tea Party sympathizers displayed an alarming indifference to facts, a property that would expand in the Trumpist movement to which many of them transferred their loyalty after 2016.'[24]

Militias rising (again)

Even more hardline than the Tea Partiers, a second wave of the anti-government militias, or so-called Patriot Movement, emerged during the first years following Obama's 2008 election.

Militia networks that had grown rapidly but withdrew in the 1990s resurged again shortly after Obama's election as leaders ginned up worries about a new Black Democratic president. They predicted deepening state tyranny, gun confiscations, and martial law to send 'true' patriots to internment camps. According to anti-government groups, President Obama and other globalists had committed to undermining the Constitution and its freedoms to benefit a shadowy international cabal behind the 'New World Order.'

Reflecting the heated populist eruption, groups like the Three Percenters and the Oath Keepers defined a growing sector of racial extremist activity during Obama's presidency and became among the largest and most notorious militias in an already crowded field. Mike Vanderboegh, an Alabama gun rights activist and 1990s militia movement veteran, initially formulated the three percent concept in 2008. He drew inspiration from the inaccurate claim that only 3% of colonists took up arms against the British during the Revolutionary War. Three percenters imagine themselves as righteous Constitutional defenders against tyranny and, in turn, formed various three percent militias and other organizations across the country with ties to law enforcement and the U.S. military members.[25]

In 2009, Yale Law School graduate Stewart Rhodes founded the Oath Keepers, claiming its focus as a vigilant adherence to the Constitution. They describe their 'oath' as an obligation among military and law enforcement members to refuse any order that is unconstitutional, which includes orders to disarm U.S. citizens, impose martial law, or set up concentration camps in U.S. cities.[26] In practice, Oath Keepers simply justify taking the law into their own hands.[27] They promote, the SPLC warns, 'their own form of vigilantism by providing voluntary armed security, not affiliated with any law enforcement entity, at various protests and venues.'[28] Like the Three Percenters, Oath Keepers rely on enlisting law enforcement and active or formerly active-duty military to join their ranks.

Second-wave militias ostensibly focused on the federal government's encroaching power and the loss of individual sovereignty.[29] But like the first-wave militia movement in the early 1990s, anti-government and white supremacist extremism significantly overlapped. Consistent with a growing and, by this time, long-term strategy, various paramilitary groups communicated a 'race neutral' politics in their public-facing propaganda. But evidence shows that, behind the scenes, individual members frequently expressed sentiments consistent with white supremacist extremism.[30] As Shane Bauer's undercover investigation with a vigilante border militia group revealed, these individuals were anything but 'race neutral': they made racial/ethnic slurs and cheerfully discussed the possibility of shooting 'illegals.'[31] We observed many of the same sentiments in our own fieldwork with individuals who not only preferred terms like 'patriot' and 'constitutionalist' but, after some prodding, also eagerly described international Jewish conspiracies and the adverse consequences of *Brown v. Board of Education*, the Supreme Court case that ruled that racial segregation in schools was unconstitutional.[32]

Second wave militia members also claimed they were responding to federal overreach during Obama's administration. But they did not mobilize during George W. Bush's presidency, despite that administration's support for the Patriot Act, which many described as the greatest threat to civil liberties in recent history.[33] Instead, it was the election of our country's first Black president that spurred their reemergence. Some people consider that a coincidence, but we don't.

Warnings unheeded, violence rising

In the years following the September 11, 2001 attack, the government redirected nearly all resources for countering terrorism toward Islamic extremism.[34] However, as extremist white supremacy grew more visible, the U.S. Department of Homeland Security (DHS) issued an intelligence brief in 2009 warning police departments about domestic terrorism and identifying white supremacist and violent anti-government groups as important threats.[35] The DHS report represented a slight diversion from the government's narrowed focus on international terror, noting that 'rightwing extremists have capitalized on the election of the first African American president, and are focusing their efforts to recruit new members, mobilize existing supporters, and broaden their scope and appeal through propaganda.'[36]

DHS identified white supremacists, anti-government militias, and radical anti-abortionists as among the most likely to carry out violent terror based on racial, antisemitic, or anti-government resentments. The report also identified disgruntled veterans as potentially susceptible to far-right recruitment efforts; a concern borne out by the federal government's own data which showed that during the 1980s and 1990s, nearly one-third of far-right extremists who were indicted on federal terrorism-related charges had previously served in the U.S. military.[37] Veterans' weapons training and leadership also attracted the far-right, helping boost their violent capabilities. And the DHS report concluded that white supremacist lone actors posed the greatest domestic terror threat as their detachment from formalized groups decreased the odds that authorities could intervene before an attack.

As if on a macabre cue, just as the DHS report came to light, and a day after President Obama's inauguration, neo-Nazi Keith Luke killed two people and was on his way to a synagogue bingo hall to kill more when police apprehended him. During questioning, when asked if he had any problems with his victims, he replied 'Every [expletive] non-White is my problem.'[38] Luke's attack represented one incident among too many violent plots and attacks spinning out from energized extremist networks.[39]

Among the most notorious attacks was Wade Page's 2012 murders of six worshippers at a Sikh Temple in Oak Creek, Wisconsin. Page, a U.S. Army veteran, explained to one of the authors (Simi) that his indoctrination into extremist white supremacy began while he was stationed at Fort Bragg, NC.[40] Following his enlistment, Page worked with the neo-Nazi National Alliance and led several white power rock bands for a decade before he attacked the Temple. In 2014, Frazier Glenn Miller, a decorated Vietnam War veteran, attacked a Jewish Community Center just outside of Kansas City, killing two people. He celebrated with a Nazi salute and 'Sieg Heil' chant. The attack was a culminating act in his four-decade-long 'career' as a recognized white supremacist leader. Miller founded the White Patriot Party in 1985 as part of a paramilitary strategy and recruited from nearby North Carolina military bases like Fort Bragg and Camp Lejeune. His new self-styled militia traded in Klan robes for army fatigues but played off the same white supremacist practices, ideas, and emotions.

All too often, reports on violent lone actors paint them as deranged wackos who kill indiscriminately, rather than as people enmeshed in a constellation of practices, ideas, and emotions that they use to motivate and justify terrorist violence to defend white supremacy. People misunderstand single-actor violence because the white supremacist movement prefers to misdirect rather than to send a clear message by taking credit for related attacks. All too often, observers explain away white supremacist violence with oversimplified accounts of unpredictable loners who 'self-radicalized' online. But the violence is predictable in that we should expect extremists to act out, given the virulent and violent culture they cultivate on and offline. Many, if not most, violent far-right attacks do not appear to be directly connected to a named group, which tells us little about how those actor(s) formed their motivations and allegiances. But it does tell us something rarely acknowledged: the broader movement prefers that outsiders do not associate these attacks with the long-term strategy to intimidate and coerce perceived enemies, inspire additional violence, and sow divisions throughout society. This is the very point of the leaderless resistance and 'lone wolf' strategies we discussed in Chapter 2.

While some of these lone attackers, such as Page and Miller, had been enmeshed in white supremacist networks for decades, others are relative newcomers. For instance, in 2015, 21-year-old Dylann Roof murdered nine congregants in Emanuel American Methodist Episcopal Church, a historic Black church in Charleston, South Carolina. Armed with a nine-millimeter handgun, he walked into a Bible study meeting, prayed with church members, and then opened fire. He imagined that his attack would galvanize Whites to start the race war that he had learned about on the vast collection of web forums that he began exploring less than two years before the shooting.[41]

Maybe Roof's descent into racial extremism would have been moderated or even stopped if authorities acted on all the evidence pointing to a resurging far-right threat. And maybe the broader political and cultural ascendance might have been thwarted had government and civic institutions devoted the appropriate resources to combatting our country's oldest form of terrorism. But too many people dismissed the threat. Powerful congressional Republicans and right-wing media outlets attacked the DHS report, President Obama, and Democrats, claiming they had disrespected the U.S. military and veterans, while surveilling and silencing conservatives. DHS Secretary Janet Napolitano first defended the 2009 intelligence brief but then quickly withdrew it, apologized, and disbanded the DHS Extremism and Radicalization unit that produced the report. According to the lead DHS analyst Daryl Johnson, his team was slowly rendered inactive as the number of analysts devoted to non-Islamic domestic terrorism dwindled from six to zero in 2010.[42] The blowback hobbled any serious public discussion about the extremist threat and turned the assessment into another partisan spectacle. It also left many questions about how to address extremist threats unaddressed. All the while, violent right-wing extremism grew with little media interest or political discussion.

This dismissal was nothing new. Since 9/11, the Federal Bureau of Investigation had focused most of its attention on 'international terrorism' and officially deemphasized white supremacist violence. In terms of domestic threats, during the early 2000s, the FBI curiously listed 'eco-terrorism' as the top homegrown risk, even though their own data showed it posed minimal dangers compared to right-wing extremists.[43] In 2010, the FBI's intelligence assessment suggested that white supremacists declined between 2007 and 2009, but most analysts tracked sharp increases as Barack Obama's presidential campaign ramped up.[44] And without a receptive audience in the White House, leadership did not prioritize efforts to stop white-supremacist violence even as homegrown threats persisted.[45]

To only blame Republican resistance tells just a part of the story about the inattention, distraction, and willful ignorance that allowed right-wing extremism to grow. The Obama administration also disregarded these warning signs. As proposals to restrict firearms' access and impose weapons bans floated through Congress, weapons and ammunition sales skyrocketed. Extremists encouraged adherents to build their stockpiles, violent rhetoric increased, and some segments of law enforcement worried about potential violence, but little concrete action was taken.[46] Far-right networks continued to grow during Obama's first term. According to the SPLC, the number of 'patriot organizations' and 'hate groups' increased substantially between 2008 and 2012. This upward trend continued a steady decade-long annual increase going all the way back to 2000, with little effort to stop it.[47]

Racial conflict grows

The far-right resurgence gained even more traction during Obama's second term in the White House. Beginning in 2012, perceptions about the quality of U.S. race relations began a steep decline.[48] The Ferguson protests offer a singular episode epitomizing the growing polarization and narrowing distance between ordinary and extremist white supremacism.

While many recognize the Ferguson protests as a moment that energized the BLM movement, few acknowledge it as a critical moment for extremist white supremacist mobilization. On August 9, 2014, an unarmed Black teenager named Michael Brown was shot to death by a local police officer. Protests started the following day and continued until November 24, 2014, when a grand jury failed to indict Officer Darren Wilson for Brown's death. During the protests, a peaceful marcher was shot in the head, non-fatally, by the police, and Vox reported a police officer shouting to a crowd of protesters, 'Bring it you fucking animals, bring it.'[49] The table was set for a confrontation between mostly Black protesters and mostly White police officers in the small Missouri town just outside of St. Louis. Meanwhile, Brown's death sparked protests across the United States and a national debate over police violence.

Before Ferguson

Part of the Ferguson story began two years earlier on February 26, 2012, when Trayvon Martin's shooting death provided the original inspiration for the phrase 'Black Lives Matter' that grew as a viral Twitter hashtag during the protests in Ferguson. Martin, a 17-year-old Black male, was walking home in Sanford, Florida, from an evening trip to a nearby convenience store where he had searched for a Skittles candy snack when he encountered George Zimmerman, an armed 28-year-old White man affiliated with the neighborhood watch patrol. Zimmerman found Martin's appearance 'suspicious'; so he phoned a nonemergency police line to report the teenager. During the call, the dispatcher instructed Zimmerman to avoid approaching Martin, as Zimmerman, by his own admission, had been following the teen. The details about the confrontation between Zimmerman and Martin following the call are murky, but what is clear is that the confrontation ended with Zimmerman killing the unarmed Martin.

The incident understandably drew widespread condemnation since it served as an example of the nation's gun-obsessed culture and long history of racialized vigilantism that helped produce the 'stand your ground' law Zimmerman used to defend himself. The 2005 Florida statute removed the requirement to retreat when possible before using deadly force to defend yourself. The law reflected the high status that guns hold in the U.S. imagination and their substantial symbolic value as a source of power and freedom, as evidenced by the unnecessarily strict popular and judicial interpretations of the Second Amendment.[50] While guns may be ubiquitous in U.S. society, gun culture is racially and gender coded in important ways. Urban gun culture prominent among a segment of Black males is often associated with street gangs and criminality. Alternatively, suburban and rural gun culture, which is associated with White males, is often considered a normative expression of masculinity, recreation, and self-defense.[51]

Florida's new law represented just a part of the nation's lethal gun politics. The gun culture had blossomed into a multi-million-dollar market that far-right extremist networks used to build bridges into mainstream society.[52] Guns are more than tools for violence. They are also used to organize social occasions at shooting ranges and gun shows, where like-minded people intermingle, form friendships, talk politics, and imagine their future.[53] The ties between gun supporters and white supremacist extremists grew even closer as extensive online spaces helped them connect and expand the synergy between the two distinct but overlapping cultures.

Martin's shooting represented yet another awful moment in the long history of anti-Black violence.[54] Zimmerman's 2013 acquittal spurred new calls for racial justice, while underscoring the nation's racial divide. A 2013 Pew survey about the incident found that 60% of White people believed that race was receiving too much attention, while only 13% of Black people felt the same.[55] The difference in perception between Black and White individuals also meant greater opportunities for extremist white supremacy to frame issues in ways that might generate bridges to the mainstream White population. A large segment of Whites shared the feeling that the liberal media were using Martin's race as a weapon to advantage Black people and foment anti-White racism.[56] This feeling was good news for extremist white supremacists who understood the close connection between emotions and effective propaganda.

In turn, extremist white supremacists portrayed the Zimmerman trial as evidence of a broader anti-white agenda. Controversial racialized events play an important role in spreading white supremacist ideas and emotions. Images of 'thuggish' Black teens and assertions that Black people 'inject race' or 'play the race card' (as it was referred to during the 1995 O.J. Simpson murder trial) bolster existing stereotypes, polarize society, and provide concrete talking points for propaganda. Racial extremists manipulate these events to find points of convergence between the ideas and emotions circulating among extremists and the White mainstream,[57] a process aided by digital technologies that enable 'inter-ideological mingling'[58] on various social media platforms. As we discussed in the introductory chapter, extreme ideas and emotions spread in a viral fashion amplified through digital networks that reduced the distance between ideologically similar but socially disconnected adherents across the United States and even the globe.[59]

Ferguson erupts

Zimmerman's acquittal also inspired Alicia Garza's *Facebook* post, 'A Love Letter to Black People,' where she coined the phrase 'Black Lives Matter.'[60] And when Michael Brown was killed two years later and protests swept across Ferguson, BLM went from being a viral hashtag to an on-the-ground social movement with an international presence. BLM signaled a new 21st-century civil rights movement and a threat to white supremacy that drew swift response.[61] As the BLM movement grew, White backlash was almost immediate. Slogans like 'All Lives Matter,' 'White Lives Matter,' and 'Blue [police] Lives Matter' emerged in a tit-for-tat game that framed BLM as exclusionary, communist, and anti-White. The White Lives Matter slogan eventually morphed into a full-blown network developing an online and offline presence across the United States and the globe.[62] And, maybe more importantly, the term became yet another meme in the extremist white supremacist arsenal-easy to understand and easy to circulate.

BLM triggered the worst fears among a segment of Whites – that electing a Black president would shift expectations among the Black population and catalyze mass mobilization.[63] Concerns about a Black-led mass mobilization in the United States date back to fears of slave rebellions during the pre-Civil War Era and continued in the 20th century when the Federal Bureau of Investigation issued memoranda about the need to suppress the rise of a Black 'Messiah' in the Civil Rights Movement (or what J. Edgar Hoover referred to in the 1960s as 'hate-type organizations').[64]

BLM became a convenient new boogeyman that extremist white suprema-cists used to define their opponents and expand their support. They embraced an identity politics that asserted that Whites were just as likely as Blacks to experience racial discrimination, a claim that David Duke and others had been pushing since the 1980s.[65] As part of this propaganda effort, white supremacists created a house of mirrors where they asserted inaccuracies dis-guised as facts to draw conclusions that fit their racist ideas and emotions. For instance, they circulated images of physical assaults on White women to claim that interracial relationships with Black men can only end in vio-lence. The images convey their view that all interracial romantic relationships should be considered unnatural and their effort to stigmatize White women who breach these racial boundaries. They also claimed that White people face extinction and Jews and demonically possessed Democrats actively seek to replace the White population by 'flooding' the country with 'nonwhite' immigrants. Donald Trump tapped into these fictional but deep-felt conspira-cies during his 2016 presidential campaign.

Racial extremists also directly responded to the Ferguson protests. Mis-souri Ku Klux Klan members communicated threats of violence and allusions to lynching the 'chimps.' When the NAACP organized a 'Journey for Justice' march through Missouri during the protests, 200 counter-protesters met the NAACP marchers with Confederate flags, racial epithets, and a display of fried chicken, watermelon, and a 40-ounce beer bottle: gunfire shattered win-dows in a van traveling with the civil rights marchers. Public displays of overt racism escalated in the wake of Ferguson as racial extremists were primed to mobilize.

Standoffs: under-policing extremist white supremacy

At the same time national protests drew attention to an old problem of racist police violence, the far-right was instigating their own confrontations with law enforcement. Echoing the early 1990s' standoffs in Ruby Ridge, Idaho, and Waco, Texas, the federal government faced two volatile confrontations during Obama's second term in office – the Bundy Ranch standoff near Las Vegas, Nevada, and the Malheur Wildlife Refuge conflict in southeastern Oregon. In both instances, the mistakes at Ruby Ridge and Waco, 20 years earlier, made authorities hyper-sensitive about violence toward civilians dur-ing these moments. And certainly, the first Black President along with the first Black Attorney General found themselves walking a proverbial tight rope as they understood that any kind of misfire with either confrontation would help ignite an enormous controversy.[66] Yet, the contrast and discrep-ancy in the policing of these two standoffs as compared to Black-led social justice protests in Ferguson and in other parts of the country could not have been clearer.[67] Even when far-right extremists pointed loaded weapons at law enforcement, they managed to survive the confrontations without so much as a scratch and, in some instances, avoided punishment altogether.

In April 2014, just months before the protests in Ferguson erupted, an armed standoff between Bundy supporters and federal authorities captured national attention in the desert north of Las Vegas. A call-to-arms sent out on social media, dubbed Operation Mutual Aid, rallied anti-government adherents from across the United States. They traveled to the Bundy family ranch to confront Bureau of Land Management officers who planned to round up the family's cattle in response to patriarch Cliven Bundy owing more than $1 million in grazing fees and fines to the federal government. A heavily armed contingent conducted what SPLC described as a 'well-organized, military-type action that reflect[ed] the potential for violence from a much larger and more dangerous movement.'[68] Paramilitary snipers lined the upper-rim of the canyon in fortified positions, pointing weapons at the officers as the Bundy's supporters stood their ground and forced the agents to back down and avoid bloodshed. Extremists capitalized on the event by generating and distributing video footage of their 'victory' which went viral on social media platforms. And four years later when the judge dismissed the charges because federal prosecutors withheld evidence, authorities appeared to have squandered the chance to firmly impede reactionary armed paramilitaries mobilizing to resist laws that they consider unreasonable or unconstitutional.[69] Across the far-right constellation, the confrontation offered proof that domestic terrorism could be effective.[70]

The video footage of armed civilians pointing loaded weapons at federal agents with no repercussions also raised important questions about what would have happened if a crowd of armed Black protesters had tried the same tactics. The answer to that question became clear in Ferguson four months later when mostly unarmed and peaceful protesters were met with military-style counter insurgency vehicles and massive swarms of militarized police units.[71] White supremacy has always been more complicated than white sheets and hoods. And police departments, from the beginning, have been used to exercise white supremacist-inspired social control.[72] That did not end with the Civil Rights Act in 1964 or the election of the first Black president in 2008. Police killings of unarmed Blacks, the pervasive lack of accountability for police violence, and the militarized response to BLM protesters all underscored this truth. The under-policing that allowed far-right extremists to brandish weapons and even point them at law enforcement with few repercussions also underscored this truth.[73] Part of the discrepancy involves the perception of extremism: White people who flocked to the Bundy Ranch in T-shirts, jeans, and ball caps were seen as 'average Americans' despite being heavily armed and adhering to ideas and emotions long consistent with the extremist white supremacist constellation. People of color and their allies, on the other hand, who gather to demand social justice are often treated as 'un-American' and dangerous.[74]

Then, in early January 2016, just a year and half after the Nevada conflict, the Bundys led a cadre to the Malheur Wildlife Refuge in Harney County, in the rural high desert of southeastern Oregon. The armed band stormed the federal refuge and illegally occupied the property for 41 days, claiming to protest the re-incarceration of two ranchers convicted of arson for setting fires on federal lands. They drew national media attention and used it to promote ideas related to sovereign citizenship, stoke animosities toward liberal elites, and resist a so-called tyrannical government. On January 25, more than three weeks into the occupation, a two-car convoy left the refuge followed by state and federal law enforcement. Lavoy Finicum drove one of the convoy cars and led authorities on a high-speed chase during which he attempted to evade a roadblock. The police shot and killed Finicum after he allegedly refused to comply with police orders, yelled for the police to 'shoot him,' and appeared to reach for a gun holstered on his side. Extremists martyred Finicum as a folk hero, but his death demoralized the remaining occupiers, and on February 11th, they surrendered to law enforcement.[75]

Attempts to prosecute the occupiers resulted in a mixed bag. Some were acquitted of the most serious conspiracy charges, raising further questions about how differently the judicial system treats White far-right extremists compared with people of color. Even a clear-cut case of domestic terrorism produced an ambiguous outcome, which helped to further embolden the extreme right during the same year Donald Trump would be elected president.

Not everyone agrees with our analysis that links the Bundys and similar types of anti-government extremists to white supremacy. The Department of Homeland Security, for example, distinguishes between what they call racially motivated violent extremists (RMVEs) and anti-government/anti-authority violence extremists (AGAAVEs) suggesting substantial differences between groups like the KKK and Oath Keepers. Various scholars and non-governmental organizations who monitor extremism also suggest the same. As we argue throughout this book, we see such hard and fast distinctions as a mistake. While we agree that substantial variability characterizes the far right, we see many underlying similarities in practices, ideas, and emotions. And we think these similarities are crucial for understanding white supremacy as the defining feature of this constellation.

Government plays catch up

As extremist violence increased, authorities acknowledged, at least partially, that right-wing extremism was a serious national concern. In 2014, the first Black U.S. Attorney General Eric Holder restarted a committee on domestic terrorism first established following the 1995 Oklahoma City bombing but then shelved after 9/11 as the federal government shifted focus to international terrorism. Holder acknowledged that for too long, the federal government had narrowly focused on Islamist threats and had lost sight of the 'continued danger we face'[76] from right-wing extremists.

When Holder announced the committee restart, however, he highlighted two Islamic-extremist attacks – the deadly shooting at Fort Hood, Texas, and the Boston Marathon bombing – as illustrating homegrown terror's danger. Holder ignored white supremacist or anti-government extremists, willfully disregarding far-right domestic terror for threats inspired by global terror networks. Even so, Holder's decision was long overdue. Since 9/11, domestic terrorists had killed more people than Islamic-inspired militants[77] while each administration, including Obama's, continued to dismiss and ignore growing domestic threats.

Columnist Jamelle Bouie[78] interprets Holder's shift to address homegrown extremism more directly as an effort to wade into racist and anti-government trends in ways that President Obama would not: 'Obama has said less on race than any other president, and when he does speak, he tends to aim for broad inclusivity.' As Holder explained,

> There's a certain level of vehemence, it seems to me, that's directed at me, directed at the President. You know, people talking about taking their country back. . . . There's a certain racial component to this for some people. I don't think this is the thing that is a main driver, but for some there's a racial animus.[79]

Even Holder's quote minimized far-right dangers. Holder most certainly understood racial animus was, in fact, a main driver for much of the anti-Obama sentiment. And though he restarted federal efforts to address domestic extremism, Holder also left much more to be done. Long-term inattention, coupled with misunderstanding, created space for racial extremism to persist and grow.

A social media racial culture war

The growing racial divisions that punctuated the Obama Era were deeply intertwined with the social media landscape that emerged during these same years. The viral nature of social media radically transformed communication in a way that earlier versions of the Internet did not. Qualities associated with social media aligned closely with extremist white supremacists' efforts to expand networks, shape public narratives, and radicalize the mainstream. In turn, social media helped strengthen the convergence between ordinary and extremist white supremacy.

In the decade leading up to Ferguson, social media offered white supremacists new opportunities to shift public consciousness, and, by the time BLM emerged, scores were active on platforms pushing narratives about anti-Whiteness, multicultural threats, and what they called 'Black on White crime.'[80] One of the most important ways that white supremacists used social media to share their practices, ideas, and emotions came in the form of memes. Coined originally by the evolutionary biologist Richard Dawkins in 1976, a meme refers to an idea or behavior that spreads among individuals within culture.[81] In the digital realm, memes reflect more deliberate or intentional efforts to construct an idea so that it is more likely to spread among people (i.e., 'go viral').[82] Extremists use memes in subtle ways where the meaning may not be obvious to outsiders as well as in more obvious hard-hitting ways where little is left for the audience to decipher. As public policy scholar Joan Donovan and her colleagues argue, 'These communities had been having a profound impact on American society for decades-mainstreaming fringe ideas through the sharing of memes, trolling celebrities and journalists and politicians, and generally getting up to all sorts of planned mayhem.'[83]

Before Facebook and Twitter, extremist white supremacists created small indigenous social networking platforms, such as the 2005 Folkcom.com, launched by the Oregon-based, neo-Nazi Volksfront. Folkcom mimicked the leading mainstream platform at the time, MySpace, and quickly grew to 2,000 members. A year later, New Saxon emerged as another exclusive extremist white supremacist platform, and, in 2007, the neo-Nazi National Socialist Movement purchased it. Extremist white supremacists also mingled on mainstream platforms like Facebook and eventually Twitter, using strategies that helped them circulate their practices, ideas, and emotions to a wider audience. For years, racial extremists cultivated private, local efforts to 'win over' neighbors or co-workers by slyly nudging conversations in racist or antisemitic directions. Extremists on web forums like Stormfront discussed ways to shift their language like touting the term 'white nationalism' and promoting styles to sanitize and legitimate extremist white supremacism which, in turn, helped them exploit the new social media technology.[84]

The role of mega platforms

Extremist white supremacists used a combination of mainstream mega platforms like Facebook and Twitter and more fringe platforms like 4chan and Telegram that started to emerge. For example, David Duke joined Twitter in 2009 and began consistently posting in 2012, while Richard Spencer, the person who coined the phrase 'alt-right,' joined Twitter in 2011. By the end of Obama's second term, terrorism scholar J.M. Berger found that extremist white supremacists were outperforming ISIS on Twitter in a number of tweets posted.[85]

Large-scale mainstream platforms provided white supremacists opportunities for real-time social interaction, which amplified their efforts to spread ideas and emotions through online and offline networks. For example,

Facebook became a major site on which extremist white supremacy spread to new levels. The social networking platform's algorithmic patterns enabled extremism to spread across the platform. By 2010, we were able to personally identify various racial extremist-related Facebook and Twitter accounts where individuals relied on similar interactional practices and claims they used offline to strengthen and grow their networks. For instance, they communicated about highly personal narratives, posted local and national news stories that helped them frame White people as victims, and shared images depicting relevant themes (some subtle and some less so).

As sociologist Nikita Carney points out, studying the digital landscape 'illuminates the speed with which discourse evolves on social media, pointing to the instability and contestability of emerging signs.'[86] Online recruitment efforts mirrored longstanding offline tactics, but the technology's scale fundamentally altered relationships between actors and the extent of white supremacist ideas and emotions that could be circulated. Digital technology helped white supremacists accelerate and amplify those ideas and emotions in ways not possible with offline face-to-face communication.

By 2015, with the presidential campaigns in full swing, Facebook had become a haven for circulating conspiracy theories. While a segment of that disinformation came from foreign government interference, the largest portion was homegrown. Relatively innocuous sounding Facebook groups like 'Friends for Trump' spread propaganda about 'illegal immigration' and 'Black on White crime' with few constraints, attracting hundreds of thousands and sometimes millions of views. For example, we observed a post on Facebook from an account known as 'Females for TRUMP' that explained the dangers of immigration coupled with an image depicting an invasion coming toward the U.S. southern border. What the post did not mention, however, was that an earlier version of the very same image was used in overtly white supremacist circles for at least a decade before. Now that same image had migrated to a much larger networking medium where it could be exposed to millions without the explicit ties to extremist white supremacy. In fact, when we interviewed the person who posted the image, they claimed to have no idea about its white supremacist origin and meaning.[87] Extremist white supremacist ideas continued to seep into the mainstream, without the stigma to hold them back.

Extremist narratives circulated widely across large segments of the population. Its proponents included people who did not realize they were helping spread extremist white supremacy. Their practices, ideas, and emotions gained a level of exposure that had previously been unfathomable. As part of the white supremacist dumpster fire burning on the Facebook platform, an especially troubling *Reveal* investigation found scores of active duty and retired law enforcement personnel participating in hundreds of racist and misogynistic Facebook pages across the country.[88]

Facebook emphasizes connecting users[89] which led the social media platform to develop policies and strategies focused on directing individuals to different ideologically aligned political groups, including well-known terrorist organizations like the Ku Klux Klan. To fulfill its aggressive efforts to connect like-minded individuals, the platform automatically generates pages that do not already exist if there is a match for users with certain interests. According to a recent Tech Transparency Project report, Facebook's automated system even generated a page for 'PEN1 Death Squad,' a well-known violent white supremacist prison and street gang linked to dozens of murders.[90] Facebook automatically creates these pages when users list employment or other interests on their profile. In this instance, a user known as 'Adolph Thewhitenosereindeer' listed their employment as 'soldier' at 'Pen1 Death Squad,' which prompted Facebook's system to auto-generate a page for the deadly white supremacist gang. But the PEN1 page is just one example; as of June 2022, 37% of Facebook's internal list of extremist white supremacists known as 'dangerous individuals and organizations' retained a presence on the platform. Despite years of Facebook claiming to address this problem, it seems unwilling to stop promoting even the most overt expressions of white supremacy like PEN1 Death Squad. Is there any reason to believe that the platform would be willing to ferret out less obvious ones?

Disinformation as edutainment

In addition to utilizing existing social networking platforms, racial extremists developed new websites like the Daily Stormer, blogs like the Right Stuff, and podcasts like the Radical Agenda that relied on high-profile personalities to help circulate its practices, ideas, and emotions without being formally affiliated with any specific group. Alex Jones provides a horrifying case in point.

By 2011, Alex Jones had become one of the Internet's most popular agents of disinformation amassing a larger following online than the right-wing talk show hosts Glenn Beck and Rush Limbaugh combined.[91] Like Oklahoma City bomber, Timothy McVeigh, Jones's radicalization was influenced by the Waco siege, which occurred just 100 miles away from his home in Austin, Texas, while he was still attending high school. Shortly after the siege, Jones, like Tom Metzger years earlier, began hosting a public access television call-in show. He eventually gained popularity as an FM radio host until 1999, when the company fired him for his wild claims related to Waco. Almost immediately, Jones transitioned to an independent broadcast for InfoWars.com, which quickly gained syndication on over 100 radio stations. Following the September 11th, 2001, attacks, Jones endorsed conspiracies about 'controlled demolitions,' referring to the idea that the U.S. government organized the plot to bring down the Twin Towers. This led more than 70% of his stations to cancel their agreements. Undeterred, Jones continued to espouse a litany of conspiracy theories and, following Obama's 2008 election, to perpetuate the Birther lie along with the bizarre claim that both Obama and Hillary Clinton were literal demons who smelled like sulfur.[92]

During this time, Jones also became widely known for the idea that mass shootings were 'false flags' staged by the government to create panic and more easily deprive individuals of their constitutional protections. In 2012, when Adam Lanza massacred more than two dozen people, including 20 children between the ages of six and seven, at Sandy Hook Elementary School in Connecticut, Jones claimed the dead bodies and grieving parents were paid actors. As part of Jones' tirades, his comments were often antisemitic, anti-Muslim, anti-gay, anti-immigrant, and misogynistic. Jones became emblematic for tried-and-true anger aimed at demographic shifts and other social change but wrapped up in a new type of multimedia savvy. At times, his 'performances' seemed staged, but that made his hatred even more entertaining for many. For a portion of Jones' viewers, tuning in was like sitting ringside at a professional wrestling match. We know from studies that radicalization often unfolds in contexts otherwise organized or associated with fun (or what sociologists Gary Fine and Ugo Corte refer to as 'dark fun').[93]

Just three years after Sandy Hook, in 2015, Jones hosted candidate Donald Trump on his wildly popular Internet-based show *InfoWars*. Trump thanked Jones for his efforts and praised the avowed conspiracy theorist. The interview was arranged by Trump loyalist Roger Stone, who also befriended the Proud Boys during this time. The presidential nominee of a major U.S. political party appearing on a documented hate-monger's Internet show foreshadowed just how mainstream extremist white supremacy would ultimately become. The mainstreaming process continued to gain momentum and intensify in the years following Trump's 2016 election as extremists used social media to push untold volumes of white supremacist ideas, emotions, and disinformation that previously existed only on society's margins.

Finding niche markets

Mainstream social media platforms are only part of the story. Extremist white supremacy's digital landscape offers a buffet of toxic options for users to enjoy. In 2013, neo-Nazi Andrew Anglin founded the *Daily Stormer* site. The *Daily Stormer*, named after Nazi Germany's propaganda sheet, known as *Der Sturmer*, relied on an image-rich platform that mimicked a journalistic tabloid style that had grown increasingly popular among online publishing sources. Anglin coupled this journalistic style with new reporting that blatantly affirmed extreme racism and antisemitism.

Anglin was also steeped in an understanding of how to cloak vitriol in humor to 'soften' the hatred and help mainstream neo-Nazism. He and his colleagues even developed a 'Daily Stormer Style Guide' which provided a playbook for how to write articles so that you could promote ideas such as 'gassing the kikes' in a style that would be unclear to readers whether you were joking or serious. The 'unindoctrinated should not be able to tell if we are joking or not . . . The ultimate goal is to dehumanize the enemy, to the point where people are ready to laugh at their deaths.'[94] The Daily Stormer quickly grew in popularity, becoming the premiere website for neo-Nazism across the globe. By April 2017, just months before the deadly Unite the Right, its site traffic ranked as one of the top 14,000 websites in the world.[95]

But white supremacists also use large communication platforms like Discord to engage a broader segment of the population. For example, they relied on Discord to access the gamer subculture, a predominantly young White male subculture that had long been a space with a substantial presence of both ordinary and extremist white supremacy.[96] Discord offered secrecy, security, and various communication options such as private messaging and conference phone calls. Extremists used the platform as the primary base for organizing the deadly 2017 Unite the Right rally in Charlottesville, Virginia, and various other white supremacist actions.

During this time, a segment of white supremacists began gravitating to the semi-encrypted platform Telegram which was originally launched in 2013 by the brothers who previously founded the Russian social media site VK, popular among white supremacists. Telegram features 'channels' that offer users instant messaging, file-sharing services, and a 'hands off' approach to monitoring calls for violence on the platform. Previously a space where jihadi extremists congregated, in more recent years, white supremacists developed a substantial presence on Telegram. Their presence includes some of the most graphic, violent videos imaginable promoting racism, misogyny, and antisemitism.[97]

White supremacy also thrives on anonymous digital image boards known as 'chans,' which is shorthand for channels. Anonymous boards date back to the earliest Internet days, but beginning around 2011, two chan boards, 4chan and 8chan (now 8kun), gained notoriety for their extremist content. In 2011, 4chan created the anonymous imageboard '/pol/,' short for politically incorrect, meant as a space to discuss contemporary political issues. Right-wing extremists quickly took it over and turned it into a hotbed for white supremacist politics. 8chan came online in 2013 as a 'free speech friendly 4chan alternative' and attracted white supremacist activity as well as pedophiles posting child pornography. 8chan members actively promoted the Gamergate and eventually the QAnon conspiracies that we will discuss in the next chapter.

During the 2016 presidential election campaign, white supremacists on 4chan's pol board began appropriating the Internet meme, Pepe the Frog, which had originated a decade earlier as part of a nonpolitical comic.

The white supremacists on 4chan often used the platform as a launching pad to push memes into wider circulation as was the case with Pepe. From 4chan, Pepe appeared in Twitter posts and eventually became widely associated with white supremacists, including at Unite the Right in Charlottesville. As part of the meme battles raging during the 2016 presidential campaign, Donald Trump joined the fray and posted images of himself as Pepe.

4chan and 8chan may be most notorious for their association with terrorism when perpetrators post written manifestos explaining their worldview and the process for planning their attack, sometimes including live recordings of the attacks that are then shared and cross-posted to other platforms.[98] The manifestos and live recordings of the terror attacks provide endless fodder to create and circulate additional memes that either directly support the violence or transform the violence into ironic sources of comic relief. In turn, 'ironic jokes' provide their culture-plausible deniability as illustrated when the *Daily Stormer's* Robert Ray shared the following, '[humor] really keeps our opponents off balance, because they can't tell, they can never be certain, what things we're absolutely serious about, and what things we're joking about.'[99]

Extremist white supremacists treat these single-actor terrorists as celebrities on social media platforms where memes express their admiration for them. Those who are still alive like Dylann Roof are listed as 'Prisoners of War' (POWs), and adherents encourage each other to write them letters and send them money. Roof's 'bowlcut' became code for terror attack, and images of Roof sporting the haircut circulated widely on platforms like Telegram and Discord.[100]

Celebrating and humorizing terror help create a culture for future attacks. Using online narratives, extremist white supremacist recruiters essentially crowdsource individuals to carry out violent attacks. As former U.S. Attorney Barbara McQuade notes, they

> exploit a variety of popular social media platforms, smaller websites with targeted audiences, and encrypted chat applications [to] recruit new adherents, plan and rally support for in person actions, and disseminate materials that contribute to radicalization and mobilization to violence.[101]

Extremist white supremacists not only reached deep into the mainstream through social media platforms, but also utilized other digital platforms including Amazon, iTunes, and, most importantly, YouTube. Created in 2005, YouTube offers users opportunities to view videos but otherwise limits them to asynchronous engagement, aside from the comment section for each video posted. YouTube also allows individual content creators to construct channels by uploading videos with the goal of building a base of followers. On YouTube, extremist personalities and networks created a subterranean landscape of 'alternative' media outlets. They pushed propaganda to strategically reinvent and rebrand white supremacy and build their followers. Although YouTube has provided extremist white supremacists with an important resource to radicalize viewers, the process is not automatic. Some former extremists have discussed the role they believe YouTube played in their own radicalization[102] with algorithms that offer users automated recommendations for additional videos that can lead them down a rabbit hole filled with extremist content.[103] Viewers usually start with an interest in conspiratorial or antisemitic content. But YouTube seems to reinforce existing biases and may introduce increasingly extreme or radical material which, in turn, helps to create interactive videos and text chains of communication.[104]

Extremist white supremacists have long embraced digital technologies from the Internet's earliest electronic bulletin boards to today's complex, globally connected, ever-changing social media platforms. Sociologist Jesse Daniels describes white supremacists as 'innovation opportunists,'[105] who rely on the Internet to grow, transform, and preserve their knowledge and tactics. They cultivate networks while avoiding, ignoring, or thriving on confrontation with counter-movement opposition. These efforts are extended to create their own social media outlets when established outlets de-platform them.[106] And, as Daniels further explains, today's white supremacy is part of an emerging media ecosystem powered by algorithms which 'deliver search results for those who seek confirmation for racist notions and connect newcomers to like-minded racists' domestically and around the globe.[107]

The Trump effect and MAGA

The time between Obama's 2008 election and the deadly 2017 Unite the Right Rally cannot be understood without examining Donald Trump's rise to the White House as both symptom and cause of extremist white supremacy's continued expansion. As Donald Trump ramped up his presidential campaign in 2015, he capitalized on and invigorated extremists by promoting a litany of themes that closely aligned with white supremacist ideology. The Ferguson conflict and anti-government mobilizations, along with growing online extremism, demonstrated that white supremacy persisted and was primed for action. The protests and rioting in Ferguson drew national attention, as did similar events involving police violence in Baltimore and New York City. Part of the nation recoiled at the images of large groups of protestors, many of them Black, demanding justice. Far-right extremists with the aid of Fox News and other media framed BLM protests as an excuse to riot and loot; social media provided a tool to help generate and amplify anti-BLM narratives widely circulated as memes, video clips, and the like.

Trump's journey to the White House began less than a year after Ferguson with racial tensions swirling and a growing sense among White people that race relations had 'worsened' during Obama's presidency.[108] Trump announced his presidential candidacy by zeroing in on immigration, a long-standing extremist issue. He claimed that Mexico was sending people to the United States who were, among other things, 'rapists,'[109] although Trump offered one of his signature qualifications to an otherwise blatant racist trope by saying, 'Some I assume are good people.'[110] But his point was clear. Mexican immigrants are dangerous and undesirable, and the United States should have fewer, not more. It was an old idea long embedded in official U.S. immigration policy that White Anglo Saxon 'stock' is threatened when too many 'non-White' immigrants enter the country. But to hear a major party presidential candidate express these ideas so openly in 2015 was striking. Many pundits assumed that this rhetoric would be an automatic disqualifier. Trump and his team, however, correctly sensed that embers of racial resentment were burning among White people that they could stoke.

It wasn't the first time Trump had seized on an opportunity to promote explicit racism. Long before Twitter, Trump took out full-page ads in four major city newspapers including the *New York Times* demanding a return of the death penalty in response to the arrests made in the case of the rape of a White female jogger in Central Park, New York City. More than a decade before the Central Park case, Trump and his father Fred were the subject of a 1973 federal civil rights investigation for racial discrimination related to their real estate practices.[111] More recently, with Trump's 2011 address to the Conservative Political Action Conference, he became the face of the Birther Movement. Trump used birtherism to gain a political foothold, which along with reality television stardom gave him name recognition and conservative cultural capital. Trump's 2015 presidential campaign announcement signaled his willingness to make whitelash his campaign's central motif.

In turn, Trump's signature slogan 'Make America Great Again,' shortened as MAGA, came to represent a movement of mostly White voters angry at the government, fearful of demographic change, and anxious at losing status and privilege.[112] In the tradition of white supremacist strategies, MAGA removed Trump from any overt association with racial extremism. According to political scientists, Darren Davis and David Wilson, 'Make America Great Again was classic because it appealed to the anxieties of change and fanned racial resentment without any explicit reference to race.'[113]

But maybe more surprising, MAGA was not very coded and, in fact, encouraged overt racism, such as Trump's campaign promise to institute a 'Muslim ban' and his encouragement for followers to commit violence at multiple campaign rallies. MAGA also provided an opportunity for extremist white supremacists to operate in plain sight. We mean that quite literally, as when prominent white supremacists like Matthew Heimbach, co-founder of the neo-Nazi Traditionalist Worker's Party, who became one of the key organizers of the deadly UTR, attached himself to the Trump campaign. Other less prominent adherents were able to serve as volunteers for the Trump campaign.[114] Trump sent a crystal-clear signal about his racism when he brought on Steven Bannon as his campaign CEO. Bannon brought extremist white supremacist bona fides directly into presidential politics as co-founder of Breitbart News, an outlet he famously described as 'the platform for the [white supremacist] alt-right.'[115] In a more figurative sense, MAGA helped further legitimize white supremacy by its connection to a successful presidential campaign. As we describe in Chapter 5, MAGA provided an opportunity structure to help radicalize the Republican Party and a growing segment of the United States.

Extremist white supremacists were listening to Donald Trump's campaign. It is easy to imagine how those who held beliefs that earlier were stigmatized felt when a powerful major party presidential candidate embraced and expressed racist tropes and called for racist policies that supported white supremacist ideals. Trump had endorsed the very core of their worldview and now had a chance to win the Republican nomination and maybe even the general election. Empowered and emboldened, extremist white supremacists rallied to support Trump.

White supremacists had long wondered whether a national political candidate could successfully run a presidential campaign that openly advocated for White grievances and racial resentment. Many believed the two major political parties were equally corrupted by Jewish-dominated interests. Surely, a candidate who spoke the 'truth' would be shut down, they said. Other extremist white supremacists saw opportunities for a candidate who could figure out a way to finesse their messages, articulating them clearly enough to set them off from the typical political talking points, but not so over-the-top that the public would mark the person as a Nazi or Klansman. Extremist white supremacists know well that U.S. society was founded, in part, on the principles of white supremacy; they believe these principles still burn deep in the psyches of many, if not most, White people. According to them, years of brainwashing and fear of reprisals cause most White people to sit on the sidelines, uncomfortable with speaking their mind but secretly hoping someone will step forward.

Some extremist white supremacists had hoped for a political figure like Trump to push white grievances to a national audience and win office. When Trump unexpectedly won, MAGA provided the symbolic cover to push extremist practices, ideas, and emotions further into the national conversation. And since most only imagined 'white supremacy' as hooded Klansmen or swastika-tattooed neo-Nazis, white supremacist practices, ideas, and emotions could fester, grow, and encroach ever more on the mainstream. Trump's campaign added an element to an existing surge of extremist white supremacy not seen in recent U.S. history. A candidate from one of the two major political parties was vying for the White House who was willing to openly speak the language of white supremacy. As we describe in the next chapter, after Trump's election, extremist white supremacists increased their efforts to seize public spaces while doing so with a new optics that had been developing for decades.

Notes

1 Simi and Futrell, 2015.
2 Anderson, 2016. Anderson argues white rage involves heightened levels of anger and resentment and is a consistent and pervasive feature throughout US history but most forcefully manifests in response to periods of progress among Black people. Similarly, the term 'backlash' has a long history of usage, but in terms of popular awareness, whitelash seems mostly closely tied to CNN political commentator Van Jones who, on the evening of the 2016 presidential election, with Trump's victory in sight, was visibly shaken and described the election outcome as a 'whitelash.' By whitelash, Jones was referring to the role racial resentment played among the mainly White voters who supported Trump's 2016 campaign.
3 Simi, 2010.
4 Tesler, 2016.
5 Barbaro, 2016.
6 CNN, 2007.
7 Törnberg and Törnberg, 2021.
8 Ibid, 2021.
9 Ibid, 2021, p. 294.
10 Ibid, 2021, p. 294.
11 Blee, interview, 2017.
12 Tarrow, 2021; Skocpol and Williamson, 2016.
13 Tarrow, 2021.
14 Williamson, Skocpol, and Coggin, 2011; Fetner and King, 2014.
15 Elliott, 2022; Taddonio, 2020.
16 Blumenthal, 2008.
17 Greenberg, 2019.
18 Lotto, 2016, p. 159; Rosenthal and Trost, 2012; Sharpe, 2010.
19 Quraishi, 2010; Barreto, Cooper, Gonzalez, Parker, and Towler, 2011; Spellman, 2009; PBS, 2010; Maxwell, 2016; Lieb, 2010; McCord, 2010.
20 Burghart and Zeskind, 2020, p. 57; Taylor and Bernstein, 2019.
21 Burghart and Zeskind, 2020.
22 Perlstein, 2013.
23 Tope, Pickett, and Chiricos, 2015; McVeigh, 2014.
24 Tarrow, 2021, p. 161.
25 Beutel and Johnson, 2021.
26 Jackson, 2020.
27 Carless and Corey, 2019a.
28 Southern Poverty Law Center, n.d.-m.
29 Jackson, 2020.
30 Farrow, 2021.
31 Bauer, 2016. For important ethnographic studies of border militias, see Johnson (2021) and Shapira (2013).
32 Simi and Futrell, 2015.
33 Lynch, 2004.
34 Smith, 2011; Johnson, 2017.
35 Department of Homeland Security, 2009.

36 Ibid, 2009.
37 Simi, Bubolz, and Hardman, 2013.
38 Murdock, 2014.
39 Extremist violence continued throughout Obama's two terms. Between 2009 and 2015, lone-actor terrorists repeatedly carried out violent massacres, while street-level violence also continued apace (Potok, 2015; Simi and Futrell; Perliger, 2012). West Point's Combating Terrorism Center confirmed a dramatic rise in the number of right-wing extremist attacks and violent plots. Although violent attacks by homegrown right-wing extremists receive substantially less attention than violence by jihadist militants, domestic right-wing extremism is more frequent and more deadly (Bergen and Sterman, 2014; Bergen and Sterman, 2021).
40 Simi, personal fieldnotes.
41 As is often the case with key events, their inspiration is multidimensional. While Treyvon Martin's shooting death in 2012 helped catalyze a new phase of the civil rights movement, his death also spurred Dylann Roof, a then 17-year-old White male intermittently living in Columbia and Hopkins, South Carolina, to Google 'Black on White crime.' Roof's search led him to various extreme white supremacist web forums where he began a process that ended with his terror attack on a historic Black church in Charleston, South Carolina. The Google results exposed Roof to a buffet of white supremacist propaganda and social networks – even if those networks were primarily in the digital realm – while nurturing the idea that his actions could spark a race war. Less than a year after the Ferguson protests started, Roof committed his deadly attack on June 17, 2015. See Ghansah (2017).
42 Bergengruen and Hennigan, 2019.
43 German, 2019.
44 Ibid, 2019, p. 239.
45 Bergengruen and Hennigan, 2019.
46 Reitman, 2018.
47 Southern Poverty Law Center, 2012.
48 Gallup, n.d.
49 Lind, Lopez, Williams, and Taub, 2014.
50 Gibson, 1994.
51 Livingston, 2018.
52 Busse, 2021.
53 Shapira and Simon, 2018.
54 Racialized violence, especially the killing of unarmed Black people, has an extensive, tragic history in the United States. The Fugitive Slave Act and its expansive amendment in 1850 were designed to provide slaveholders with complete authority to capture and discipline with whatever means they saw fit any person who escaped bondage. Those means could include death by burning or any other method that would effectively communicate the consequences for running away. Long after the Emancipation Proclamation, unarmed Black people faced attacks by White mobs enforcing segregation codes in the former Confederacy as well as the northern, midwestern, and western states. Some mobs were indistinct from law enforcement, as civilians coordinated with officers or received little or no scrutiny from authorities. This was the case in the 1964 murder of three civil rights activists in Philadelphia, Mississippi, when members of the White Knights of the Ku Klux Klan and the Neshoba County Sheriff's Department coordinated to assassinate James Cheney, Michael Schwerner, and Andrew Goodman for registering Black people to vote. Two years later, the founding of the Black Panther Party for Self Defense (BPP) in 1966 marked a new phase in a longstanding effort among Black activists to demand an end to police brutality and extra-legal killings such as lynchings. The founding of the BPP also unleashed a torrent of government

violence aimed at squashing those the FBI deemed public enemy number one. The war on the Panthers culminated in the 1969 assassination of Chicago Panther leader Fred Hampton, who was executed while sleeping in his own apartment by members of the Chicago Police Department with the aid of a FBI confidential informant. The line between extremist and institutional white supremacist violence has always been hard to distinguish (O'Reilly, 1989).

55 Pew Research Center, 2013.
56 Ibid, 2013.
57 Bail, 2016.
58 Graham, 2016, p. 1.
59 Hsiao and Pfaff, 2022.
60 Cobb, 2016.
61 Della Porta, Lavizzari, and Reiter, 2022.
62 ADL Report, 2022f.
63 Geschwender, 1964.
64 O'Reilly, 1989.
65 Berbrier, 1998.
66 Our point here is not to criticize the cautious government response but rather point to the biased and selective nature of that cautiousness.
67 Wood, 2020.
68 Southern Poverty Law Center, 2014b.
69 There were multiple cases prosecuted by the federal government related to the Bundy Ranch standoff that did result in relatively severe penalties. We are not suggesting the court's decision was absent merit but rather focus on how the decision further amplified a perception on the far right.
70 Shortly after spending time at the Bundy Ranch, a romantic couple traveled to Las Vegas and murdered two police officers at a local pizza parlor, covering the bodies with a swastika and a Gadsden Flag, representing their anti-government views. Other related instances of radicalized action were fortunately thwarted. For example, a month after the Bundy standoff, Retired Army Colonel Harry Riley organized 'Operation American Spring,' an action designed to remove President Obama, along with various Congressional leaders, from office so they could be tried for treason. While Riley's plans did not come to fruition, these ideas foreshadowed the attempted insurrection at the nation's capital seven years later.
71 We recognize that some of the Ferguson protests were violent and included substantial rioting and looting.
72 Cunningham, 2022; Ward, 2018.
73 Ibid, 2022; Ibid, 2018.
74 Reid and Craig, 2021.
75 Pogue, 2018.
76 Kindy, Horwitz, and Barrett, 2017.
77 Bergen and Sterman, 2021.
78 Bouie, 2014.
79 Grier, 2014.
80 Donovan, Dreyfuss and Friedberg, 2022.
81 Dawkins, 1976.
82 Donovan, Dreyfuss and Friedberg, 2022.
83 Ibid, 2022, pp. 4–5.
84 Berlet, 2001.
85 Berger, 2016a.
86 Carney, 2016, p. 182.
87 Personal interview.
88 Carless and Corey, 2019b.

89 Nix, 2022.
90 Ibid, 2022.
91 Southern Poverty Law Center, n.d.-a.
92 Southern Poverty Law Center, n.d.-a.
93 Fine and Corte, 2021; Blee, 2002; Simi and Futrell, 2015.
94 Blee and Simi, 2020, p. 42.
95 SPLC, n.d.-b.
96 ADL, 2022e.
97 Gais and Squire, 2021; Anti-Defamation League, 2019d.
98 Ware, 2020.
99 Brathovd, 2017.
100 Blee and Simi, 2020.
101 McQuade, 2022.
102 Gough, 2021.
103 See Chen et al. n.d for an important study that questions the overall impact of YouTube algorithm but still confirms the important role the platform plays in spreading extremism and disinformation.
104 See Pluegers-Peters, 2022; Anti-Defamation League, 2022g.
105 Daniels, 2018, p. 62; Donovan, Lewis, and Friedberg, 2018.
106 Donovan, Lewis, and Friedberg, 2018.
107 Daniels, 2018, p. 62.
108 Pew Research Center, 2013.
109 Gamboa, 2015.
110 Silva, 2019, p. 199.
111 Mahler and Eder, 2016.
112 McVeigh and Estep, 2019.
113 Lempinen, 2022; Davis and Wilson, 2022.
114 King, 2016.
115 Posner, 2016.

4

CHARLOTTESVILLE

In August 2017, hundreds of avowed racists invaded the small city of Charlottesville, Virginia, our second moment. They marched in tight formation, shouting the most offensive words in the English language. Some openly branished weapons, while others concealed them. Insignia on their clothing, signs, and bodies extolled white supremacy and slavery. Antisemitism was on full view with swastikas and chants of 'Jews will not replace us.'

The display of racial intimidation advertised as 'Unite the Right' (UTR) left a staggering toll of destruction. One white supremacist murdered a young woman in a vicious car attack. Others brutally beat scores of observers and counter-protesters, including college students on their own campus. Jewish congregants hid their Torah scrolls and slipped out the back door as extremists passing by shouted 'There's the synagogue' and 'Sieg Heil.' The long-standing call for 'race war' by proponents of extremist white supremacism had moved from slogan to bloody reality. Racist extremism had come out of hiding in full force.

UTR was the largest open demonstration of white supremacist extremism in this country since 30,000 robed Klansmen brazenly marched down the streets of the nation's capital in 1926.[1] To those watching around the world, 'Charlottesville' – as it came to be known – was shocking. It was also puzzling. How could this happen in a quiet college town, seemingly without warning? How did extremist organizers and protestors create the spectacle of raw, violent hatred on the streets and campus lawns of Charlottesville, and what did it mean?

History teaches that racial extremists come out of hiding when they are emboldened to do so. The Ku Klux Klan, long known for operating secretly and under the cover of darkness, boldly strutted in front of cameras and in

DOI: 10.4324/9781003322337-4

broad daylight in 1926 because it had enlisted millions of members and felt protected by friendly government officials. When racist extremists marched into Charlottesville nearly a century later, they too had a growing base of supporters and sensed a newfound openness to racist messages at the highest level of government. Crucial but less visible was the vast ecosystem of media and communications that gave white supremacist extremism a staggering reach into the homes and lives of average citizens.

Emerging from hiding

This chapter maps how white supremacist extremism came out of hiding in Unite the Right. External shifts made it possible for racial extremism to become more visible, while strategic decisions within the movement pushed some of its factions toward ever more violent expression. These set the stage for the explosive events of UTR. But a massive surge of extremists didn't just appear in Charlottesville. They were recruited in a carefully planned campaign that took advantage of a media and social media ecosystem cultivated to convey white supremacist practices, ideas, and emotions. Although Unite the Right lasted only two days, its effects reverberated into the next decade.

Opening the door

Whitelash against the Black Lives Matter (BLM) movement was one factor that opened the door to a more visible racist extremism. In the years leading up to Charlottesville, BLM formed chapters across the country and gained a level of support unusually strong for a movement focused on racial equity. Even 56% of the White population approved of BLM, compared to only 40% who had supported the civil rights movement in 1966.[2] BLM also was highly successful in drawing attention to the symbols of institutional racism that sprawled across the nation's landscape. Its efforts, including 1,700 protest events, were central to the removal of nearly 100 Confederate commemorations during this period.[3] Activists successfully pushed to have schools, roads, and hiking trails renamed; flags taken down; Confederate holidays no longer sanctioned; and Confederate flags removed from statehouses.[4]

BLM's growth and success unleashed considerable reaction from White citizens, especially when conservative media repeatedly broadcast images of looting and property damage associated with some of its protests.[5] White counter-protestors began to show up at BLM rallies, shouting that 'all lives matter' and 'White lives matter' and demanding harsher police treatment of suspects. This backlash extended to the campaign to remove Confederate symbols, resulting in clashes such as the May 2017 confrontation between 700 pro- and anti-monument forces in New Orleans over whether a statue of Confederate General Robert E. Lee should remain standing.[6]

The expansion of right-wing echo chambers also opened the door to extremist white supremacism by intensifying racial outrage among White people. These echo chambers resulted, in part, from geographic sorting, as finance, technology, and health care industries boomed in cities to which the young and educated flocked, while rural areas and smaller towns lost jobs and a viable economic future. In the overwhelmingly White, Christian, older, and less-educated populations of declining places, the complexities of global economic change were reduced to a simple tale of white victimization that reverberated in communities of the like-minded.[7] Similar echo chambers grew among consumers of right-wing media which pulsated with white resentment and rage. Fox News was a main contributor. Fox increased its viewers considerably from 2015 to 2017, as its commentators generated a steady stream of outrage against Muslims, immigrants, and people of color, which stoked fear and anger among White viewers.[8] Shortly after Trump's 2016 election, the incendiary Tucker Carlson was given his own show on Fox News, quickly reaching stardom as the voice of white grievance. The Fox echo chamber thrilled and expanded its audience by its march to the extreme, as Carlson dispensed such inflammatory nuggets as the warning that removing Confederate monuments signaled the onset of 'the destruction of America's delicate social fabric.'[9]

Surging white racial resentment in mainstream society facilitated the expansion of extremist white supremacism by blurring the distinction between extremist practices, ideas, and emotions and those circulating among ordinary Whites. As extremism started to seem, well, less extreme and less stigmatized, it appealed to a broader range of White persons. The prediction that the white population would soon be a minority in the United States took on an ominous cast as it was transformed into a white supremacist message that George Soros and other Jewish conspirators were intentionally encouraging immigration from Africa, Asia, and Latin America to destroy the future of white people in this country.[10] Similarly, broad anxieties about globalization and government overreach spread widely among Whites, becoming portals through which white supremacist propaganda that Jews controlled global society could be pumped.[11] And messages about the Confederacy refashioned nostalgia for antebellum southern society into a defense of white rights in the North and South, mirroring a long-standing tactic against minority populations, which dates back at least to Christian campaigns against Muslims in premodern Europe. A vivid and chilling example of nostalgic support for white domination was a call to supporters of the Confederacy to join Unite the Right:

> The defense of Confederate monuments is not only an issue for Southern-
> ers, it is one that impacts all White men and women in America. . . . The
> Confederate flag has also become a symbol of White resistance around

the world. . . . At Tours, the Reconquista, the Crusades, and at Vienna, our men answered the call to defend their Faith, Family, and Folk. In the modern age, young men are called to once again rise up in defense of all that they hold dear.[12]

In the lead up to Charlottesville, these and other extremist white supremacist messages flooded into online spaces,[13] especially those in which they could operate anonymously and covertly.[14] Online gaming was an especially successful arena, with about 10% of players in a survey a few years later reporting that they were exposed to extremist racist messages,[15] including, disturbingly, those playing children's games such as the very popular Roblox.[16] Social media was similarly inundated with extremist white supremacism. According to an outside investigation, by 2018, Twitter had more than 100,000 self-identified alt-right accounts in which 'overt white nationalists were extremely influential,' and 'white nationalist hashtags and websites were widely shared.' Racial conspiracy theories had become 'marbled into the network' of these Twitter accounts, broadcasting hostility to immigrants and people of color and encouraging trolling as a political tool.[17]

In addition to working through existing media and virtual communities, racial extremists expanded their own communication ecosystems in the years leading up to Charlottesville. The multimedia company *Red Ice* extended into Internet radio and television, hosting racist extremism and Holocaust-denying content, and covering events such as Richard Spencer's Holocaust-winking speech after Trump's election. *The Daily Shoah* (*shoah* is Hebrew for Holocaust) podcast premiered with hosts collectively named the 'death panel,' while the web-based *Daily Stormer* blasted headlines such as 'All Intelligent People in History Disliked the Jews' along with violent racist and antisemitic ideas, memes, and images. Moreover, *The Daily Stormer* was a pioneer in the transition from online to offline activism, rallying readers, known as the 'Stormer Troll Army' or 'Stormers,' to mount harassment campaigns and, starting in 2016, organizing in-person groups across the country to 'prepare for the coming race war.'[18]

Finally, Donald Trump also opened the door for a resurgence of extreme white supremacism. His campaign, election, and presidency lent legitimacy to racially extremist practices, ideas, and emotions that had been relegated to the political margin for decades. In the words of psychologists Steven Roberts and Michael Rizzo, Trump's barrage of racist slurs, ridicule, and conspiracy-laden attacks 'normalized racist behaviors and may have inspired others to view such behaviors as acceptable.'[19] He broadened the scope of those who merited attack to include transgendered persons, progressives (who he frequently labeled 'Marxists'), and those whom he characterized as violence-prone affiliates of an ill-defined group he termed 'antifa.' With reckless disregard for the consequences, Trump promoted the extremist idea that there was a yawning chasm between 'us' and 'them' and insisted that even seeking to reduce social inequality (later described as being 'woke') was not merely incorrect but also a dangerous idea that would only be espoused by enemies. As he declared in a national television appearance, 'political correctness is just absolutely killing us as a country.'[20]

Looking back, it might not be surprising that racist extremists would find Trump a natural ally. But at the time, it was as unusual for such groups to publicly engage with electoral politics as it was for mainstream politicians to publicly ally with racist extremists. With rare exceptions, such as David Duke's 1991 run for Governor of Louisiana or scattered efforts by Nazi candidates to compete for low-level offices, white supremacist extremists had mostly eschewed electoral politics since the heyday of the 1920s' Klan. But Trump was difficult to pass up. His audiences were packed with disaffected White supporters receptive to racially extreme ideas and practices, while his frequent efforts to stir up racial fury aligned with the emotional basis of white supremacism. His speeches echoed extremist ideas with a thin veneer of political respectability. White supremacists wielded antisemitism to attack mainstream media by, among many tactics, using the typographical echo mark (((()))) to indicate that a writer or reporter was Jewish and therefore connected to a global conspiracy to control information to undermine white power and is, by implication, an appropriate target for extremists. Trump's attacks on the mainstream press as an 'enemy' that was promoting 'fake news' conveniently overlapped and gave credibility to extremist assaults on mainstream media. Also, his presidential administration served as a portal through which extremist messages flowed to white audiences. Bridge figures such as Steve Bannon of *Breitbart News*, the anti-immigration zealot Stephen Miller, and the Hungarian far-right-connected Sebastian Gorka linked the Republican Party, especially Trump's MAGA movement, to practices, ideas, and emotions of extremism that were circulating in the United States and abroad.

Despite the clear advantages of siding with Trump, racist extremists initially were wary. Many worried that he might betray their cause; others regarded him as too chummy with Israel and Jews (including his son-in-law Jared Kushner). Although supporters of extremist white supremacism seemed to favor Trump more than any mainstream politician since George Wallace, their support was not overwhelming at first. Posts about Trump on the white supremacist forum Stormfront in 2016 never rose above 50% favorability, and posts on the Discord server that was used to organize Charlottesville rarely mentioned Trump, and then mostly negatively.[21] Yet, white supremacist concerns about Trump tended to be short-lived, muted by the marked synergies that racial extremists found in Trump and his MAGA movement around practices of brutality and division, divisive racial ideas, and emotional styles of belligerence and rage. That racist extremists vacillated in their assessment of Trump points to an aspect of white supremacism that is often overlooked – its adaptative and pragmatic nature. Although rigid dichotomies of us/them and White/non-White permeate extremist white supremacism, its specific understandings and strategies can be surprisingly flexible as they adapt to changing circumstances. Over the last century, racial extremist movements have maligned U.S. Catholics as a national enemy and later recruited Catholic members, both deplored and embraced rights for White women, and sought electoral office as well as tried to collapse the political system. To some observers, these opposite stances may seem paradoxical. But within extremist white supremacism, such apparent contradictions are inconsequential strategic adjustments necessary to secure white racial domination.

Visible violent extremism

Racial extremists' effort to broaden their appeal and hide in plain sight by rebranding themselves as moderate continued in the years before Charlottesville, with ideas modeled on European Identitarianism that, in public, emphasized white identity and the culture of Western civilization,[22] and a public style of smooth respectability meant to contrast with the thuggish practices and raw emotions of neo-Nazis and Klans.[23] As discussed previously, such distinctions were apparent, not real, differences, a front stage deception that hid the vicious racism and violent aspirations that operated in the backstage.[24]

Alongside a rebranded racial extremism, a more openly muscular and violent racism became increasingly visible in the years before Charlottesville, perhaps influenced by those European far-right groups that were promoting fighting in the streets.[25] As we noted earlier, a strength of white supremacist extremism, and a factor in its persistence across remarkably different economic, political, and social time periods in U.S. history, is its strategic flexibility. This flexibility is also evident in the varying emphases or currents of racial extremism that co-exist within the same time period. In the mid-2010s, white supremacist extremism offered both violent and moderate, both action-focused and quasi-intellectual forms of engagement. The currents in which Richard Spencer was involved are an example. Generally regarded as having coined the term 'alternative right' (from which 'alt-right' later emerged), Spencer previously had been a vocal advocate of rebranding racist extremism, although it didn't take much to decode how hollow his intentions were. To Spencer, image was everything. 'We have to look good,' he insisted, 'being part of something that is crazed or ugly or vicious or just stupid, no one is going to want to be a part of it.'[26] Yet, while he served as president of the National Policy Institute, a self-styled think tank whose mission included 'to elevate the consciousness of whites,'[27] Spencer co-authored a report that argued for white racial superiority in intelligence, a biological propensity to prefer one's own race, and other long-standing white supremacist fallacies.[28] His 'alt-right' facade of moderation was further punctured in 2014 when Spencer was arrested in Hungary for attending a racist gathering that violated the country's prohibition against expressions that injure the dignity of racial and other communities. It collapsed when a video caught him toasting the victor of the 2016 presidential election and giving a shout out to 'Hail Trump, hail our people, hail victory!' [in German, 'hail victory' is 'sieg heil'] in a crowd in which several presented fascist stiff-armed salutes. His extremism now fully out of hiding, Spencer then delivered a speech at a Texas university that proclaimed that America 'belongs to White men. Our bones are in the ground. We own it.'[29]

Other openly violent racist extremism appeared in the form of the paramilitary practices of race-focused militia, patriot groups, and gun enthusiasts; dangerous ideological currents from neo-Nazi satanism and antisemitic conspiratorialism; and the emotional power of a swaggering, intimidating style of hypermasculinity harnessed to racist ends. Some racist extremists shifted from race talk to actively preparing for race war. Like much that happens in a movement that draws from a consistent but evolving constellation of practices, ideas, and emotions, the turn from idle boasting to terrorist action followed the playbook of earlier extremist-instigated plans for catastrophic violence. Only decades earlier – well within the memory of some racist extremists who came to Charlottesville – The Covenant, the Sword and the Arm of the Lord (CSA), a paramilitary group steeped in the racist ideas of Christian Identity, transformed their Arkansas compound into a guerrilla training camp. Their ample supplies of weapons, ammunition, and explosives were used to attack several Jewish and gay-identified institutions and central to their unrealized plan to attack the Oklahoma City Federal Building a full decade before Timothy McVeigh planted a bomb that destroyed it. CSA also stockpiled massive quantities of potassium cyanide, allegedly intended to poison the water supply of several large cities. In the same period, persons associated with the neo-Nazi National Alliance engaged in bank robberies and shoot outs with police and designed a plan to bomb the main approach to Disney World. An affiliate of the white supremacist terrorist group 'The Order,' also known as The Silent Brotherhood (*Bruders Schweigen*), used a machine gun to assassinate the Jewish talk show host Alan Berg.[30]

The trajectory of UTR organizer Christopher Cantwell illustrates the escalating violent aspirations of white supremacist extremists in the time between Ferguson and Charlottesville. Raised in a prosperous area of Long Island, New York, Cantwell had an extensive history of arrests and incarcerations early in his life which might account for his deep animosity toward a government he described as 'a violent, evil monster.' For a brief time, he leaned toward electoral politics and announced his intention to run for the U.S.

Congress on the Libertarian Party ticket. When he was not able to garner the support needed to have his name on the ballot, he became fiercely and violently anti-government, urging others to 'kill government agents . . . until their jobs simply become so dangerous that they seek other lines of work.' By the time he began broadcasting the podcast *Radical Agenda* in 2015, Cantwell was visibly allied with racial extremism, appearing in public with Spencer and at a demonstration with the neo-Nazi National Socialist Movement (NSM), where he told a reporter that 'it's worthwhile for white people to organize for their interests.'[31]

New racist extremist groups with explicitly terroristic agendas also advanced the move toward preparing for race war, drawing from a white supremacist constellation whose core was essentially unchanged since the first Ku Klux Klan. The most notorious of these new terrorist groups was Atomwaffen Division (AWD), which emerged in 2015 from the Iron March Internet forum, a transnational network for neo-fascists that advocated accelerating the destruction of society by creating social chaos, including through violence. AWD's ideology was broadly based on Nazism, with a focus on the decentralized of genocidal violence as recounted in the book *Siege* by James Mason. In contrast to what it regarded as ineffective online extremism chatter, AWD announced itself in this way:

> We are very fanatical, ideological band of comrades who do both activism and militant training. Hand to hand, arms training, and various other forms of training. As for activism, we spread awareness in the real world through unconventional means. [keyboard warriorism is nothing to do with what we are.][32]

Another group that became more visible in this period was the Order of the Nine Angles (O9A), a neo-Nazi occult-based organization that originated in Britain, embraced Satanism, and expressed admiration for both Hitler and Osama Bin Laden. Ethan Melzer, who was connected to 09A, infiltrated the U.S. Army and sent sensitive details to members of 09A about his unit's planned deployment to Turkey, hoping to provoke a prolonged armed conflict in which U.S. soldiers would be killed.[33]

More regionally based hyper-violent racist groups also appeared during this time, such as the Rise Above Movement (RAM), a network of racist street fighters that drew from segments of the white power skinhead movement of Southern California but adopted a contemporary fitness-focused style influenced by European Identitarianism. RAM operated as a battle force on behalf of what they regard as a victimized white race.[34] Multiple murders were linked to AWD and multiple violent assaults to RAM members. Both had a presence at Charlottesville, and, although now defunct, each group spawned and inspired international and national networks.

Unite the right

Thus far, we have focused on the context – who and what made Charlottesville possible. Now we turn to *how* UTR happened, examining the dynamic flow of practices, ideas, and emotions[35] – some hidden and others in full view – that characterized its preludes, organizing steps, events, and aftermath.

Preludes

To many politicians, government terrorism-monitoring agencies, and media observers, UTR seemed to come out of nowhere, but there were foreshadows of how it would unfold. Particularly telling was a series of unusual alliances and moments of cooperation among the sometimes adversarial neo-Nazi, Confederate, and Klan currents of racist extremism, which hinted that unifying the right might be possible. Self-described 'alt-rightist' Spencer appeared at rallies with Klan members and neo-Nazis. A new group, Nationalist Front (NF), was created by the neo-Nazi NSM and the Traditionalist Worker Party (TWP). Soon after, the neo-Confederate League of the South (LoS) appeared with neo-Nazis at an April 2017 rally in Pikeville, Kentucky, a small town in the Appalachian Mountains. The Pikeville event prefigured another feature that would play out in Charlottesville – extreme white supremacists' efforts to reach out to Trump voters as a constituency likely to listen to their explicitly racist ideas, an example how the constellation of extremism circulated in mainstream audiences. Matthew Heimbach, a TWP leader and later a UTR organizer, described the county of Pikeville as being perfect for the rally, as it is '98.35% White and went over 80% for Trump in the recent elections,' continuing that

> 2016 was the year of the Great Meme War, but 2017 is when we begin taking back the streets. The White working class has been abandoned for decades and it is time they know they have an advocate in the White Nationalist movement.[36]

The month before the Pikeville rally, Elliott Kline – also later an organizer of UTR – broadcast the idea that

> we have moved into a new era in the Nazification of America. Normie Trump supporters are becoming racially aware and Jew wise. They are willing to stick up for themselves side by side with Nazis without being averse to violence.'[37]

It is difficult to imagine a clearer example of how extremist practices, ideas, and emotions can become packaged for mainstream consumption.

Escalating violence was another extremist practice that prefigured Charlottesville. Extremists at rallies in Sacramento and Anaheim, California, in 2016 stabbed multiple counter protestors. In 2017, they engaged in conflict in what became known as the 'Battle of Berkeley,' about which Spencer reflected that it was 'a day to remember because it reveals to us this new normal that we are living in . . . this world of politicized violence.'[38] Such open violence fed on itself. White supremacists basked in the publicity that violence attracted, which caused more racists to flock to the action. Some individuals known to be violent but not identifiably affiliated with extremist white supremacist groups, like Kyle 'Stickman' Chapman who was at Berkeley and reappeared at J6, became heroes whose aggressive provocations solidified a new racist style. It is little wonder that Andrew Anglin, the earlier-mentioned proprietor of the *Daily Stormer*, announced to his followers that the summer of 2017 would be known as the 'Summer of Hate.'[39]

In Charlottesville itself, a series of smaller racist events in 2017 established a template of action for UTR. In May, Spencer led a protest against the town's decision to remove a statue of Robert E. Lee from a downtown park, an event later dubbed 'Charlottesville 1.0.' Marchers sported the white polo shirts and khaki pants of the rebranded alt-right, held lit torches, and chanted 'White Lives Matter,' 'You Will Not Replace Us,' the German Nazi slogan 'Blood and Soil,' and what would echo later as yet another example of the adaptation of white supremacism, 'Russia is our friend.'[40] Extremists splashed news of the May march across their media, presenting it as a model of the needed unity of neo-Confederates and those worried about white racial genocide:

> We see where this is going. That is the reason why there were Northerners in attendance at that vigil last night in Lee Park. This is about wiping all of us out – all of us for being White. . . . This cultural genocide isn't going to end with monuments. It never does.[41]

A short time after the May event, a local racist activist, Jason Kessler, messaged Spencer with his ambitions for a violent confrontation to be known as 'Charlottesville 2; Unite the Right; Battle of Charlottesville'[42]:

> I think we need to have a Battle of Berkeley situation in Charlottesville. Bring in the alt-right, Proud Boys, Stickman, Damigo, Spencer and fight this shit out . . . They bring everything they've got and we do to [sic].[43]

As planning began for UTR, the Charlottesville council voted to rename Lee Park as Emancipation Park. A contingent of Proud Boys descended on the city, followed by a rally of 50 Klan members in July. All was set for a massive display of unified racial hate that would terrify its opponents and draw in its admirers. Charlottesville would also test the water for the future: how much extremist hate and violence could be enacted in full public view?

Organizing steps

We've argued that thinking of racial extremism as the set of people and groups that promote white supremacy is too narrow, as it neglects the less visible segments of its constellation of practices, ideas, and emotions. Yet, the actions of people and groups do reinforce and modify the constellation in particular times and places. For the most part, however, it is difficult to pinpoint precisely how actions are fashioned and carried out in white supremacism as the movement keeps its inner workings hidden, fearing exposure, infiltration, and prosecution. But we have unusual insight into the dynamics that led up to and exploded in Charlottesville because two of us (Blee and Simi) served as expert witnesses in *Sines v Kessler*, the federal civil lawsuit later brought against the UTR organizers. Communications among white supremacists intended to be secret were revealed as part of the court case, allowing us to reconstruct in detail how coordinated actions by white supremacists staged the bloody events at UTR.

UTR's early key players were Jason Kessler, a member of the Proud Boys and Charlottesville local known for espousing antisemitic conspiracy theories and for his racist attacks on the town's Black vice mayor, and the more prominent Richard Spencer. Some of the nation's most vicious white supremacists quickly joined the effort, bringing their specialties. Christopher Cantwell added anti-government and anti-police ideas along with a virulent antisemitism that is summarized in his comment that 'America will never be free until the last kike is strangled with the entrails of the last male Democrat.' Nathan Damigo, who founded Identity Evropa to appeal to college-aged students, gained notoriety for physically assaulting a female counter protester during the Battle of Berkeley. Elliott Kline, also from Identity Evropa, who used the name Eli Mosley to honor his hero, the notorious British fascist Oswald Mosley, referred to himself as a 'Judenjager,' a snide reference to a German Nazi 'Jew hunter' and called for the creation of a 'Jew-detecting app' to allow neo-Nazis to ferret out Jewish persons. Although he had mostly been involved in online racism, Kline talked of Charlottesville as an opportunity to go beyond: 'I came to the realization around the inauguration [presumably of President Trump] that we must take this from an online activist movement to a real-life activist movement. . . I decided that was my calling.'[44]

Other organizers included Robert 'Azzmador' Ray, who wrote for the *Daily Stormer* and had been involved with the 'Stormer Book Clubs,' the on-the-ground gatherings of white supremacists, a 'troll army' which he encouraged to engage in firearms training and 'prepare for the coming race war.'[45] Matthew Heimbach and Matthew Parrott, who espoused extreme antisemitism and Holocaust denial, cofounded the TWP to establish an independent white ethno-state in North America, and viewed Adolf Hitler as an inspiration, were also central actors. So were Michael Hill and Michael Tubbs from LoS. Hill, its founder, claimed that White people are endowed with a 'God-ordained superiority' and decried 'the perfidy of the organized Jew.'[46] Tubbs, his right-hand man, had a long history of racist violence, including robbing two African American soldiers at the Fort Bragg, North Carolina Army base in 1987 during which he and a partner yelled, 'This is for the KKK.' A subsequent investigation of Tubbs found five stockpiles of weapons, tapes of Hitler's speeches, and lists of targets including businesses owned by Jewish and Black people.[47] That Tubbs wasn't the first, or the last, white supremacist extremist to operate at Fort Bragg is a window into how white supremacist extremism persists over time. Frazier Glenn Miller, the notorious leader of a North Carolina Klan and White Patriot Party who we discussed in Chapter 3 and who later would murder three people he mistakenly assumed were Jewish, joined the Klan as an active-duty soldier at Fort Bragg and, according to court testimony, paid soldiers at the base to smuggle military weapons off the base in the mid-1980s. The year that Tubbs staged his racist robbery, Miller issued a 'Declaration of War' that called on his supporters to murder 'our enemies' and provided a point system for selecting targets. A decade later, Fort Bragg was back in the headlines for racist activity as three soldiers who were part of a cluster of nearly two dozen neo-Nazi skinheads were convicted in the killing of a Black couple.[48]

Media and online organizing

The organizers of Charlottesville did not belong to the same groups, nor did they even all know each other, before they started mobilizing for UTR. They didn't need to. Because white supremacist extremism operates as a constellation, they were interconnected through practices, ideas, and emotions that were spread through its media and online networks and employed these to recruit for Charlottesville. On white supremacist-friendly media and online platforms such as *Political Cesspool*, *Red Ice*, *Daily Stormer*, and Storm-front, they declared that the time had come for racist extremism to come out of hiding. The news traveled swiftly. A member of the Three Percenters, Virginia's anti-government militia, messaged the 'Mountaineers Against Antifa' Facebook group that 'I can assure you there will be beatings at the [UTR] August event. . . . That day we finish them all off.'[49] A post in the *Occidental Dissent* stressed the need to practice racist activism in the real world:

> It is fun to engage in troll storms, swarms and raids online. We should aim to demonstrate *how much more fun it is* to break taboos as a real[-]world movement with likeminded people. I can't emphasize enough the

importance of *practicing* your beliefs in public space. . . . As the movement rolls from place to place beyond Charlottesville, it will absorb new people who will come out and act on the beliefs they already hold in private.[50]

In June 2017, UTR organizers created the Charlottesville 2.0 server on the online Discord platform to mobilize attendees. Although Discord was initially used for online gaming, UTR organizers found it appealing as a mechanism for recruiting because of its secrecy and security features and because the platform, which tolerated extremist content, had already attracted a base of white supremacists.[51] Through their posts on the open server – and on a hidden leadership channel – UTR's organizers shaped how the event unfolded.[52]

White supremacism has long been successful in using what seems commonplace for extremist ends, as our earlier discussion of white power parenting suggests. The Charlottesville 2.0 server is another example. On the surface, it seemed set up for routine logistics, with subunits ('channels') for users to share information on such topics as carpooling, local laws, medical and legal assistance, and funders for those who needed assistance to attend.[53] But the discussion of logistics easily slid into more provocative talk. The channel *gear and attire* hosted discussions of wielding shields as offensive weapons, and *laws* offered legal guidance about carrying concealed weapons and attacking counter-protestors. On the *flags_banner_signs* channel, Discord users, including one using the Holocaust-themed name 'kristall.night,' demonstrated how to fashion a hidden weapon by fortifying a flag pole with an interior axe handle, with a helpful link to the Amazon site selling 36-inch ax/maul handles.[54] Users across Discord posted references to employing vehicles, from cars to tractors, to attack counter protesters, preparing and forecasting the car attack that killed a protestor at UTR. Even carpooling channels became venues for encouraging online racists to transition to offline collective action, as shown in a post by SCnazi encouraging riders to sign up for the 'Carolinas Hate Van' to 'buy us more time together. It's hard enough in our busy wage cucking lives to find quality time with each other, and this should be a particularly High Energy point in time to do it,' closing with 'Hail Victory'[55]

The sociologist Paul Lichterman argues that activist communities come together either around a sense of common identity or around plans for action.[56] Both strategies – forging a sense of a racist 'us' and directing what the group should do – were present in the Charlottesville Discord community. Users quickly formed a sense of common identity, as they swapped racist words, symbols, memes, and interpretations that have been the hallmark of white supremacist culture in the United States since the Civil War.[57] But a shared identity does not automatically make people interested in taking racist action, especially violent action. For that, people need to have specific types of understandings: that there is a catastrophic threat to the White race; that a definable group is behind the threat; that the threat needs to be stopped immediately; and that there are opportunities to stop it. These were exactly the messages that spiraled through the Discord server.

The Charlottesville Discord community was awash with posts on threats to the white race, especially the 'great replacement' theory – the idea that Jewish elites and their national and global coconspirators intentionally back policies such as unchecked immigration of people of color to extinguish the white race. On Discord and elsewhere, UTR's organizers pushed this idea of racial catastrophe. They urged White people to 'join us in Charlottesville' to

> send a message to the Jewish oligarchs and their hordes of minions that we will not go silently into the night as they desire – no, we will fight them, we will defeat them, and we will secure our people's destiny.[58]

Hill wrote,

> [W]e are compassed around with enemies who seek our destruction. From above, in the form of the international Jew and his white gentile traitor allies, to below, in the dark shape of the negro, Mestizo, and Muslim street thug, we are beset by those who despise us and all we hold dear. The time has come when white men of the West must put aside their petty differences and unite for our very survival and well-being.[59]

UTR's organizers and other Discord users targeted as enemies anyone who they viewed as being in league with Jewish conspirators. In addition to all those they regarded as not White, their enemy list included 'antifa,' 'commies,' 'race traitors,' and 'the left.' The focus on antifa was a shift from Ferguson – where BLM was the primary rallying cry and target – but represented a similar opportunity. In much the way that extremists might attack any counter-protestor – or anyone walking near a white supremacist event – for being a 'commie' or a 'Jew,' they could denounce anyone who advocated militant action, acted provocatively, displayed insignia associated with the left, or simply dressed in black as 'antifa.'[60] As a primary organizing document for Charlottesville put it, 'This rally, like the Battle of Berkeley, will be a chance to show the left in one of their central power hubs that they will no longer go unopposed like they are used to.'[61]

Previewing a shift that burst into public view in the J6 insurrection and underscoring how specific extremist strategies adapt to changing circumstances, the chatter on Discord more often lumped police into the category of antagonists of the white race than, as in Ferguson and anti-BLM protests, as a force to protect white people against militant Black protestors. This may seem surprising, given the long history of racism in law enforcement, but the highly dynamic relationship between white supremacism and law enforcement may be best illustrated by demonstrations with 'back the blue' signs that quickly turn against the police when law enforcement attempts to manage the protest. For many of those girding for the battle to come in Charlottesville, the police would not necessarily be allies.[62] One post declared that 'Cops are soldiers of ZOG'[63]; another elaborated how cops should be treated at UTR:

> Im [sic] not saying you should do the Antifa 'all cops are bastards chants' but doing the 'blue lives matter' chants and bootlicking is equally as bad. Cops are not our friends. Just act professional and respectful.[64]

Organizers openly promoted Charlottesville as an opportunity for a practice of violence, to fight the enemies of the white race and end the urgent threat they posed. Michael Hill of LoS tweeted 'if you want to defend the South and Western Civilization from the Jew and his dark-skinned allies, be at Charlottesville on 12 August.' Samantha Froelich, Elliott Kline's ex-girlfriend and former Identity Evropa member, testified that Kline announced that 'he couldn't wait to crush Jews' and 'he couldn't wait to stomp Jews.' Discord users took up the theme of urgency, with thousands of posts spreading the alarm that at UTR, 'we're fighting for the very survival of our race.'[65]

Perhaps the most striking feature of the Charlottesville 2.0 server was the escalating number of posts that glorified violence in text, photos, memes, jokes, and coy asides that gave not-so-subtle nods to Charlottesville as an opportunity for violent action. Heimbach encouraged his followers on Discord to support 'our POWs like Dylann Roof,'[66] the mass murderer of African American churchgoers. Other users tagged themselves with emojis of Roof's bowl cut hair and posted wishes that they could join in UTR, such as 'I'm headed down to free Dylann Roof and we are going to head to cville in a parade formation.'[67] Posts featured genocide-promoting cartoons of ovens for Jews and nooses for Black persons. Users shared photos of themselves dressed for a military-level assault and images of how counter-protestors could be mowed down with heavy agricultural machinery. And they recycled a mind-numbing litany of dehumanizing slurs against their targets, assigning a massive segment of the world's population to the category of noxious animals or nonhuman demons toward whom violence was permissible, encouraged, even required.[68] Not surprisingly, the culture of Discord was highly masculinist, infected with misogynistic memes that encouraged attacks on women, even white supremacist women, who were not sufficiently respectful toward men.[69]

The barrage of violent posts shaped a shared identity and interest in the Discord community around the notion of all fighting as one. Coded language was particularly effective in forging a culture of racist violence. Some codes were accessible to those with even a passing knowledge of white supremacist extremism, such as the pervasive allusions to 88 for 'Heil Hitler' [H is the eighth letter in the English alphabet] and 14 for the infamous slogan of the U.S. racist terrorist David Lane that signals the threat of genocide of the white race, 'We must secure the existence of our people and a future for white children.' Less common phrases appeared as well, such as the post at the onset of UTR that 'We're all earning our red laces this weekend,'[70] referring to a practice of allowing those who attack an enemy of the white race to wear red shoelaces. The post illustrates how adherents of white supremacist extremism simultaneously invoke and mock previous iterations of racial extremism (in this case, the racist skinhead culture of the 1980s and 1990s), thus creating touchpoints of continuity that help white supremacist extremist culture persist over time while adapting to current trends.

Extremists on the Discord platform posted countless examples of specific opportunities for engaging in violence, such as instructions on how to tape hands to deliver knockout punches or how to deploy mace as a weapon. Vendors stepped in too. The company, Resistance Tools, urged UTR attendees to buy weapons from 'fascist small businesses' like theirs. Their ad was a compact lesson in the strategies of Charlottesville: carry concealed weapons; load up on weapons that could injure and disable enemies while seeming to be 'self-defense stuff;' and remember that the goal – in the coded language of 14/88% – is race war and genocide[71]:

** FOR PEOPLE NOT CONCEALED CARRYING IN C'VILLE **
I sell stun guns, tasers, pepper spray, batons, and other self-defense stuff at www.resistancetools.com/. Use the coupon code ** UNITE THE RIGHT2017** at checkout and get **14/88%** off! Free shipping on orders of $35 or more. *Please help support fascist small businesses.

Momentum

Virtual communities seem to have their own momentum. One aspect of this momentum is that on sites that cluster people with a particular point of view or experience, people reinforce their similarities with each other, which further exacerbates tendencies toward group polarization.[72] Another aspect of momentum in virtual communities is that they tend to drift toward the most extreme expressions. As anyone who spends time on Facebook or Twitter will recognize, a single inflammatory post can change the direction of an entire conversation.[73] The Charlottesville 2.0 server is an example. It was strongly self-reinforcing at the same time as its conversational threads tended to follow – and thus precipitate – the most outlandish, brutal, and shocking posts, including ones that urged that Jewish persons be gassed, African Americans hung, and African children used as a shield during UTR confrontations.

Collective momentum affects individuals, as well as a virtual community, as we see in posts by 'Aaron' on the Vanguard American (VA) channel of the Charlottesville 2.0 server. Aaron's early posts showed excitement that UTR would allow neo-Nazis like him to make a stance in public. Two months out, and more infused with the extremism on Discord, Aaron predicted 'I'm expecting a full nazi party again. I missed the first one so we need to make sure this one is the cause of the race war.' His next posts mused about how thrilling it would be to wear a swastika in the open. But soon, presumably swayed by the expanding conversation on the server about the importance of optics at UTR, Aaron started posting instructions on how to disguise adherence to national socialism in the light of day and display full-on Nazism only under the cover of darkness. 'Bring your national socialist apparel in another bag' and 'Polos during the day. Swastika shorts at night.' Along with this shift in focus, he expressed an increasing interest in violence that he could enact on the streets of Charlottesville. On the eve of UTR, Aaron posted 'I am triggered tonight. I'd be surprised if I don't go full 14/88 on the 12th,' followed by the alarming post 'Daily reminder that nazis kill people daily. No days off, even on Christmas.' After this dramatic acceleration, his reaction to the death an activist at UTR might not be unexpected but is deeply chilling: 'My man ran over people and is still relaxing in a hotel? Respect.'[74]

The emotional appeal of spectacle and titillation, long part of the repertoire of white supremacist organizing,[75] was also key to the violent momentum that built in the UTR Discord community. For example, 'Dr. Ferguson,' who claimed to be a military veteran, wrote a series of posts in which he expressed that he would like to use the same tactics in Charlottesville that he thought were effective against BLM in Ferguson:

> I would like to bring my megaphone that can play mp3s. I used it when i was in ferguson to harass black lives matter and color the narrative to our favor. Of course i wont be using it while the speakers are speaking, but of course if/when violence erupts and we want to control the atmosphere with music i can blast shadilay or something we enjoy. I will be filming as well so i enjoy giving these moments a cinematic quality.

Racist insiders would understand the reference to Shadilay, a song from an Italian band that gained attention among white supremacists for its songwriter's pseudonym 'Manuele Pepe.' The name echoed the earlier-mentioned white power-appropriated meme Pepe the Frog, a symbol that also appeared at pro-Trump rallies. Dr. Ferguson's subsequent posts were more direct about his violent game-plan for Charlottesville: 'I can calm or enrage. Also give a certain cinematic spectacle to those watching at home' and, slightly rephrasing the 14 worlds of U.S. racist terrorist David Lane, 'I am about securing the existence of my people and a future for white children.'[76]

Although the UTR online community had significant internal momentum, organizers seeded conversations with timely interjections under their own names, such as Robert (Azzmador) Ray's 'I want to invest in race-specific bio-weapons and n***** [asteriks added] killing robots.'[77] However, they often employed double-speak to preserve plausible deniability against legal consequences. By ostensibly cautioning participants *against* violence, organizers were able to *encourage* it as they reminded attendees to 'bring your burner phones'[78] and to remember that they should *appear* to be nonviolent. They frequently used humor as a form of double-speak, with a seeming joke conveying a serious message. Their strategy of double-speak spilled into offline racist culture as well:

[Y]ou would ask if you've seen my friend Kyle. 'Did you see Kyle,' that was the joke, is that you're Sieg-Heiling in plain day. . . . [i]f someone were to call you out on it and say, 'Hey, that's – that's really disgusting ideology,' you can say, 'It's just a joke. We don't mean it,' even though you did.[79]

Events

Approximately 600 white supremacist extremists from 39 states invaded the town of Charlottesville in mid-August. Most were from nearby states, but some traveled from as far away as Alaska, Arizona, California, and Washington as well as South Africa, Canada, and Sweden. The organizers saw that their vision of drawing together a wide swath of extremist white supremacism had been realized, as neo-Nazis, Klan members, racist skinheads, neo-Confederates, adherents to Christian Identity and Odinism, and many more generic racist extremists arrived.[80]

UTR was unusual in being a multi-day racial extremist event. Friday the 11th of August was its first act, a nighttime march through the University of Virginia (UVA),[81] a campus designed by Thomas Jefferson and designated a UNESCO World Heritage Site.[82] Although organizers kept the Friday event secret from many who had descended on the city, hundreds of white supremacists moved unimpeded through the heart of the campus. The clean-cut men in white shirts wielding fire torches echoed images of KKK night riders and Nazi soldiers as they chanted 'You will not replace us' and 'Jews will not replace us,' giving an intimidating political performance that signaled the gloves were off.[83]

The marchers' aggression accelerated as they approached UVA's iconic statue of Thomas Jefferson. Screaming threats, they encircled the small group of students and counter protestors who surrounded the statue and attacked them with fists, boots, torches, and mace.[84] Afterward, Jason Kessler announced that 'what we accomplished on Friday night shook the rafters of the entire political establishment' and declared the torch march an 'incredible moment for white people who've had it up to here & aren't going to take it anymore.'[85]

Organizers similarly choreographed plans for Saturday's event: march to a rally at Lee Park to hear a roster of speakers advertised to include Spencer, Kessler, Cantwell, Heimbach, and Hill.[86] Although the rally was supposed to start at noon, militia members in camouflage with semiautomatic rifles and pistols arrived much earlier,[87] as did vans that delivered racist extremists to locations throughout the town. A fearsome column of helmeted LoS and TWP members sporting flagpoles and shields strutted down the main street in formation[88]; others paraded into town with taped fists, wielding PVC pipes and yelling about taking the country back. Threatening speech does not always end with aggressive action, but at UTR – as planned – extremists rapidly started violently assaulting counter-protestors and bystanders. A particularly gruesome beating of an African American man who was trapped in a downtown parking garage was just one of many brutal outcomes.[89]

The City had planned to separate extremists and counter-protestors by ushering them into separate quadrants of Lee Park. But the plan collapsed when white supremacists forced their way into the small park 'throwing punches, stabbing at the crowd with flagpoles, shoving people with shields.'[90] As its downtown spiraled into violent chaos, the City issued an emergency order just after 11:00 am to end the event and disperse all participants. Saturday would be a day of intimidation and violence, not of speeches.

After the disbursement order, Spencer, Kline, and other organizers returned to a more distant park that they had used earlier in the morning as a staging area, held a brief rally, and left.[91] Tragically, the violence that UTR organizers had fomented did not leave with them. Later that afternoon, as townspeople and counter-protestors milled around the downtown mall, a car deliberately barreled through the crowd in a tight alleyway at high speed, reversed, and drove through the crowd again, killing Heather Heyer, a local paralegal, and leaving many others injured. UTR organizers predictably denied any connection to James Fields, the driver, but photos showed him dressed in the recommended UTR attire and standing with members of Vanguard America. Earlier, he had shared images on Instagram of a car hitting protestors.[92]

In the days that followed, UTR organizers celebrated the bloody chaos they had engineered, including a helicopter crash that killed two state police officers who were monitoring the event. Far from expressing remorse, Kessler tweeted that 'Heather Heyer was a fat, disgusting Communist. Communists have killed 94 million. Looks like it was payback time.' Fields confided to his mother from jail that Heather Heyer's death 'doesn't fucking matter' because she was 'the enemy.' Kline told his girlfriend that UTR was a 'success overall' and that he was 'a fucking war hero.'[93] Following organizers' lead, Discord users also celebrated the violence in Charlottesville: '1 dead antifa supporter 2 dead cops 35 ppl injured International coverage. This is a failure how?'[94]

Aftermath

Despite organizers' predictions, the immediate effect of UTR was to undermine – not supercharge – the momentum of racist extremism. Spencer could only muster a handful of followers to return to Charlottesville in October to film themselves chanting slogans in Lee Park. An attempt to stage Charlottesville 3.0 in 2018 drew a tiny crowd, as did rallies in Tennessee, Florida, Massachusetts, and elsewhere. A year after UTR, Cantwell declared the movement 'a catastrophe' and 'leaderless.'[95]

Although racial extremism garnered massive publicity from UTR – and proved its supporters could form an angry and violent mob – the costs to the white supremacist movement were considerable. Organizers faced multiple civil suits from plaintiffs seeking damages for their injuries; several were ordered to pay large sums in the $26M judgment in *Sines v Kessler*. Platform and payment companies blocked UTR's organizers. Media and anti-racist activists exposed the organizers as racist extremists – and some as frauds – in part through the publication of a large trove of posts from the Charlottesville Discord server by the media collective Unicorn Riot.[96] Some extremists turned their attention to raising funds for those arrested for movement activities.[97] Others distanced themselves from the movement and UTR, even renaming their groups. Some claimed to have defected from the racial extremist movement altogether. Those remaining split over whether it should stage more public actions or retreat into covert organizing.

Unite the Right seemed to leave white supremacist extremism in organizational disarray. Despite their success in creating a vast online Discord community and attracting hundreds for a violent attack on Charlottesville, the movement appeared to be in retreat – shedding affiliates and splintering, its followers demoralized. Organizers who sought visibility at UTR slid out of sight. Support in the mainstream media vanished, and many politicians dissociated themselves. Racial extremism looked as if it had suffered a serious setback. But, once again, the collapse was more apparent than real.

In the wake of the carnage in Charlottesville, public opinion might have been expected to turn fully against extremist white supremacism.[98] That did not happen. When Trump made his infamous statement that 'there were very fine people on both sides' of the clashes in Charlottesville, many public officials and ordinary citizens rushed to disagree. But, in an eerie foreshadowing of how disinformation and polarization would shape views of the January 6 insurrection, it didn't last. Less than two weeks after Charlottesville, only a minority of those who identified as Republicans regarded white supremacists as responsible for the violence at UTR. This was especially true of men and those without a college education.[99] The window of opportunity for the nation to decidedly disavow racial extremism had slammed shut.

UTR was an inflection point. In almost no time after Charlottesville, extreme white supremacists resurfaced to take advantage of a quickly radicalizing White population and became a driving force in the country's growing polarization and acceptance of political violence. In the months and years that followed, the viral growth of extremist white supremacist practices, ideas, and emotions would become tragically evident, especially in the attack on the nation's capitol.

Notes

1 Gordon, 2017; Blee, 1991.
2 Setter, 2021. BLM had such deep infusion into popular culture that the Twitter hashtag #BlackLivesMatter was used nearly 12 million times (Ruffin II, 2015; Hillstrom, 2018).
3 Williamson, Trump and Einstein, 2018; Elephrame, n.d.
4 Southern Poverty Law Center, 2019; Elephrame, n.d.
5 Smolla, 2020. Property damage is especially influential in raising fears and stimulating political backlash and even violence by creating an image of protests as out of control and of cities as needing to be defended. See Nassauer (2019), Liberman (2020), Hillstrom (2018), Ruffin II (2015), Scheuerman (2021), Williamson, Trump, and Einstein (2018).
6 CBS News, 2017.
7 Goldman and Mutz, 2014. Of course we recognize that tales of white victimization are far from being limited to rural, less educated, and economically depressed areas and, as we show throughout our book, have an extensive presence across time and place in white supremacist extremism.
8 The Fox viewership was more than double the number who tuned into CNN (Otterson, 2017; SportsBusiness Daily, 2016; Walker and Forman-Katz, 2021).
9 The quotation from Tucker Carlson is in Confessore, 2022b; see also Confessore, 2002a, 2022c; Miller-Idriss, 2020.
10 Joffre, 2022; Reuters, 2023. An excellent account of how such rumors operate in ordinary society is found in Fine and Turner (2001).
11 Racial extremist messages were also directed to some progressives in the form of a racist environmentalism (later termed 'eco-fascism') that married ecological purity and racial purity and a revival of White Aryan Resistance leader Tom Metzger's 'third position' that combined anti-Semitic, anti-globalist, and anti-capitalist ideas (Berlet, 2016).
12 *Sines v. Kessler* plaintiff exhibit, 1827.
13 In particular, these were virtual communities with encrypted messaging and 'delete everywhere' features that made it difficult for authorities to monitor extremist content. Lawrence, Simhony-Philpott, and Stone, 2021.
14 Nagle, 2017; Blee, 2020.
15 Anti-Defamation League, 2019a. The survey asked respondents about messages that white people should dominate other identities, that there should be a 'whites-only' nation, and that 'white culture' is superior to different cultures.
16 Keierleber, 2021; Farivar, 2019.
17 Berger, 2018a, p. 7; Edison Hayden, 2021b; Wendling, 2018; Reid and Valasik, 2020.
18 Southern Poverty Law Center, n.d.-b; Squire and Gais, 2021.
19 Roberts and Rizzo, 2021.

20 CNN 1018; also Caesar, 2017; Conway, Repke, and Houck, 2017; Epstein, 2015; Weigel, 2016.
21 Törnberg and Törnberg, 2021.
22 Mylonas and Tudor, 2021.
23 Rebranding occurred in other areas of white supremacist extremism, such as the efforts of groups like the Keystone State Skinheads to present themselves as a working class movement to restrict immigration rather than a violent racist gang (Vysotsky and Madfis, 2014).
24 Eliasoph and Lichterman, 2003.
25 Aasland Ravndal, 2021; Blee and Simi, 2020.
26 Fox, 2013.
27 Southern Poverty Law Center, n.d.-q; Barrouquere, 2020.
28 Devlin and Spencer, 2016.
29 Woodrow Cox, 2016; Southern Poverty Law Center, 2017.
30 Ford, 2022; Southern Poverty Law Center, n.d.-l, n.d.-e; Huang, 2021; Southern Poverty Law Center, n.d.-d.
31 Southern Poverty Law Center, n.d.-d.
32 Southern Poverty Law Center, n.d.-c; Soufan Center, 2020.
33 US Department of Justice, 2022b; Neumeister, 2023.
34 Newhouse, 2021; Anti-Defamation League, 2018.
35 Paul Lichterman (2020) makes this point about political action more generally, as does Kent McClelland (2014), who notes the advantage of 'examining the ongoing flow of events.'
36 Post to *the Daily Stormer* website by Matthew Heimbach, February 9, 2017.
37 Southern Poverty Law Center, n.d.-h; Kline's remarks were on the website of the Daily Stormer, cited in Sheffield, 2017; also see 'Elliott Kline,' 2017.
38 'What Berkeley Means,' 2017; German, 2020.
39 Morlin, 2017; Squire, 2018.
40 McCausland, 2017; Smolla, 2020.
41 Wallace, 2017a.
42 *Sines v Kessler* plaintiff exhibit, 1455.
43 *Sines v Kessler* plaintiff exhibit, 8652.
44 Cott, 2018; Southern Poverty Law Center, n.d.-h.
45 Zaitchik, 2018; Southern Poverty Law Center, n.d.-b.
46 Southern Poverty Law Center, n.d.-j.
47 Southern Poverty Law Center, n.d.-k; *New York Times*, 1990.
48 New York Times, 1990; Broder, 1997; Belew, 2018; Keating and Assael, 2021; Southern Poverty Law Center, n.d.-g; *Chicago Tribune*, 1997.
49 Signer, 2020, p. 134.
50 Wallace, 2017b.
51 The activist group Unicorn Riot's website posted screenshots from the Charlottesville 2.0 server. [Our access to Discord through the legal case gave us the confidence in the accuracy of the Unicorn Riot release].
52 Kline cautioned on the private leadership channel that 'sharing information publicly from this discord or about this event or who is attending outside of closed circles or this discord will get you immediately banned from all future all right events' (Schiano, 2017a).
53 Schiano, 2017a, 2017b.
54 *Sines v. Kessler* plaintiff exhibit, 1060.
55 *Sines v. Kessler* plaintiff exhibit – SCnazi post.
56 Lichterman, 2020. The particular effectiveness of extremist virtual communities in fomenting conflict and violence may reflect the finding by Kent McClelland (2014) that solidarity increases the likelihood of engaging in conflict when solidarity is achieved at extreme positions.

57 Adams and Roscigno, 2005.
58 *Sines v. Kessler* plaintiff exhibit, 1827.
59 *Sines v. Kessler* plaintiff exhibit, 1554.
60 Also see Daniel Koehler's (2021) discussion of the long-time focus of far-rightists on anti-fascism.
61 Blee and Simi, 2020, p. 38.
62 Cunningham (2022) finds that law enforcement underestimated the danger posed by white supremacists and overestimated the danger posed by counter-protestors at UTR, leading police to respond passively during the event, even when police themselves were the target of their aggression.
63 Post on the Discord platform July 7, 2017.
64 Post on the Discord platform July 30, 2017.
65 Froelich deposition, p. 32; *Sines v Kessler* plaintiff exhibit, 2101; *Sines v Kessler* plaintiff exhibit, 1827; Post on the Discord platform August 7, 2017.
66 Deposition of Matthew Heimbach, cited in Blee and Simi, 2020, footnote 234.
67 Post on the Discord platform by Ignis Faatus, August 7, 2017.
68 In addition to egging on attacks directly, such vicious torrents can suppress the instinct to avoid engaging in violence and further engage users in extremism.
69 Post on the Discord platform by 卐 Heimdulf – VA 卐 June 30, 2017.
70 Post on the Discord platform by Stannismannis, August 11, 2017.
71 Post on the Discord platform, July 15, 2017.
72 Iandoli, Primario, and Zollo, 2021.
73 This also happens in the early times of mainstream activist groups: Blee, 2012.
74 Posts on the Discord platform by Aaron.
75 For the 1920s' Klan's use of spectacle and titillation, see Blee (1991).
76 Posts on the Discord platform by Dr. Ferguson.
77 *Sines v. Kessler* plaintiff exhibit, 0502.
78 *Daily Stormer* post by weev, July 31, 2017.
79 Samantha Froelich, former girlfriend of neo-Nazi Elliott Kline, provided sworn testimony in *Sines v. Kessler*, which peeled back the artifice of white supremacist joking by citing Kline's *Daily Stormer Style Guide*, an instruction manual for white supremacist writing. See Froelich Deposition; also Marantz, 2018.
80 Anti-Defamation League, 2019b, 2021d.
81 This was not the first time that UVA provided the setting for a national display of right-wing extremism. On October 7, 1948, Senator Strom Thurmond addressed a crowd gathered at UVA's Old Cabell Hall to renew his acceptance of the nomination to be the presidential candidate of the Dixiecrat Party, a third-party effort to defend the practice of racial segregation: Smolla, 2020.
82 Signer, 2020.
83 Women and children were cautioned against coming to what organizers predicted would be a violent event. On the power of political performance, see Taylor, Kimport, Van Dyke, and Anderson (2009).
84 Cunningham, 2022; Smolla, 2020.
85 *Sines v. Kessler* plaintiff exhibit, 2082.
86 *Sines v. Kessler* plaintiff exhibit, 348.
87 International Association of Chiefs of Police, 2017.
88 Smolla, 2020, p. 262.
89 Cunningham, 2022; Shapira, 2019.
90 Smolla, 2020, p. 259.
91 Smolla, 2020.
92 Andone and Dolan, 2018.
93 *Sines v. Kessler* plaintiff exhibit, 1448; *Sines v. Kessler* plaintiff exhibit, 0219A; Kavanaugh, 2019; Froelich deposition, p. 34.
94 Post to the Discord platform, August 13, 2017.

95 McWhirter, 2018. Simko, Cunningham, and Fox (2022) find that UTR gave new impetus to the struggle to remove Confederate monuments by making clear that these were symbols of white supremacy.
96 Cott, 2018. Snow (2018) reports on the consequences to a Marine who was exposed for doing extremist white supremacist activity on the Charlottesville Discord server and other arenas.
97 For example, the Global Minority Initiative (Berkowitz, 2021) claimed to be raising money for arrested white supremacists.
98 Studies show that extreme and disruptive protests such as UTR can reduce support for social movements and have negative impacts, even on those who were not directly affected. Valentino and Nicholson, 2021; Williams et al., 2021.
99 Quinnipiac University, 2017.

5

INSURRECTION

In the decade from Obama's first presidential election to the violent melee in Charlottesville, an increasingly emboldened and visible white supremacist extremism pushed into the mainstream. After Unite the Right, it made even more headway into the nation's civic life, leading to our third moment, the volatile mix of extremist Trump supporters who endorsed his 'Big Lie' about the election and full-fledged white supremacists, which was on public display in the insurrection of January 6, 2021 (J6). This chapter traces how racist extremism gained traction in the years immediately after Charlottesville and how it was able to accelerate further by taking advantage of the COVID pandemic and 2020 presidential election.

After Charlottesville

One route by which white supremacist extremism gained traction in the mainstream after Charlottesville was through the Republican Party. White supremacist extremists moved into the GOP as it drifted further into extremism, while, in the reinforcing spiral of electoral politics, the Republican Party became a more attractive platform for racial extremists.

Consider the trajectory of Nick Fuentes. Starting out as a minor player in white supremacist talk radio, Fuentes hosted a live video feed from Unite the Right that secured his reputation in racist circles and boosted his Twitter following. This newfound celebrity status allowed Fuentes to bring a base of followers with him as he was kicked off major Internet platforms and migrated to more obscure ones. He also parlayed his fame into high-profile offline extremism, gaining a speaking perch at the 2018 American Renaissance annual conference with proponents of Identity Evropa; the anti-immigrant,

DOI: 10.4324/9781003322337-5

racist multimedia *VDare*; the white supremacist publishing outlets *Counter-Currents* and *The Occidental Quarterly*[1]; and a Swedish YouTube blogger speaking on 'The Defense of the West Begins with You.'[2] Such celebrity gave Fuentes broad reach to rally people to protest what Trump termed 'election fraud' and to join the J6 insurrection. Fuentes also had the ability to operate in the interstices between extremism and the Republican Party, evident in the America First Political Action Conference (AFPAC) that he organized, featuring speeches by both elected officials and extremist white supremacists and held alongside the GOP-dominated Conservative Political Action Conference (CPAC). Despite AFPAC's proximity to GOP members, Fuentes did little to obscure its racist agenda. At its 2021 conference, he declared that 'White people founded this country. This country wouldn't exist without white people. And white people are done being bullied.'[3] Raw white supremacist vitriol was sharing a stage with the members of the nation's governing party.

Cuban American extremist Christopher Rey Monzon took a different path into the GOP. He participated in the League of the South (LoS)'s 'show of force' to defend a Confederate statue in New Orleans as well as their assault on Charlottesville. Monzon also pursued racist confrontation on his own, allegedly denouncing Florida city commissioners as 'a cancer on the face of the earth! All Jews are!' As might be expected, Monzon's Hispanic background drew concern from some racist extremists, but LoS head Michael Tubbs defended him: 'Chris has done more fore [sic] Southern nationalism, Florida's independence and White supremacy in one 24-hour period than 99.9999% of Florida's native White population have done in their life [sic] times.' Monzon, using his online avatar name 'Chris Cedeno,' followed up with a chilling addition: 'Except lynching negroes, I unfortunately have yet to do that.' Despite his history of violent extremism and continuing ties to LoS, Monzon ran for city council in Florida (unsuccessfully) and in 2022 became vice president of the Miami Springs (Florida) Republican Club.[4]

Extremism didn't expand its footprint in mainstream society only by individual white supremacists aligning themselves with the GOP. The Republican Party itself shifted sharply toward extremism. Only a short time after several GOP leaders spoke against racial extremism at Charlottesville, vast swathes of the party were openly embracing elements of its constellation, including conspiratorial bigotry and raging anger, even violence. Republicans nominated candidates associated with racist extremism for public office,[5] and, in at least one case, the direction was reversed: extremist groups used Republican Party talking points to recruit members.[6]

Even as some racist extremists slipped out of Charlottesville and into hiding, their core ideas were moving onto center stage. In this, President Trump played a central role. At his rallies and through his social media, Trump broadcast stories taken with little modification from conspiratorial fantasies spewing forth from the extremist ecosystem that predicted 'white genocide,' including a Black-led campaign to murder South African White farmers (a lie featured also on Tucker Carlson's Fox News show) and a plan by migrants at the Mexican border to attack the United States. Once trumpeted (no pun intended) by the highly visible president, these false tales blasted across friendly media, the perfect 'digestible elements of new racist rhetoric' to energize those Whites increasingly receptive to extremist and conspiratorial beliefs.[7]

Shock value can ensure media coverage and heighten a crowd's emotions. Trump's messages followed the template. He depicted migrants in the most startling and dehumanizing manner, as coming to 'invade' and 'infest' the nation and later, in another malicious flourish, tweeted a video seeming to show cash being distributed to Spanish-speaking migrants.[8] Far-right GOP U.S. Representative Matt Gaetz tweeted the same video, also suggesting that George Soros was the source of the money.[9] Trump left it to his friendly right-wing media world to decode the video. It complied, broadcasting messages such as the statement by the racial extremist and former presidential candidate Patrick Buchanan that ending the migrant crisis was 'critical to the future of our civilization,'[10] as well as multiple stories suggesting that Soros was central to a global Jewish conspiracy that was deliberately engineering the destruction of the white race.[11] For decades, white supremacist extremists had nurtured this conspiratorial antisemitic racist trope. Now it was out in the open.[12] Trump did more than spread the ideas of white supremacist extremism. He also employed its bombastic style of communication to whip up emotions of fury and fear and amp up the resolve of his audiences to take action to protect the White race. At his MAGA rallies and on Twitter, Trump said out loud what had been unmentionable, titillating his followers and signaling that racist, dehumanizing, and conspiratorial talk no longer needed to be hidden or spoken furtively.[13]

Just days after Trump's tweet about cash being distributed to migrants, 11 Jews were slaughtered in a Pittsburgh synagogue by an attacker who screamed, 'All Jews must die.' Just two hours before attacking, the shooter posted on the racist-friendly platform Gab that a Jewish refugee agency 'likes to bring invaders in that kill our people. Screw your optics, I'm going in.'[14] Undeterred by an outpouring of criticism that linked his words to the murders, Trump continued his assault on migrants, reinforced by a torrent of ads that appeared on Facebook between January and August 2019 warning of the effects of an 'invasion.' Less than nine months later, 21 people were murdered and dozens injured by a white supremacist shooter at an El Paso Walmart. The shooter posted a manifesto to the online message board 8chan that included the words: 'this is a response to the Hispanic invasion.' A few days later, Tucker Carlson pronounced white supremacy to be largely a 'hoax.'[15]

Trump also introduced more visibly antidemocratic practices. His repeated efforts to flout norms of governing and the rule of law and attack democratic institutions and rights[16] led to descriptions of the United States as a 'backsliding democracy' and the Republican Party as a far-right party.[17] Trump's abuses were not unprecedented; they were a more explicit version of five decades of antidemocratic strategies enacted by the GOP. What the historian Nancy MacLean describes as the party's 'stealth plan' of increasing privatization, restricting voting, reshaping the courts by appointing judges favorable to conservative and right-wing causes, and reducing the clout of unions was core to Republicans' success in winning elections in Southern states and capturing the presidency.[18] Even Trump's embrace and encouragement of far-rightists were nothing new for the GOP. As political scientist Joseph Lowndes notes, over the past three decades, Republican

> party insurgents enlisted the energy and ideas of radicals outside the system to ignite and direct the passions and resents of White Christian voters inside it. Their success depended on the ability of activists to provoke racial resentments without openly embracing white supremacy.[19]

Despite identified militia and white supremacist inspiration for the 1995 Oklahoma City bombing, for instance, some in Congress continued to cultivate ties to anti-government extremists, 'even engaging them on their campaigns and events, much like today,' as Wendy Via and Heidi Beirich note.[20] As we have shown, homegrown extremism was blended into Republican messages and campaigns throughout Obama's presidency[21] as movements, including the Tea Party and Oath Keepers, latched onto conspiracy theories around Obama's citizenship that were spread by Donald Trump, as well as fears related to immigration, gun confiscations, and a globalist 'new world order.'

Another factor that aided the expansion of racial extremism into the mainstream after Charlottesville was the continuing growth of online extremism. Even as some offline white supremacist groups faded from sight after UTR, the digital ecosystem of racial extremism flourished. Undeterred by platform companies' meager efforts to remove violent content and ban those who repeatedly posted such messages, hate-filled virtual communities continued to spring up on Internet web forums, anonymous message boards, and social media platforms, stoking white rage, resentment, disinformation, violence, and fear.

As we discussed in Chapter 3, the development of dozens of smaller niche platforms more closely aligned with extremism had diversified the landscape of online extremism. Gab, connected to the massacre at the Pittsburgh synagogue, was one of those platforms, and its history serves as a microcosm for the broader story of how white supremacy operates in the online universe and how it overlaps with offline extremism. Founded in 2016, Gab branded itself as a 'free speech' haven and 'alt-Twitter' social network but quickly emerged as a space where white supremacists and other far-right extremists found a welcoming environment. Andrew Torba, Gab's founder, instituted little moderation on the platform, even as age-old antisemitic tropes flourished, such as tales that Jews are responsible for the death of Jesus and use the blood of non-Jewish children in religious rituals.[22] The platform benefitted when prominent figures like right-wing provocateur Milo Yiannopoulos and Andrew Anglin, the founder of the *Daily Stormer*, became early adopters.[23] Although its connection to the hatred-fueled rampage in the Pittsburgh synagogue led several large tech companies including Apple Apps Store, GoDaddy, PayPal, and their hosting provider Joyent to deplatform Gab, it found other ways to remain online.

Extremist white supremacism also spread through misogynist forums and blogs on the Internet.[24] Control over women is core to the white supremacist goal of maintaining white dominance,[25] so racist virtual communities are typically rife with woman-hating. Advocating and celebrating violence against women are long-standing themes, recently supplemented by support for creating a 'White sharia,' a fascist-patriarchal state.[26] 'White sharia,' it should be noted, is intended as a meme[27] (a catchy slogan) that combines seemingly unconnected elements of whiteness and a particular version of Islamic law to shape a message that will grab readers by playing off the long-standing white supremacist idea that white women are supposed to have many babies to prevent white genocide.

Online communities are complicated, even those dominated by racist extremism. Notwithstanding the soaring misogyny in extremist online spaces, a handful of women were able to become prominent recruiters, influencers, and propagandists. Some spun out far-right conspiracy theories, like supposed attacks against white South African farmers, the tale also broadcast by Trump.[28] Others found success as media personalities (also mirroring Trump). Male-dominated online forums even created virtual women's spaces (users are sometime termed 'wheatfield dwellers') to bring women together online and attract additional women to the cause.[29] Like many aspects of white supremacist extremism, openings to women had mixed results. Women who promoted white causes in online racist spaces found themselves attacked and threated with violence and sexual assault from the virtual community.[30]

Many commentators have noted that misogyny is a feature of white supremacism, but it has proven difficult to identify the exact role that women-hating plays in generating racial extremism. However, an online conflict in the mid-2010s that came to be known as 'Gamergate' provides an unusually clear example of how this happens. Gamergate began on the 4chan platform with a loosely organized group of men who engaged in rape and death threats, doxing, and other forms of harassment against women, especially those who criticized the sexism and violence of gaming culture. As the tech commentator Angela Nagle reports, 4chan had long been 'teeming with racism, misogyny, dehumanization, disturbing pornography, and nihilism.'[31] When the most egregious Gamergate men were pushed off 4chan, some migrated to the less controlled 8chan, where they could post vicious and dangerous messages with little resistance. Gamergate subsequently ballooned across platforms, politicizing and unifying men from disparate corners of what came to be known as the 'manosphere.' It drew together right-wing men who identified with the transgressive gamer culture, men who were dedicated anti-feminists, and hard-core far-rightist men. A familiar pattern of extremist acceleration followed: less violent manosphere virtual communities such as men's rights activists lost ground to more hate-based and conspiratorial communities such as Incels (Involuntary Celibates) and MGTOW (Men Going Their Own Way). At the same time, the cycle of male grievance and conspiratorial thinking generated in Gamergate opened the door to other forms of grievance and conspiratorial thinking in the manosphere, especially the talk about the victimization of White men by Jews and people of color.[32]

The expansion of extremism in the mainstream also was pushed through cultural forms, including an exclusionary White Christianity that sought to establish as core national principles the claims of a specific form of Christianity largely practiced by politically right-wing Whites. On the surface, this might seem a purely religious movement that would fade as fewer Americans found religion an important aspect of their lives. But history shows that the fusion of Christianity, nationalism, and racial extremism is not likely to be fleeting. To the contrary, this dangerous mix has repeatedly scarred the nation. It has appeared in the 'fiery cross' of the Ku Klux Klan since the 1870s.[33] It took form as the 'religious right' that emerged in the last decades of the 20th century as White Southern evangelical Christian leaders strategically wielded the emotionally-tinged issue of abortion to forge a voting bloc that would not only ban abortion but also prevent the federal government from compelling racial integration of White Christian schools in the South.[34] And, in recent years, it rebounded as Christian Nationalism that pushes the fiction that White Christians are the most persecuted group in the United States. Sociologists Phillip Gorski and Samuel Perry argue that in Christian Nationalism, whiteness is 'the link that connects the deep story and political vision.' Surveys show the political effect of this unified identity today. One of many revealing findings is that the more that White U.S. residents regard Christianity as central to civic life, the more likely they are to oppose the removal of Confederate monuments.[35]

The power of Christian Nationalism was not unleashed to protect white racial privilege alone. Riding the tide of a burgeoning global anti-gender movement, Christian Nationalists and their political allies pushed legislators, libraries, school boards, and politicians to ban books; change curriculum; restrict assistance to LGBTQ+ students and gender transition health care; and take other extreme measures meant to bolster traditional family structures, male authority over women, and rigidly dichotomous and fixed genders.[36] Their successes reflect what religious studies scholar Jessica Johnson describes as 'the fear that white Christian male supremacy and American exceptionalism are no longer givens, fomenting an urgency to do spiritual and worldly battle against racial, gendered, and religious enemies – the collective conviction in the need for revolutionary violence.'[37]

The spread of extremism into the mainstream also coincided with more public visibility of offline white supremacist extremist groups that brought intense practices of intimidation, aggression, and violence into civic life across the nation.[38] No longer did racist extremism seem a footnote in history or something tucked into backwoods America. It was showing up on campuses, city streets, and local councils. Patriot Front was organized as a successor to Vanguard America (VA) after its association with the UTR car attacker became known, carrying forward VA's goal of a white ethnostate. Patriot Front's first public appearances were low-risk actions such as distributing threatening material on campuses and in neighborhoods and unfurling banners with thinly coded messages such as 'European roots American greatness' and 'James Fields did nothing wrong.' It then took on more visible and risky actions: creating pop-up protests and threatening protestors at a Texas border detention center.[39] The Proud Boys, a deeply misogynist group of self-identified 'Western chauvinists' that claimed to be fighting to save Western civilization, was another extremist group that gained additional visibility at this time for their confrontational and often violent clashes with their opponents as well as for the provocative attire at their public appearances, such as the T-shirt emblazoned with 6MWE ('Six Million Wasn't Enough'), a reference to the Holocaust, and RWDS ('Right Wing Death Squad'), a reference to the Chilean dictator Augusto Pinochet, that appeared at a DC event.[40] Proud Boys claimed to welcome members of all races, sexual identities, and religions. In reality, most members were White, and the Western civilization they were dedicated to defending was decidedly rooted in white culture.[41] The Oath Keepers, which as we discussed in Chapter 3, initially gained visibility in the 2014 Bundy Ranch standoff,[42] also became more visible after Charlottesville with 'Stop the Steal' actions such as patrolling voting places, acting as armed security for Trump's voter fraud rallies, and staging paramilitary activities on the U.S.–Mexico border to deter immigrants.[43]

Finally, the encroachment of extremism into the mainstream in the post-Unite the Right period intersected with public attention to racial violence.[44] The callous murder of George Floyd, a 46-year-old African American man, by Minneapolis police in May 2020 – yet another in a long string of police killings of Black men – gave new urgency and momentum to the BLM movement nationwide. The protests and riots that followed Floyd's murder also sparked a white backlash similar to what emerged in response to the Ferguson protests. But the extent to which violence had been legitimated as a racial tactic was evident in laws passed in three states that provided levels of immunity to drivers who injured or killed protestors engaged in actions deemed to be part of a protest or riot.[45] Once again, as an opportunity for social justice emerged, institutional forces and extremists converged to resist any progress and to mount their own vision for a more racialized, patriarchal, and authoritarian system, a vision that echoed in nostalgic pleas to 'Make America Great Again.'

New opportunities

The penetration of extremism into the mainstream was well underway when two 2020 events allowed white supremacists to sow additional chaos and conspiracies across civic life. These were the onset of the COVID-19 pandemic and the presidential election campaign.

The pandemic

The COVID pandemic was a *black swan* event, one that couldn't be predicted and had a profound impact.[46] It was a gold mine for white supremacism, generating conditions that extremists have long found advantageous, such as widespread economic distress and loss of faith in leaders and institutions. Also, pandemic-induced social isolation suppressed the scale of social justice protests after Floyd's murder, while spurring huge increases in Internet and social media usage just as the virtual world of racist extremism was proliferating.[47] Zoom meetings, classes, and events offered new places into which racist and antisemitic messages could be pushed, a phenomenon that came to be known as 'Zoom bombing.'

The pandemic was an opportunity to spread conspiratorial stories about its origins and thereby heighten a sense of victimization and fear, a strategy used to great effect by extremists in earlier tales of black helicopters surveilling rural areas to seize power on behalf of a new world order and of false documents generated to hide the truth about President Obama's birthplace.[48] When Trump repeatedly blamed China for the virus and described COVID in racist language such as 'kung flu,' he set off another racist conspiracy narrative, one that played on long-held White fears of a 'yellow peril' and a general impurity of Asian immigrant populations in the United States.[49] Racist extremists seized on Trump's rhetoric, integrating it into their usual attacks on Jews, elites, and immigrants, and expressing the hope that COVID would target minority groups.[50] Acts of hatred and violence, especially against Asian, Asian American, and Pacific Island (AAPI) persons, predictably increased.[51]

A further opening for racist extremists was the Trump administration's chaotic and contradictory responses to the spreading pandemic, which were peppered with attacks on state and local efforts to contain COVID through public health measures. Quickly, health care workers and government officials became targets of abuse and violence. Timothy Wilson, a white suprema-cist, was caught while planning a car bomb attack on a Missouri hospital with COVID patients. He planned the attack for March 24 – just days into national recognition of the pandemic – a graphic example of how quickly a perceived grievance can spur terroristic action.[52]

The development of a vaccine against COVID in early 2021 was met by a highly polarized public with both relief and alarm. As battles over masking and vaccine requirements in workplaces, on transit, and in schools broke out across the nation, racist extremism had another opening. Protests against the COVID vaccine swept people from the broader anti-vaccination movement, as well as from alternative health, anti-corporate, and libertarian movements, into contact with racist extremists and heavily armed militia. Warnings of conspiratorial Jewish elites blended with messages about a tyrannical federal government. It was an ideological stew that opened the door to what historian George Mosse termed as the 'scavenger' politics of the far-right,[53] allowing extremist practices, ideas, and emotions to mutate in protests that terrorism scholars Bruce Hoffman and Jacob Ware described as 'a heterogeneous col-lection of extremist actors . . . all seeking to press their own unique agendas and independently pursue their own strategies.'[54] Extremist expert Heidi Beir-ich captured the moment: 'The barriers that once existed between divergent forms of far-right extremism are dissolving.'[55] To a remarkable degree, white supremacist extremists had succeeded at their long-standing strategy of creat-ing confusion about who they were and what they were trying to achieve.

COVID also boosted the visibility of extremist groups. As early as April 2020, anti-pandemic restriction rallies (as well as anti-BLM rallies) featured members of the Oath Keepers standing guard[56] along with Proud Boys as well as members of the Three Percenters, a group dedicated to fighting what they regarded as a tyrannical U.S. government. The Oath Keepers even tried a new venture, offering protection for businesses that reopened in defiance of pan-demic guidelines.[57] During this unsettled time, Boogaloo Bois, a decentralized anti-government and anti-law enforcement network that predicted a second civil war (a 'boogaloo') and sought to bring down the U.S. government, also came into visibility. Although Boogaloo Bois had been around for nearly a decade, its unusual politics – some adherents assert white supremacism while a few stand with BLM against the police – positioned it to gain strength from the simultaneous spread of protests against COVID restrictions and for racial justice. Boogaloo Bois also joined anti-lockdown and anti-govern-ment demonstrations where they made a striking appearance, arriving heav-ily armed, sporting their signature Hawaiian-themed shirts, and reportedly pushing crowds toward violence and chaos.[58] Its affiliates were associated with a variety of terroristic plots and violent actions, including shooting into a police precinct in Minneapolis, murdering a federal security officer in Oak-land, California, and planning to firebomb a power substation in Nevada.[59]

Presidential election

The presidential election provided a second opening for racist extremism in 2020, as Trump sought to remain in office for another term. During the campaign, rumors that Trump's opponent, former vice-president Joe Biden, intended to seize guns from civilians if he won the election brought visibly armed and intimidating militia, paramilitary groups, and seemingly unaffiliated gun-toting citizens to Trump's campaign rallies. Trump supporters took up other thuggish actions as well, including a well-documented incident in which dozens of vehicles formed a self-designated 'Trump Train' on a Texas highway and were accused of terrorizing a Democratic campaign bus.[60]

As the 2020 election grew closer, the engagement of extremists in Trump's electoral efforts became even more visible. Trump's late September call-out to Proud Boys to 'stand back and stand by' during a nationally televised debate was memorable in retrospect, as Proud Boys appeared at Trump's post-election Million MAGA protest marches – where their violent encounters with counter-protestors drew Twitter praise – and played a central role in the J6 insurrection. But they were only one of numerous extremist groups that circulated around the Trump campaign and its aftermath. Two days after the election, for instance, Oath Keepers founder Stewart Rhodes texted his supporters that 'We aren't getting through this without a civil war.' A month later, in a speech at a pro-Trump rally a month after the election, he called on Trump to invoke the Insurrection Act, arguing that if he didn't, others would be engaging in 'a much more desperate, much more bloody war.'[61]

Anti-government extremists and Trump supporters also found common cause with those involved in the online QAnon conspiracy. QAnon began on 4chan and migrated to the similar 8chan (now 8kun) Internet forum, bringing together a dizzying amalgamation of ideas in a loose narrative about the anonymous figure (Q) who leads a struggle against a Satanic apocalyptic plot. As in most conspiracies, evidence was not provided; indeed, the lack of evidence is understood to prove its accuracy. QAnon had an unusual, and effective, structure. Its followers were grouped into smaller online communities that forged their own interpretations of events within a QAnon framework, what Peter Forberg describes as 'a constant play between collective narrative and personal projection – no two QAnons are alike.'[62] This unique interpretive structure left ample room for racist extremism and Trump narratives of electoral fraud, especially since QAnon positioned Trump as a central figure in the struggle against demonic forces and the hidden ('deep') administrative state under the control of a pedophile cult of prominent Democrats.[63] Moreover, QAnon's visualizations appeared to create a coherence among random data that could elicit strong emotions of anger and outrage from viewers.[64]

The rapid rise in conspiratorialism and disinformation and its entanglement with racial extremism had consequences far beyond the presidential campaign. An example is the creation of Kyle Rittenhouse as a victim-hero; a characterization that reappeared when Ashli Babbitt was killed by Capitol police as she tried to break into the U.S. House Chambers on J6. Rittenhouse was young when he linked up with a group of armed self-proclaimed defenders of 'lives and property' engaged in confronting racial justice protesters in the small Wisconsin town of Kenosha in August 2020. He may have been fueled by President Trump's exaggerated claims about the destructiveness of BLM protests or perhaps by the circulating 'riot porn' videos that engaged viewers in the fantasy of protest battle. In any case, Rittenhouse fatally shot two people and seriously injured another, acts celebrated by racial extremists and gun rights advocates. He was later acquitted of all charges.

The Kenosha conflict displayed many features of the increasing overlap between extremism and mainstream. According to extensive reporting in the *New Yorker*, at least one armed defender appeared to regard the police as his enemy, mirroring the shift of some extremists away from support for the police. The same article noted Rittenhouse's connections to Trump and his media allies. According to his social media history, Rittenhouse had attended a Trump rally. After the Kenosha incident, Tucker Carlson, the Fox News commentator, glorified Rittenhouse as someone who 'decided they had to maintain order when no one else would.' The *New Yorker* article also revealed that Rittenhouse received support from Lin Wood, the attorney who had a role in multiple moments of this book: he represented the White couple who pointed guns at BLM protestors in the aftermath of the Ferguson protests and acted as a central figure in Trump's election denial efforts. And, unsurprisingly, the Proud Boys made Rittenhouse part of their messaging.[65]

At the close of 2020, the gap between extremist white supremacy and ordinary white supremacy was considerably narrower than when Obama assumed the presidency, or even when Trump had. Extremism had not moderated or rebranded itself to appear more moderate. Rather, those who embraced Trump's angry and bigoted politics had marched toward the extreme, illustrating Cas Mudde's 'pathological normalcy.'[66] The expanding space of extremism in the mainstream provided an opportunity for both. J6 was the result.

Insurrection

Charlottesville was organized by racist extremists coming out of hiding. J6 was set in place by the world's most visible politician, with the hidden help of white supremacist extremists. Six hundred persons, nearly all white men, marched in Charlottesville; far more (an estimated 2,000, mostly white and including many women) assaulted the Capitol on J6. Yet, the events of

UTR and J6 unfolded in remarkably similar fashion. Both were organized in online forums, although Charlottesville was mainly coordinated on a single platform, while messages about J6 spread across multiple platforms. In each event, a rally the preceding day heightened expectations among the gathering crowd that the main event would be a battle. Although far fewer sported insignia or clothing that identified them with a white supremacist group on J6 than in UTR, conspiratorial theories, especially the 'great replacement' theory and an accompanying sense of victimization and resentment over the declining place of Whites, swirled around both events.[67] In each event, participants turned shields and flagpoles into offensive weapons, and both events ended in death and multiple, grievous injuries. And, in both, the reality of the event was almost immediately re-narrated across disinformation campaigns that blamed its violence on 'antifa' and BLM.[68]

In one significant way, UTR and J6 were quite different. UTR was organized by extremists for extremists, more dramatic than other protest events but with a familiar form. J6 was a singular, shocking, unpredictable episode that destabilized political meanings and redrew political boundaries.[69] It was the most deadly attack on a federal government property since the 1995 bombing of a federal office building in Oklahoma City. But the Oklahoma City bombing was the product of a relatively isolated racist movement committed to striking out against the U.S. government. The J6 attack involved a largely white extremist network attacking the government, with the clear endorsement of a sitting President, key presidential advisors, and other core Republican officials, while a sizable number of military and law enforcement personnel blended into the vast angry crowd of ordinary citizens. The constellation of practices, ideas, and emotions animating the Oklahoma City and J6 attacks was virtually identical, but a sea change had transformed white supremacist extremism between 1995 and 2021. No longer confined to challenging from the sidelines, it was asserted from the highest corridors of power in the country.

Some observers of J6 mistakenly focused on the 'ordinary' appearance of the J6 insurrectionists rather than the mass radicalization that brought 'ordinary' people to the capital. As Senator Ron Johnson's comments following J6 indicate, perceptions of who is ordinary and who is extremist are shaped by race and politics. When asked about his reaction during the siege, the Senator explained he did not feel scared because, 'I knew those were people that . . . truly respect law enforcement, would never do anything to break the law, so I wasn't concerned.' He continued, 'had the tables been turned, and President Trump won the election and those were tens of thousands of Black Lives Matter and antifa protesters, I might have been a little concerned.'[70]

Efforts to distinguish ordinary from extreme at J6 missed the underlying constellation that squarely placed that event within the long history of white supremacist extremism in this country. J6 was an example of what

Tőrnberg and Tőrnberg describe as a 'complex interplay between online-mobilized far-right movements and mainstream politics,' with extremist groups – most notably, large contingents of Proud Boys and Oath Keepers – marching alongside radicalized 'ordinary' folks, from fervent MAGA Trump supporters to adherents of Christian Nationalism and QAnon and advocates of the Confederacy.[71] Jacob Chansley, the insurrectionist who came to be known as the 'QAnon Shaman' for his posturing to cameras inside the Capitol, exemplified this ideological blend as he thanked God for 'allowing us to send a message . . . that this is our nation, not theirs.'[72] He was later sentenced to 41 months in prison for his role in the insurrection although he was recently released from custody. Oath Keepers and Proud Boys who led the attack drew stiffer sentences. Steward Rhodes was sentenced to prison for 18 years after his conviction for seditious conspiracy. As of this writing, two other Oath Keepers were sentenced to eight and four years, respectively, for obstructing Congress' certification of Biden's election. Enrique Tarrio and three other Proud Boys were convicted of seditious conspiracy and other charges and received sentences ranging from 10 year to, for Tarrio, 22 years.

Aftermath

The story of what followed J6 is still being written. But it is already clear that a significant number of mainstream people – especially those in the Trump-allied GOP – continue to move ever more sharply into racial extremism. Elaborating on sociologist Cynthia Miller-Idriss' observation of 'the extreme gone mainstream,'[73] we note that, simultaneously, the mainstream went extreme. By 2022, 6% of adults in this nation (more than 15 million people) regularly turned to what sociologist Daniel Karell and his colleagues term 'hard-right social media' such as Gab, Telegram, Parler, and the Trump-affiliated Truth Social for their news. It is hardly surprising that fairly large segments of Americans, especially in the Republican Party, embrace false ideas about immigrant invasions, Democrats operating pedophile rings, and networks of transgendered persons 'grooming' children as well as the emotions elicited by these threatening tales. Nor is it surprising, given the constellation of white supremacism, that increased hard-right social media activity is associated with increased incidents of offline civil unrest.[74]

Normalized extremism

Once marginalized and stigmatized, racial extremism has become normalized in society as well as institutionalized in a major political party, with alarming results.[75] Racial extremists and other far-rightists are attacking, and diminishing, democratic rule in the United States and around the world. They paint the institutions of democratic rule as tyrannical – Trump's denunciation of the 'deep state' is an example – and offer racist, authoritarian govern-ance instead. Although Trump did not create authoritarianism, he weak-ened democratic checks and balances, including media autonomy, freedom of expression, and rule of law, and exacerbated and capitalized on politi-cal divisions. Like dictators do, he allowed, even encouraged, members of extremist and right-wing paramilitary groups to intimidate those he regarded as his enemies, including Democratic Party officials. He intimidated Repub-lican politicians into pledging fealty to him and his MAGA vision or risk his wrath and that of his emotionally charged followers. His blatantly racist and bigoted statements as president amped up old hatreds and gave them a shine of legitimacy. Trump's most extreme loyalists in Congress even proposed an 'Anglo-Saxon based 'American First Caucus' (AFC) to promote nativist, anti-immigration policies' and 'uniquely Anglo-Saxon political traditions.'[76] And, when the 2020 election failed to go his way, Trump stoked an insurrection led by his loyalist extremists, with Proud Boys, Oath Keepers, and neo-Nazis in the mix.

White supremacist extremism thrives amid chaotic political division and mistrust. Chaos is precisely what Trump's former political advisor Steve Ban-non encouraged to move politics further to the right. His 2013 goal, to emulate Vladimir Lenin, founding head of Soviet Russia, who 'wanted to destroy the state, and that's my goal too. I want to bring everything crashing down, and destroy all of today's establishment,'[77] would be followed by a new Christian-racial nationalism anchored in whiteness, patriarchy, and a Christian identity hostile to pluralism, egalitarianism, and secularism.[78] By 2016, Bannon was a presidential advisor in the Oval Office, along with aide Stephen Miller, both of whom used the intensely grotesque racist French novel, *Camp of Saints*, as a metaphor to justify xenophobic immigration policy. Their vision aligned directly with the white supremacist 'great replacement' narrative that imagines an existential attack on the white race. As Trump's stranglehold on the GOP strengthened during his presidency and beyond, a shocking number of high-level politicians relied on white supremacist extremist strategies and ideas to develop laws and policies.

Trump's bridge between the GOP and the most dangerous sectors of right-wing extremism had stunning results. Republicans openly courted far-rightists outside the United States, including in autocrat-dominated Hungary.[79] Back at home, former president Trump dined with the notorious white supremacist Nick Fuentes at his Florida Mar-a-Lago club. Online spaces also facilitated exchanges between GOP officials and voters and extremists. As an example, nearly 12% of all state legislators serving in the 2021–2022 legislative ses-sion, from all 50 states, had joined at least one far-right Facebook group.[80]

Some platform companies also linked the GOP and extremists. Gab is an example. After J6, Gab was catapulted with an infusion of new users; by the end of January 2021, its registered users totaled just over three million. This new traffic generated an influx of revenue and resources for its owner, the avowed Christian Nationalist Andrew Torba, to support his favorite causes, including a meeting of Fuentes' America First Political Action Conference that featured two sitting members of Congress as guest speakers.[81] But even as Gab became one of the most influential platforms that catered to far-right extremism, the GOP did not shy away. To the contrary, when Doug Mastriano, an election denier and part of the mob at the Capitol on J6, won the 2022 Republican nomination for governor of Pennsylvania,[82] his campaign paid Gab – the platform used by the synagogue shooter in Pennsylvania's second- largest city – $5,000 for 'consulting' services, and Mastriano praised Torba, declaring 'Thank God for what you've done.'[83] The story of Gab embodies what we have observed repeatedly with white supremacist extremism: it knows how to persist.

Extremism in government

Extremism has been gaining a deeper reach into government, at all levels. Legislators in Congress and statehouses across the country have sponsored bills to undermine democracy and human rights – to suppress voting, curtail reproductive freedoms, limit LGBTQ+ rights, and outlaw efforts to teach about racism and slavery. Voter suppression efforts have been among their most impactful strategies, especially insidious laws intended to impede voting by citizens of color and tilt political power toward their base of aggrieved Whites. In Texas, a GOP-supported voter suppression bill stated its intention to maintain the 'purity of the ballot box' – the precise language used during the Jim Crow era to disenfranchise Black citizens as unfit to vote.[84] Republicans, aided by the judicial branch, have sought numerous other measures to narrow freedoms over bodily autonomy, sexual preference, and religious liberty. The U.S. Supreme Court, dominated by right-wing judges, three appointed by Trump, used a specific set of Christian values to take the unprecedented step of revoking abortion rights. It also undermined secularism, ruling that public tax dollars can be used to fund private religious education and that school employees can pressure students to attend group prayers. The Arizona state legislature approved a plan to provide taxpayer dollars for children attending private religious schools even as voters overwhelmingly voted against a similar measure just four years earlier. And state officials across the nation moved to overturn same-sex marriage, erase facts about systemic racism from textbooks and classrooms, and strip human rights and dignity from transgendered citizens.

Idaho stands as one bellwether for state-level antidemocracy efforts by the extreme right. The state's Republican party has 'openly allied itself with extremists' who have amassed power in the state legislature, county commissions, and school boards and target opponents with 'frightening cruelty and harassment, embracing a strategy called "confrontational politics" which has helped drive more moderate officials across the state to resign or retire' as they pursue their goal to create authoritarian, White, Christian theocracy.[85] Their goal fits seamlessly with the state's history as a refuge for white supremacists, such as the Christian Identity Aryan Nations, Christian Patriots, and the Northwest Front. It also fits with these supremacists' Northwest Imperative fantasy that imagines joining Washington, Oregon, Idaho, and western Montana into a white country to which racist patriots can migrate.[86] That white supremacist extremist groups continue to operate in the state is evident in the Patriot Front's attempt to stage a violent large-scale disruption of a LGBTQ+ Pride event in northern Idaho[87] and in Idaho's Lieutenant Governor Janice McGeachin's unapologetic efforts to ally herself with white supremacists and other far-right extremists.[88] In a playbook that does not get enough attention, '[h]er extremism has endeared her to the Idaho Freedom Foundation, a powerful dark money organization receiving bundles of donations from out-of-state billionaires,' writes journalist Christopher Mathias. Unfortunately, Idaho is just one of many states where similar developments are unfolding.[89]

Not only once-fringe ideas like 'great replacement' theory have been broadcast to audiences of millions through Fox, one of the world's major media outlets,[90] but also once-unacceptable practices like political violence have become widespread as a major political party gives them the nod. To take just one example, consider the New York Young Republican Club (NYYRC), which began in 1856 as the New York Young Men's Republican Union with the abolitionist Cassius Marcellus Clay as its first speaker and Abraham Lincoln's name inscribed on its banner. How things have changed. At its December 2022 gala, which attracted far-right European party members, GOP congresspersons, U.S. racial extremists, former president Trump's son Donald, Jr., and other 'Stop the Steal' promoters, the NYYRC president declared that 'We want total war. We must be prepared to do battle in every arena. In the media. In the courtroom. At the ballot box. And in the streets.' The call to violence was echoed by Republican U.S. Congresswoman Marjorie Taylor Greene who instructed the crowd that if she and Steve Bannon had organized J6, 'we would have won.' 'Not to mention, it would have been armed.'[91] Greene's response to Democratic and progressive backlash the next day was the standard racist extremist canard that she had been joking. The same tactic, as you'll recall, was used by the organizers of the deadly UTR rally.

In this context, the extremism of Proud Boys, Oath Keepers, Patriot Front, and League of the South can appear less extreme, providing new opportunities for organized white supremacism to push ever-more explicit racism, xenophobia, and antisemitism into the mainstream. This slideway into extremism has been further facilitated by the onslaught of disinformation from Trump's post-election lies and the conspiratorialism swirling through social media, creating an 'up is down, down is up' world in which it is difficult to assess claims made by political figures, even racial extremists.[92] The result is an astoundingly widespread acceptance of political disinformation. In April 2021, when arrests of insurrectionists were well underway, the majority of Republicans agreed that J6 'was led by violent left-wing protestors trying to make Trump look bad.'[93]

The nation may be at a point at which the flow of politics is reversed. Earlier, racist extremists worked to infiltrate and influence the mainstream. Today, parts of the GOP are in danger of becoming a conduit into white supremacist extremism. Cas Mudde argues that in 2022, 'the Grand Old Party has become a far-right party that advances racist arguments in both implicit and explicit form. And many organizations within the broader 'conservative' movement have followed suit, from Fox News to Turning Point USA.'[94]

The Republican Party has spent decades giving openings to racist and far-right extremists. Trump's ability and willingness to stoke white rage at whatever cost accelerated the move toward extremism, with tragic consequences. Large proportions of the white population, especially those connected to the GOP, now openly embrace outlandish racist ideologies. Fully one-half of Republicans (but less than one-fifth of others) believe that people of color will have more rights than Whites will have in the future, fueling a fierce backlash against anything that exposes or addresses racial inequities.[95] More than a third of Republicans feel they are losing influence to immigrants. Nearly one half think that there is a group working to replace current U.S. citizens with immigrants who will support that group's politics, a key point in the 'great replacement' theory.[96] This is a legacy of Trump, rooted in decades of Republican fealty to an ever-shrinking proportion of the population that is White, Christian, male, and concentrated in rural and suburban areas of the South, Midwest, and Northwest.

Even more shocking, Republican voters increasingly accept violence as a viable means of achieving goals in mainstream politics. A January 2021 survey sponsored by the conservative American Enterprise Institute found that the majority (56%) of Republicans support the use of force to stop the decline of the traditional way of life, and 39% agree that if elected officials do not protect America, 'the people must do it themselves even if it requires taking violent actions.' Far fewer Democrats or Independents took this position.[97] Four percent of respondents in a March 2021 national survey (by extrapolation, nearly 10 million people) both regarded the 2020 election as stolen and were willing to engage in violence to protest.[98] In June 2021, only three months later, a full 26% reported that the election was stolen and 9% that force was justified to restore Trump to office. The following May, a national survey found that an alarming 36% of Republicans agreed that

'It may be necessary at some point soon for citizens to take up arms against the government.'[99]

Threats of violence

Not surprisingly, the rhetoric of violence has mushroomed, with escalating threats of violence across society. This is a form of terrorism long practiced by extremist white supremacists. Communicating threats is a fairly low-cost, low-risk practice. Despite the significant intimidating effects of violent threats, the likelihood of arrest and prosecution for making threats is fairly low. In many cases, both law enforcement and the public at large regard these as more of a nuisance – isolated incidents by otherwise-harmless individuals simply 'blowing off steam' – than as a criminal harm to the targeted person or institution and the broader community. And the line between protected speech and criminal threats can be blurry. Yet, threats of violence – even in the absence of acts of violence – can substantially erode democracy by undermining institutions and making targeted individuals and groups fearful of participating in civic life.

Threats to public officials by those exhibiting anti-government and racial extremism have increased since Trump's 2016 election, communicated in phone messages, letters, and digital media.[100] Elected officials are one target.[101] Threats investigated by the U.S. Capitol Police against members of Congress increased by 144% between 2017 (the first year of Trump's presidency) and 2021 (the first year of Biden's presidency).[102] Consistent with the misogyny of far-right extremism, women officials are targeted more often than men.

Since the 2020 presidential election, election workers, especially those regarded as hampering Trump's efforts to stay in office, have been targeted by threats of violence in 21 states. A particularly vivid example is the 62-year-old Black election official in Georgia who fled her home after Trump falsely accused her of election fraud. She received death threats, including messages calling for her to be hung. An FBI agent informed her that an arrested suspected J6 insurrectionist had a list of names of people to be executed, including the election worker and her daughter.[103] And this was just one case – a fraction of the torrent of death threats and harassing messages sent to election officials after J6.[104]

Health and education officials are facing increasing threats of violence. During the COVID pandemic, the top public health official in Orange County, California, resigned after receiving death threats. Similar threats occurred across California and various other states. Education officials, including school board members, administrators, and even teachers, are threatened by extremists who believe they are inculcating critical race theory and transgenderism in children.[105]

Extremists have also escalated threats directed at their traditional targets, such as Jewish day schools, synagogues, and community centers, which have had multiple bomb threats, threatening phone calls, and communications praising Hitler and alluding to a 'Holocaust 2.0' in recent years, as well as reproductive care centers whose medical professionals and escort workers have faced threats and acts of violence.

In the flurry of the moment, it is tempting to regard what has happened – the threats, the violence, the visibility, and mainstreaming of extremism – as novel and unexpected. That is a dangerous mistake. The constellation of practices, ideas, and emotions that burst into view on J6 and that continues to nourish the movement of extremists into mainstream politics and the movement of ordinary people into extremist politics has been stunningly constant since the 1870s. To take but one example, the acts of intimidation at polling places that Trump whipped up through accusations that Black voters were committing electoral fraud are eerily similar to the racist attacks on Black voters in the Reconstruction era and then again during the civil rights movement. Details changed. Today's claims of online attacks on electronic voting machines would have been fanciful earlier. But the core animating practices, ideas, and emotions are remarkably stable.

Since the constellation of racial extremism is persistent, not episodic, we need to avoid assuming that what isn't seen doesn't exist – to watch carefully for extremism when it is submerged and gathering steam; to pay attention not only to current events, but also to the steps that lead to them; and to recognize the dangers of both extremist white supremacism and the ordinary white supremacism in which it grows.

The United States must avoid the tragic model of European Nazism in which 'Germans did not so much display a startling lack of "civic courage" as demonstrate a surprising readiness to accept and to participate in the new civic aims of the regime. They were stepping up, not cowering down.'[106] The country needs to be clear-eyed about the threat it faces, as well as the opportunities to counter that threat and move society in a more progressive direction. Our final chapter focuses on solutions, with a dose of healthy skepticism about the public's will to do what is necessary.

Notes

1 Southern Poverty Law Center, n.d.-n.
2 American Renaissance, 2018.
3 Miller and Carroll Rivas, 2022.
4 Hatewatch Staff, 2017; Mazzei and Feuer, 2022.
5 Mazzei and Feuer, 2022; Mathias, 2022.
6 Martin, 2022.
7 Berbrier, 1999, p. 428; Confessore, 2022c.
8 Griffiths, 2018; Kelly and Rizzo, 2018; Confessore, 2022c.
9 Confessore, 2022b, Peters, 2018; Kelly and Rizzo, 2018.

10 Buchanan, 2018.
11 Albright, 2018; Lind, 2018.
12 Berger, 2018a.
13 Cammaerts, 2021; also see Zeller, 2021.
14 Robertson, Mele, and Tavernise, 2018.
15 Confessore, 2022c.
16 Gary Alan Fine and his colleagues argue that there is a 'dark fun' associated with violating social norms, which creates a collective *esprit de corps*: Fine and Corte, 2021.
17 Ben-Ghiat, 2020, p. 267; MacLean, 2017; Chinoy, 2019; Economist Intelligence, 2018.
18 MacLean, 2017.
19 Lowndes, 2021a. See also Lowndes (2021b).
20 Via and Beirich, 2022.
21 Jenkins, 2016.
22 Anti-Defamation League, 2021a, 2021b.
23 For its first few years, Gab had only modest growth and minimal revenue, even as it was adding to an already enormous online ecosystem of hate.
24 Ribeiro et al., 2021.
25 See for example, Blee (2020); Blee and Yates (2017); Latif, Blee, DeMichele, and Simi (2023); McRae (2018).
26 Lawrence, Simhony-Philpott, and Stone, 2021. One study found a 180% increase in posts containing both misogyny and antisemitism from 2015 to 2017: Antisemitism Policy Trust, 2019.
27 Donovan, Dreyfuss, and Friedberg, 2022.
28 Anti-Defamation League, 2022a.
29 Darby, 2020; Squire, 2019.
30 Llanera, 2023.
31 Nagle, 2017, p. 105; Blee, 2020.
32 Lawrence, Simhony-Philpott, and Stone, 2021; Nagle, 2017.
33 Kruse, 2015; Jones, 2021.
34 Balmer, 2021; Smith, 2021. Many white supremacist extremists shied away from the religious right because of its roots in Judaism and, instead, embraced symbols of pre-Christian Nordic religions or the pseudo-religion known as Christian Identity.
35 Gorski and Perry, 2022, pp. 17, 26; also Whitehead and Perry, 2020.
36 Kuhar and Paternotte, 2017; Kováts and Pető, 2017; Köttig, Bitzan, and Pető, 2017. The Proud Boys have also appeared at school board meetings and libraries where they form an intimidating presence. See Harris and Alter (2022).
37 Johnson, 2022.
38 See Edwards and Rushin (2018).
39 Anti-Defamation League, 2019b; Southern Poverty Law Center, 'Patriot Front,' n.d.; Ryan, 2022a.
40 Anti-Defamation League, 2020c.
41 Stern, 2019; Campbell, 2022.
42 Jackson, 2020.
43 Jackson, 2020; Southern Poverty Law Center, n.d.-m.
44 Smith, 2021; Ayal Feinberg and colleagues found that the month after Trump held a political rally within a county in 2016, the number of hate incidents significantly increased: Feinberg, Branton, and Martinez-Ebers (2022).
45 International Center for Non-For-Profit Law, n.d.
46 Taleb, 2010. Della Porta (2022) refers to the COVID-19 pandemic as an 'emergency critical juncture' which produced a lasting legacy.

47 Bates, 2021; Awan et al., 2021.
48 Barkun, 2003.
49 Wu and Nguyen, 2022; also Takaki, 1998.
50 Anti-Defamation League, 2020a, 2020b.
51 Corpus Ong, 2021.
52 Anti-Defamation League, 2020a; Williams, 2020.
53 Mosse, 2020.
54 Hoffman and Ware, 2020.
55 Beirich, 2022.
56 Anti-Defamation League, 2020a, 2020b.
57 Southern Poverty Law Center, n.d.-m.
58 Hoffman and Ware, 2020.
59 DeVargas, 2020; Thompson, 2021.
60 *Cervini v. Cisneros*, 2021.
61 Ryan, 2022b; Reuters, 2022a; also see DFRLab (2021).
62 Argentino, Marc-André, 2022; Forberg, 2022.
63 Forberg, 2022; PRRI Staff, 2021.
64 Hannah, 2021.
65 Williams, 2021; Donovan, 2020.
66 Mudde, 2010, p. 1168.
67 Saturday's invasion of Charlottesville was preceded by the Friday night torch march and assault on counter-protestors on the UVS campus. J6 was preceded by an eight-hour event the day before at Freedom Plaza at which highly incendiary statements were reported, such as the statement of Bikers for Trump Chris Cox that he would 'take the first bullet' and claims by others that they would act as an army the next day: DFRLab (2021).
68 The German right-wing media re-narrated the J6 insurrectionists as what Doerr and Gardner (2022) describe as 'non-violent . . . morally righteous . . . and facing the "real" violence of the police and left-wing movement actors,' what they term the 'mobilization of hatred and self-pity through re-narration.' The publication of the Final Report of the Select Committee of the US House of Representatives (House January 6th Committee, 2022) that investigated the January 6th attack includes a vast amount of evidence and commentary collected during the investigation.
69 Swidler, 1986.
70 Levin, 2021.
71 Kutner, Ihler, and Murray, 2022; Törnberg and Törnberg, 2021, p. 285.
72 Gorski and Perry, 2022, p. 15.
73 Miller-Idriss, 2018.
74 Karell, Linke, Holland, and Hendrickson, 2023.
75 New scholarship has focused on joint efforts of electoral and social movement actors on the far-right in Europe (Castelli Gattinara, Pietro, Caterina Froio, and Andrea Pirro, 2022).
76 Rajghatta, 2021.
77 Radosh, 2016.
78 Guilford, 2017.
79 Tavenner, 2022.
80 Institute for Research and Education on Human Rights, 2022.
81 Thiel and McCain, 2022.
82 Mastriano was defeated by the Democratic candidate in the general election.
83 Ramirez, 2022.
84 Knowles, 2021.
85 Mathias, 2022.

86 Anti-Defamation League, n.d.; Blee, 2002; Simi and Futrell, 2015.
87 Ryan, 2022a.
88 Brunner, 2022.
89 Mathias, 2022; Michel, 2015; Edsall, 2023.
90 Kranish, 2021.
91 Gais and Hayden, 2022; New York Young Republican Club, 2022.
92 Via and Beirich, 2023.
93 Reuters and Ipsos, 2021.
94 Mudde, 2022.
95 Pape and Chicago Project on Security and Threats, 2021.
96 AP and NORC at the University of Chicago, 2022.
97 Cox, 2021.
98 Pape and Chicago Project on Security and Threats, 2021.
99 University of Chicago, 2022a, 2022b. This area is likely to continue to be debated. For example, Westwood, Grimmer, Tyler, and Nall (2022) argue that the estimates of support for political violence in the cited studies are inflated by methodological decisions in the survey instruments, but we also have concerns about Westwood and colleagues' alternative measures of political violence. Setter and Nepstad (2023) find that situational variation alters public attitudes toward political violence, as conservatives and Republicans report low levels of support for political violence after the George Floyd protests (during which media focused on violence from the left) and higher levels of support for political violence after J6 (when media focused on violence from the right).
100 Simi and Hughes, 2023.
101 Hsiao and Pfaff, 2022.
102 Solender, 2022.
103 So and Szep, 2021.
104 ADL, 2022b, 2022c; Reuters, 2022b.
105 Simi and Hughes, 2023.
106 Fritzsche, 2020, p. 349.

6

THE PATH AHEAD

White supremacist extremism endures, and it gravely threatens the core of U.S. democracy. It always has. From the beginning of the Republic, white supremacy has been the elephant in the room, an antidemocratic force that limits the true potential for freedom enshrined in the Declaration of Independence. With the Three-fifths Compromise in 1787, the U.S. Constitution *institutionalized* white supremacy in a way that hasn't been eradicated despite legislation and various forms of progress.[1] Today, the extremist white supremacist threat is more pervasive than it has been in over a century, in part because it has expanded and occupies a greater portion of the mainstream. This expansion has also meant less distance between extremist and ordinary white supremacy as extremism is both becoming more prevalent and commonplace. In many respects, the problem seems so large, so intractable that many solutions may seem hopelessly incomplete. And they are. The nation has waited far too long to directly deal with this problem, and now most solutions are insufficient.

But threats to democracy are even more dangerous when proponents lose hope and conclude that fighting back is pointless. Antidemocratic forces seek to bend people's will toward their goals. They want their opponents to voluntarily surrender and to forego using the very process under attack – in short, to give up on democracy. They want a less representative segment of the U.S. population voting and fewer engaged in politics from Congress to local school boards. Extremist white supremacist proponents accomplish these goals through intimidation and fear – practices enmeshed in a constellation of hostile ideas and hateful emotions.

Getting a deeply divided America to take the white supremacist threat seriously is a difficult task. For years, white supremacists bided their time,

DOI: 10.4324/9781003322337-6

holding onto their racist and antisemitic ideas in spaces where they could hide. They stayed under many people's radars until new opportunities offered them a route to prominence in political and public life.

Throughout the book, we have emphasized a constellation of practices, ideas, and emotions because this framework helps us understand just how persistent, and intractable, white supremacy is in the United States. Our explanation moves beyond focusing on leaders and organizations or small cadres and networks that emerge and recede in the extremist landscape. We highlight the lasting cultural features that adherents learn, interpret, use, and transmit over time. We demonstrate how extremist currents ebb and flow, and how extremists change their image and style as they angle for wider societal acceptance for their ideas.

Our framework also highlights the convergence between extremist and ordinary white supremacy – a dynamic sometimes overlooked. In fact, extremist white supremacy requires the broader cultural infrastructure that ordinary white supremacy provides, from racist institutional practices to hateful jokes and racist stereotypes that divide and dehumanize. Most importantly, we also demonstrate that the core practices, ideas, and emotions do not just fade away. At times, extremists may shift how they express their racism, reframe their ideas to garner wider support, and play down their most hateful emotions to appear less threatening. But their foundational views – racism, antisemitism, misogyny, and the use of violence and intimidation to secure white power – remain constant.

It is vital to understand this constancy, that is, how practices, ideas, and emotions persist and how extremist white supremacy is connected to and reinforced by ordinary white supremacy, if we are to confront and counter this problem. By broadening our focus to capture decades of change, we show how policy makers, law enforcement, journalists, and citizens underestimated and misconstrued white supremacy's persistence. Ignoring the warning signs left adherents in position to grow as they took advantage of political, technological, and cultural opportunities during the Obama and Trump years. Our cultural approach also helps clarify that this broad constellation includes anti-gay, anti-trans, and misogynistic violence, as well as militia mobilization that some observers separate from extremist white supremacy.

Our emphasis on culture also helps anticipate the extremist white supremacist constellation's ever-expanding targets meant to attract new adherents and sustain old ones. For example, the 'anti-woke' campaign is based on the premise that progressives in Hollywood, public education, and various other social institutions seek to enforce authoritarian dictates related to diversity, inclusion, environmental responsibility, and various other perceived left-wing issues. This so-called wokeism is rarely defined, however, and even proponents of ending wokeism struggle to define it.[2] Perhaps, Florida Governor and 2024 presidential hopeful Ron DeSantis' comment to the Telegraph summarizes anti-woke propaganda best:

> We look at woke infiltrating schools as a problem, woke infiltrating bureaucracies as a problem and woke infiltrating corporate America as a problem. We say that Florida is where woke goes to die. . . . It is fundamentally at odds with reality.

And true to form, DeSantis' Florida is quickly becoming the most anti-woke state in the country, banning books by the hundreds and even terminating an elementary school principal who allowed sixth-grade students to view images of Michelangelo's David without parental permission. Apparently, David's flaccid penis was just too woke for Florida.[3] The zeitgeist of anti-wokeism reflects the broader desire for negation at the core of the extremist white supremacist constellation we have described throughout this manuscript. And negation is a fire that historically often burns everything in its path. The desire for negation we are battling will destroy the planet in the form of climate denialism; public health in the form of anti-vaccination; democracy in the form of voter suppression; women's control of their own bodies in the form of anti-abortion and so many other cornerstones of a modern society.[4]

The solutions to confronting extremist white supremacy that we suggest later in the chapter reflect our focus on the constellation rather than groups and individuals though that strategy also has a place. We discuss broader essential changes that require a systemic, multi-faceted, and long-term effort, in contrast to solutions that reflect haphazard shots in the dark with little or no fit between the nature of the problem and proposed fixes to the problem. Unfortunately, there are many examples from related fields – such as the ill-fated 'just say no' campaign to reduce teen drug use or the poorly conceived 'scared straight' programs designed to prevent kids engaged in juvenile delinquency from transitioning to more serious adult criminality – that underscore the importance of designing solutions with the full complexity of the problem in mind.[5] As authorities and citizens consider the most promising measures to address extremist white supremacy, we need to intelligently include measures that can disrupt the cultural transmission of the practices, ideas, and emotions that we address in this book.

What to do?

So, what should this country do about white supremacist extremism? Of course, this question assumes that people really *want* to do something about it. Many do not. They either do not acknowledge white supremacists, do not see extremism as a problem requiring scrutiny and action, or are aligned with one or more extremist viewpoints. As more and more U.S. citizens absorb ideas that mobilize the far right, such as the 'great replacement' narrative and Trump's stolen election lies, and support the use of threats and violence against their political opponents, the country moves further away from a just, reasonable, and resilient body politic. Those who see racism, antisemitism, authoritarianism, and violence as fundamentally immoral, unjust, and antidemocratic face a daunting task.

The problem now is that the nation is playing a complicated game of catch-up. For more than two decades, law enforcement, elected officials, journalists, and citizens mostly ignored or dismissed the danger emanating from extremist white supremacy. The uncomfortable reality is that our current intensifying extremist threat was, in the words of extremism experts Wendy Via and Heidi Beirich, 'entirely foreseeable and likely preventable.'[6] Time and again, watchdog groups such as the Southern Poverty Law Center (SPLC) and Anti-Defamation League (ADL), the few political activists and researchers that focused on the topic, and scattered voices among law enforcement warned about white supremacist extremists active in our midst. And time and again, those warnings were ignored, written off, and shut down. Even in our scholarly circles, fellow researchers asked us not-so-subtle questions about why we focus on white supremacy, making clear that they thought the topic was bizarre, unsophisticated, and unimportant. After Trump's election in 2016 and the Unite the Right rally in 2017, we no longer heard those questions. Instead, we heard and read about the shock and surprise that people expressed as they began to come to terms with what we already knew. White supremacist extremism is neither bizarre nor unimportant. On the contrary, it is a common and powerful facet of our political system, and new players have again emerged to attack tolerance, trust in democracy, and social inclusion.[7]

To be frank, we do not feel very optimistic about the likelihood the United States and the world will do what is necessary to effectively combat extremist white supremacy, nor do we see its appeal losing ground. We do not have much sugar to coat the bitter pill that white supremacy forces us to swallow. The United States is in a bad place, facing an overwhelming challenge to democracy, and any possibility of diminishing the threat requires a sober assessment that refuses our unrelenting desire to see the glass half full. The glass is nowhere near half full, and anyone who cares just even a little about the future of democracy should see the desperation in the current situation.

Part of what we need to ask each other involves the most basic questions: What kind of country do we want to live in? Is it a place where only the 'fittest' survive? And, by fittest, do we really mean the most privileged people with the biggest guns or the most resources, and who are willing to use them to get their way? Do we really want to live in a country where authoritarian dictators are admired as strong and decisive leaders rather than as bullies and despots? This kind of social Darwinist survivalism is exactly what white supremacists fantasize about, and, clearly, this dystopian vision has attracted growing segments of mainstream society. We need to collectively reject this worldview as a first step in the broader, massive undertaking required to fully realize the potential for a true multicultural democracy.

Simultaneously, we need to affirm alternatives to extremist white supremacy, which embrace community with the principles of peace, inclusion, empathy, and equality. Extreme white supremacists create a community of sorts. But those opposed to them are much larger and can be more powerful. We need to commit to develop a broad-based community of mutually supportive diverse people, bent on inclusion rather than exclusion, more peaceful than conflictual, and ultimately healthier – in all the ways we think about health (mental, physical, and spiritual) – than presently exists. It is a big unwieldy goal, an 'end in view' as the philosopher John Dewey called utopian visions that may be impossible to fully reach.[8] But, what other options are there then to try?

A multidimensional approach

Right-wing extremists do not yet control broad swaths of the U.S. government, though that is their goal, and they have made worrisome inroads. As we write this, the presidency is in Democratic Party hands, and the Biden administration has developed a long-overdue plan to combat far-right extremism. Known as the National Strategy for Countering Domestic Terrorism, the plan lays out four 'pillars' around which to build a 'government-wide strategy' to 'address violence and reduce the factors that lead to violence, threaten public safety, and infringe on the free expression of ideas.'[9] After several administrations ignored and dismissed extremist white supremacy, it is remarkable that President Biden even offered a strategy on domestic terrorism. Unfortunately, it took dire circumstances to recognize that domestic terror is now commonplace in U.S. society and that it flows from what the White House terms 'biases against minority populations' and 'perceived government overreach.'[10]

In theory, the 'Strategy' addresses important matters. One pillar calls for enhanced research, information sharing, and analysis to better understand extremist threats and risks. Better understanding should, in theory, help inform the second pillar of prevention – resources and services to build resilience among people who might be targeted by extremists. Research and prevention efforts should then support the third pillar that seeks to disrupt and deter domestic terror activity before it occurs. Rather than just responding to terror attacks after the fact, this 'pro-active' stance works to prevent terrorism by enabling federal law enforcement, along with state and local authorities, to track and disrupt extremist activities. The fourth pillar emphasizes the need to confront the long-term and deep-seated contributors to domestic terrorism, such as racism, misogyny, and hatred of religious and sexual minorities; gun violence; mental health issues; and economic disparities. In short, the Biden plan calls for a multidimensional approach that beefs up and reimagines law enforcement and builds a long-overdue prevention infrastructure.

Of course, any time the government tacks into domestic extremism waters, it must navigate complications with civil rights and liberties, particularly the U.S. Constitution's First, Second, and Fourth Amendments. On the one hand, public safety must be protected. On the other hand, it is dangerous to compromise Constitutionally protected civil liberties, including the right to free speech (on social media and in the public square); the right to free assembly/association; the right to bear arms; and rights protecting against unreasonable search, seizure, and surveillance. And there are real worries to consider, including a long history of FBI abuses related to counter-intelligence operations that relied on covert and often illegal means to surveil, infiltrate, discredit, and disrupt domestic political organizations, mostly on the left but occasionally on the right.[11]

The dichotomy between public safety and civil liberties may be a false one. Constitutional protections have never been absolute, and the government at the local, state, and federal levels is responsible for investigating, arresting, and prosecuting those who violate criminal statutes. As law professor Mary Anne Franks argues, a certain obsessive 'constitutional fundamentalism,' especially about free speech and the right to bear arms, works to create less – not more – democracy.[12] There has been a misunderstanding in the public aided by certain legal interpretations that the First Amendment provides individuals immunity to engage in an 'anything goes' type of speech with complete protection. In fact, the First Amendment is primarily a protection against government restrictions of speech. Nongovernmental entities like social media platforms are well within their rights to restrict hate and offensive speech, as outlined in terms of service agreements. One outcome from the confusion over freedom of speech is that politicians and media figures like Alex Jones[13] are allowed to use rhetoric that goes well beyond 'fiery'.

Right-wing extremists have effectively shrouded themselves in constitutional protections while violating laws against making criminal threats and fomenting criminal conspiracies. The government can and should do more to curtail the illegal activities associated with extremism while, at the same time, preventing domestic terrorism through legal reforms such as common-sense gun legislation. This legislation could require national waiting periods and reduce access to the literally hundreds of millions of firearms in circulation across the United States.[14]

Unlike some observers who seem hesitant to invoke the need for law enforcement strategies to address white supremacy, we see this arena as vital to stemming the current threat to democracy.[15] But rather than creating new laws to address domestic terrorism, as some claim is necessary,[16] we see greater efficacy in applying existing laws that already provide the government with tools to respond to domestic terrorism.[17] While strategies based on prosecuting each individual group can be helpful in certain respects, they tend to limit law enforcement by treating each extremist group independently and conducting investigations in isolation.

Understanding extremist white supremacy through a constellation framework could provide law enforcement with better ways to identify its underlying networks and actions. The offline and digital network connections that link extremists within the United States and across the globe provide opportunities for prosecutors to apply various criminal conspiracy statutes such as the Racketeer Influenced and Corrupt Organizations Act (RICO). Federal law enforcement has used this statute successfully against white supremacist prison gangs and white supremacist street-based networks such as Blood & Honour – Tampa Bay.[18] In recent years, despite a surge of domestic terror activity, surprisingly few federal prosecutors have employed RICO or other criminal conspiracy statutes against the racial extremist threat. Although the January 6th sedition prosecutions are an important exception, the federal government has been exceedingly slow to pursue legal actions for national and international threats tied to extremist white supremacy. The absence of criminal conspiracy charges filed against the organizers of the violent UTR is one important case in point. The exceedingly lenient punishment given to Brandon Russell, the founder of the international terror cell Atomwaffen Division, is another. Even though Russell had explosives and preparatory material that indicated he was making plans to attack a nuclear power plant, he received a five-year sentence. He was released in 2021 with virtually no conditions preventing him from associating with white supremacists either online or offline, a standard condition typically imposed for known gang members.[19] Even more shocking, on February 3, 2023, Russell and one of his associates, Sarah Beth Clandaniel, a 34-year-old convicted felon who previously served prison time for an armed robbery charge, were arrested for conspiring to destroy an energy facility underscoring a longstanding desire among extremist white supremacists to attack critical infrastructure in the United States. If convicted, both Russell and Clandaniel face a maximum of 20 years in federal prison.[20]

These cases highlight the need for law enforcement and the judicial branch to aggressively investigate, prosecute, and punish racial extremists' criminal violations. But the problems cannot be fixed with a new law. Federal judicial branch members need more resources for training about the threat of domestic terrorism. The Federal Bureau of Prisons and U.S. Probation and Pre-Trial Services need more resources to investigate and monitor domestic terror threats, and the Department of Justice needs greater capacity to conduct federal hate crime investigations and prosecutions.

There are also opportunities to apply existing laws that limit paramilitary activity. For example, former U.S. Attorneys Barbara McQuade and Mary McCord have each argued that the government should enforce statutes that criminalize paramilitary militia activities.[21] All states have laws that prohibit private militia activity, and 25 states make it a criminal offense.[22] But authorities have failed to address and prosecute these activities. Part of this failure results from the perceptual problems we identified in previous chapters, which help produce very different responses to far-right extremism as compared to perceived threats from racial minorities or the far left. Understanding the constellation helps to address these perceptual problems and bring extremism into clearer focus.

The recent verdicts in the seditious conspiracy case filed against J6 insurrectionists including Oathkeepers' founder Stewart Rhodes and his accomplices underscore the importance of the legal system to help stem the antidemocratic, far-right extremist surge. The verdicts create an official record that J6 was more than an overexcited mob but was rather planned violence even though it is unclear if those at the upper echelons, including Trump himself, will be charged. Insurrection verdicts are also a necessary precondition for long-term prevention strategies. Prevention strategies, such as those emphasizing public health, can only take root if justice is meted out against those who violently attack the government and private citizens.

Civil lawsuits can also be an effective deterrent against racial extremists, as exemplified by *Sines v. Kessler*. In contrast to criminal cases, which are brought by state or federal prosecutors and can result in the imprisonment of the defendants, civil cases are filed by private parties to receive monetary judgments as compensation for damages incurred from the defendants' actions and, in some cases, also punitive financial judgments. Many of the most prominent U.S. civil cases filed against racial extremists in recent decades were initiated by the Southern Poverty Law Center and resulted in judgments that splintered or imploded groups and forced them to forfeit property they held. The effectiveness of civil lawsuits can be limited when groups and individuals are able to hide their assets. Government efforts to trace fund transfers, including in cryptocurrencies and across national borders, could provide a useful tool.

The longstanding presence of extremist white supremacists, including racist militia, in law enforcement must be another focal point. Congressional committees have drawn attention to this issue but, to date, have taken very little action.[23] Various initiatives could be implemented to disentangle law enforcement from racial extremism. The initial screening process to ferret out extremists before they become police officers requires revamping, and officers unwilling to comply with policies that prohibit discriminatory practices should be terminated. A national clearinghouse style database that includes all known officers who have extremist affiliations and/or who have expressed agreement with extremist ideals (something not allowed by most departmental policies) would provide much needed data about the scope of the problem. This type of intelligence gathering also has relevance for law enforcement hiring across the country and could spur additional research to help understand different facets of the long-overlooked problem of extremism in police ranks. Maybe most importantly, if law enforcement is going to play a role in defending democracy, police need to establish much deeper levels of trust with communities than they have now, especially communities that have been victimized by unlawful and unjust policing practices. To put it bluntly, it is difficult for law enforcement to build community trust when many citizens suspect these agencies of having extremist white supremacists in their ranks.[24]

Those who try to address racial extremism in law enforcement must also challenge and find ways to transform the overlap between policing culture and extremist white supremacy. In this respect, white supremacists do not need to infiltrate police department ranks because white supremacism is already part of the policing culture, as illustrated by informal communiques such as text messages among police officers that involve racist and other hateful discussions.[25] We can also see the overlap in policing and white supremacist culture in the long history of racist police gangs such as the Lynwood Vikings. This gang flourished in the Los Angeles Sheriff's Department during the 1980s and 1990s, and one federal judge referred to it as a 'white supremacist neo-Nazi street gang.'[26] Of course, any type of police reform faces an uphill battle in the United States because the decentralization of policing and reactionary police unions makes any recommendations difficult to implement.

Invoking law enforcement to address domestic terrorism also means reimagining law enforcement with greater emphasis on public health strategies such as mental health support and social work services.[27] While controversial, we know that a major part of the extremist white supremacist problem involves unaddressed mental health issues and unresolved childhood and adolescent trauma.[28] Clearly, most people living with mental health problems are not involved in extremism, but having mental health problems does seem to create certain vulnerabilities that may increase a person's susceptibility to racial extremism. White supremacist involvement, in turn, may generate or exacerbate mental health problems, given the high levels of trauma related to different types of violence and the generally toxic nature of extremist environments. We also know that better resourced and more responsive mental health interventions could prevent terror attacks like we saw in Buffalo, New York, in 2022 and elsewhere across the United States.[29] It is important to address untreated mental health issues that, when neglected, make us all less safe, especially those in communities most likely to be targeted by white supremacist terror.

A new deal

One of the most immediate needs is to transform the U.S. criminal justice system to align more closely with the ideals of democracy, fairness, respect, and equity. Too much discussion about criminal justice poses these ideas as competing with the needs for safety and security. We regard a radical transformation of policing, courts, and prisons to be essential to countering white supremacy and sustaining a robust democracy. However, we are concerned about calls to abolish the criminal justice system wholesale. As the current attack on democracy intensifies, advocating the elimination of the police and closing prisons is music to the ears of white supremacist demagogues and their political allies.

Short- and long-term commitments from law enforcement are needed to provide additional monitoring, investigation, and prosecution of criminal activity including hate crimes and domestic terror. But we also acknowledge truth in the saying, 'You can't only arrest your way out of a problem.'

Since it was established shortly after the 9/11 attacks, the Department of Homeland Security (DHS) has been at the center of addressing the terrorism threat. The agency's focus on prevention has been very uneven. The Obama administration contributed their 'countering violent extremism' initiative (CVE) to help shift federal focus toward prevention. What followed was a period where CVE routinely came under fire for narrowly focusing on Islamic extremism while ignoring far-right extremism. Some critics claimed CVE was a front for a covert surveillance system aimed at the Muslim community.[30] With good reason, concerns about CVE intensified during Trump's administration, as the DHS became associated with his policy of keeping '[immigrant] kids in cages.' Following the police murder of George Floyd, Trump made efforts to use DHS as his own private policing agency to attack BLM protesters and those he characterized as antifa.

During the Biden administration, DHS established the Center for Prevention Programs and Partnerships (CP3) as part of an effort to change perceptions and revamp their priorities. CP3 embraced an early prevention and public health framework that focuses substantially on extremist white supremacy. The new approach emphasizes partnerships with local governments and nongovernmental organizations to build a patchwork or consortium-style network across the United States with the federal government serving as a facilitator that directs resources to each community based on their unique needs. This valuable approach is 10, if not 20, years overdue and faces a major problem of scale. Solutions must take account of the enormity of the problem. Given the current prevalence of extremist white supremacy, the federal government must take a much more proactive and involved approach. Distrust of the federal government may taint these efforts, but being passive will not increase the government's legitimacy. Many of those who distrust the federal government will do so no matter how innocuous the federal government tries to appear.

Our country needs a major effort, something akin to earlier 'New Deal' and 'New Frontier' federal campaigns, to rebuild trust in government and reduce polarization with an emphasis on 'truth and reconciliation.'[31] By reconciliation, we are not suggesting appeasement of antidemocratic and oppressive forces. Truth, morality, and justice cannot be sacrificed to achieve some mutual agreement that colludes with injustice. But as alliances are built, it is vital to be strategic and empathetic toward different perspectives about how to best achieve the ideals of a multicultural democracy.

A national campaign to attack the far-right constellation must center on uprooting white supremacy in all its forms: hatred, violence, discrimination, and exclusion. As our explanation of the constellation and its persistence shows, the current crisis is far more entrenched than is often acknowledged. Authorities must disrupt the most pernicious groups, like the Proud Boys, Patriot Front, and every other unsavory flavor of the week. But it is also necessary to uproot the practices, ideas, and emotions that drive extremist white supremacy to stave off its spread into the mainstream. People and groups that violate the law need to be investigated, with culpable individuals arrested and, in some cases, sentenced to lengthy prison terms, but these efforts must be coupled with a broader attention to the underlying constellation that sustains extremism.[32]

A national campaign must double down on democracy, justice, inclusion, and equality. Advocates should embrace these ideals to the same extent that Steve Bannon wanted his followers to embrace being called a racist.[33] Of course, this means accepting disagreement about what these ideals should look like and how best to achieve them. Fighting over different approaches for achieving these goals only furthers antidemocratic efforts.

Prevention and intervention

In addition to challenging extremist white supremacy through the legal system, we also see a dire need for a sustained, multidimensional focus on prevention and intervention efforts in four areas: civic education, deradicalization, Internet, and counternarratives. We then conclude with recommendations about things to avoid, an often-overlooked aspect of policy making, followed by a short discussion about specific acts individuals can take to help stem the antidemocratic tide sweeping the country.

Civic education

Rebuilding civic life is essential. Civic education that promotes the virtues of democracy should be a national focus. Such an effort must engage difficult issues such as past failings of democracy (both home and abroad), limitations of democracy, and alternatives to democracy, while avoiding jingoistic nationalism. Given the growing influence of digital culture, rebuilding civic life must engage online hate and extremism in ways that not only include but also move beyond deplatforming efforts. Such efforts should include bipartisan, nongovernmental organizations attempting to rebuild civic infrastructure in the wake of attacks by the Trump administration and continuing antidemocratic disinformation campaigns. Unfortunately, the divided government seems far from partisan cooperation on this and other vital issues.

Rebuilding civic culture is a long-term project and will need to start with helping children of all racial/ethnic backgrounds learn the value of intergroup relations, diversity in all its forms, and emotional and social intelligence. Children should learn about bigotry and hatred to help them understand and resist the vitriolic ideas and discriminatory behaviors that flow from white supremacist culture and that they will likely confront, even in childhood. Such education can serve as a catalyst for self-discovery and self-assessment for all children.[34] To avoid intentionally or unintentionally reinforcing essentialist ideas, it is important to emphasize that racism, misogyny, and other forms of bigotry are in no way natural or inevitable. Children should not only understand the stark realities of our society, but also be helped to imagine a different, more inclusive, and inviting future.

To be clear, many challenges stand in the way of implementing any school-based initiatives. In the past several years, the far right has mobilized around school concerns, stoking fears and anger on issues related to the COVID public health measures required in many schools, curriculum content informed by critical race theory, something the far right describes as 'anti-White' and anti-American,' and 'groomer' conspiracies, which exploit long held anti-gay hatred by claiming that 'pedophiles' and liberals are allegedly trying to 'convert' young children toward an LGBTQ+ lifestyle. One of the most recent incarnations of the groomer madness involves the false claim that schools are using litter boxes to accommodate students who are 'furries' (a subculture interested in the anthropomorphic qualities associated with animal characters). Like many of the lies spread online and offline, there are shreds of truth that become deeply distorted and perverted. In this case, several schools in 2018 did begin issuing students litter boxes, but the purpose was to address bathroom needs during a school shooting. The fact that schools need to consider such measures should by itself be a national scandal, but these measures were then turned into opportunities for extremists in alt-media such as podcasting giants like Joe Rogan to peddle disinformation. The resulting outrage, in turn, discourages schools from enacting progressive measures that address the very hatreds that give life to conspiracy theories[35]: a catch-22, to say the least.

Extremists have targeted schools in other ways. Across the country, the age-old tactic of book banning has reemerged.[36] Educational officials also face death threats and angry mobs at their homes over policies that extremists do not like. For example, an elementary school principal in California was confronted at his private residence by parents who believed he was trying to harm their children with COVID measures.[37] It is not clear that pro-democracy supporters understand the extent to which schools have become a major front in the war against justice and equality. Our schools require resources and support to protect students and teachers from threats and attacks. Society needs to support school efforts to teach children the value of democracy.

Deradicalization

Prevention and intervention also come in smaller doses, like programs that support people trying to disengage and deradicalize from their support for extremist white supremacism.[38] European-style 'EXIT' programs, first developed in Norway and then in Sweden, Germany, and other countries, inform the current efforts in the United States. Yet, compared to their European counterparts, U.S. disengagement programs tend to be underdeveloped, under-resourced, and, quite frankly, often operated by untrained individuals ill-prepared to address the complexities involved in exiting extremism. The programs too often rely on so-called 'formers' – individuals who were formerly involved in extremism – with little vetting and no formal training to provide interventions or advise on such efforts. Intervention programs aimed at helping high-risk individuals, such as extremists who may be suicidal or homicidal, need careful assessment and close monitoring and evaluation. These programs often lack these elements, which puts service providers, their clients, and the public at risk.[39]

Despite these limitations, well-designed and appropriately implemented intervention efforts can and should be an important tool for reducing hate and extremist-fueled violence. White supremacist adherents who completely deradicalize by withdrawing from racist networks and their violence-ridden practices, ideas, and emotions may even embrace the ideals of a multicultural, inclusionary society. Even those who cannot fully break from extremist movements and activities or who continue to embrace some extremist ideas and emotions tend to engage in less violent behavior.[40] Although deradicalization can be a long-complicated process,[41] intervention programs that adopt best practices and professional standards from the fields of social work and mental health have track records of success.

The need for well-run intervention services far exceeds what is available now or in the foreseeable future, especially considering the vast and growing numbers of individuals radicalizing in online spaces. Moreover, U.S. disengagement programs are primarily designed for adults, although many of those who are 'falling down the extremist rabbit hole' today are teens and even younger children. And there are no clearly effective strategies to bring people out of conspiratorial thinking except through long-term work with a trusted friend or relative. Research and action in this area need to be prioritized.

Confronting digital extremism

The Internet is a 'true accelerant' for white supremacy[42] and poses major challenges to preventing and countering extremism. As we show, extremists use the Internet to spread their malicious narratives, coordinate actions, monetize their content, and attempt to radicalize both long-timers and new joiners. Observers have long known about the Internet's importance to extremist persistence. But major platforms ignored their role in spreading online hate and failed to enforce anti-hate regulations. And few platforms have any meaningful policies to address disinformation. As the ADL demonstrated, even more than six years after implementing its first policy against hateful conduct, Twitter continued in 2022 to ignore many blatantly anti-Semitic posts.[43] With Twitter's new owner, Elon Musk, at the helm, the platform now accepts openly neo-Nazi users like the *Daily Stormer*'s Andrew Anglin whose account had previously been closed. Twitter has relaxed standards related to hate speech which unsurprisingly produced an exponential increase in the use of racist slurs.[44]

Slowing extremist white supremacy's spread requires more systematic and comprehensive strategies and more focused enforcement than we have seen to this point. And clearly, the stakes are high. Limiting the spread of online narratives would likely curb violence and limit recruitment. But the reactive strategies that authorities tend to pursue do not suppress extremist narratives nearly enough. Efforts such as removing content producers from online platforms, blacklisting keywords or websites from web-based search results, and hiding information through web search protocol designs so that racial extremist content is more difficult to find are all potentially helpful in solving the dilemma. But the massive quantity of material already circulating on the Internet minimizes the effects of these reactive efforts.

In any case, most digital platforms demonstrate only limited commitment to these strategies and do not coordinate suppression efforts internationally, which leave too many openings for extremist content to proliferate. If the public continues to rely on private tech companies to surveil and decide who and what is 'extreme' and should be deplatformed, then we will see more white supremacy, not less. That said, we have seen deplatforming used successfully against Islamist extremist groups[45] after U.S. politicians demanded that major technology platforms remove ISIS and al-Qaeda and make other efforts to diminish their online presence. Yet, as Heidi Beirich and Wendy Via argue, 'it would be inconceivable for social media platforms to allow ISIS propaganda to grow and spread unchecked, or to be monetized, but that is exactly what happens with white supremacy.'[46]

Domestic efforts to monitor, intervene, and disrupt online extremism will likely remain inadequate, but technology platforms should still be held responsible for the content they publish. Lawmakers would need to alter civil liability statutes for that to happen, and any regulatory strategy would run up against challenges related to the First Amendment. Indeed social media regulations have been written in ways that open opportunities for extremists to exploit. For instance, Texas passed a law to deregulate online content and allow full autonomy for expression on major social media platforms.[47] Such complete unrestricted expression opens the floodgates even wider for extremist narratives and calls to violence. That said, opportunities exist to compel social media companies to monitor whether their platforms amplify extremist content. Companies, however, need to more fully commit to systematic strategies to monitor and deal with extremist content, something they have been unwilling to do thus far. To complicate matters even more, many Internet sites with extremist content are licensed outside of the United States and thus beyond the reach of U.S. law.

Efforts to curb online extremist content mostly focus on centralized Internet services used by major social media companies such as Facebook, Twitter, YouTube, and TikTok. Rightly so, since they are the major drivers behind the growth in hate and far-right extremism movements, conspiracy theories, and radicalization. They also serve as spaces for organizing violent events. But, as these major platforms took actions to moderate and limit disinformation and extremist content, white supremacists increasingly moved their online activity to more niche platforms, such as Telegram, Gab, Parler, and Truth Social, which offer havens to those spreading conspiracies, disinformation, and calls for violence. Their tolerance for messages promoting hate, bigotry, and violence opens the door wider for real-world violence, as demonstrated by the Pittsburgh synagogue murderer who interacted frequently on Gab before he lashed out. These niche platforms also draw far-right politicians who deepen their connections by interacting with committed extremists. As we noted earlier, the 2022 Republican candidate for governor of Pennsylvania engaged Gab to advertise his campaign and predictably generated antisemitic posts on the platform.[48]

Counternarratives

Countering extremist narratives is an essential, complex, and long-term strategy for challenging racial extremism. White supremacists are adept at exploiting factual events by twisting interpretations to fit and justify their worldviews and fabricating conspiratorial fantasies that rile emotions and encourage followers to lash out. Their core claims have not changed much over time, drawing from common emotionally evocative ideas such as that White people are culturally superior, White people deserve power and privilege, race-mixing is dangerous, and racially conscious White people must save their race from cultural and biological extinction. Their ideas inspire wide-ranging fantasies, from 'great replacement' and new world order conspiracies to claims that may seem less obviously white supremacist, such as the Big Lie election conspiracy, Gamergate, or Pizzagate.[49] Some narratives evoke the righteousness of God's will to justify racism and hatred, creating an almost intractable foundation for these beliefs while other narratives rely on secular underpinnings to argue for the biological and cultural superiority of the white race.

Efforts to counter extremist ideology cannot just focus on pushing back or promoting more virtuous messages. In some cases, pushing back against extremist messages can unintentionally reinforce extremism as the very efforts to counter them are often used as evidence of the conspiracy's 'truth.' Moreover, there's no clear way to find agreement on specific virtues to support that would counter racist narratives. Often, extremists use ideas that seem virtuous to hint at or justify quite troublesome meanings and practices. James Chase Sanchez notes that both the KKK and Trump have used the terms 'patriotism,' 'heritage,' and 'security' with 'textual winks' to construct a civic version of white supremacy over the last few years.[50] The versatility and ambiguity of such terms make it possible for audiences, including racist audiences, to ascribe a meaning that matches their goals.[51] For those trying to counter extremism, virtue messaging is not very effective. Moreover, as J.M. Berger argues, virtue messages 'must seek the lowest common denominator, resulting in a value set that is nebulous, non-cohesive and ahistorical. While not entirely pointless, values-oriented messaging is necessarily limited.'[52]

Those trying to counter extremist narratives face a long-term struggle over broad cultural and political meanings. Extremists work to deconstruct prevailing progressive ideological and cultural mindsets and replace them with racist traditionalism, hierarchy, and inequality. As historian Alexandra Stern explains, white supremacists want 'to become the hip counterculture of the twenty-first century [using] a semiological hall of mirrors that careens from righteous militancy to misanthropic irony [and] has insinuated itself in the American imagination. . . .'[53] They strategize ways to build soft power by creating rival alternatives to mainstream institutions, including academia, arts, news, and entertainment media, to shift people's judgments about what's politically desirable and possible. Through strategic messaging by varied means that range from academic-looking journals, music, podcasts, talk shows, blogs, and social media networks to clothing, hairstyles, and coded symbols, they seek to normalize extremist practices, ideas, and emotions to further their expansion.[54]

Countering extremist narratives requires recognizing and naming them as such across the entire multimedia ecosystem. It also requires a proactive approach, instead of the current approach of trying to fight such narratives as they emerge in 'whack-a-mole' fashion. For example, Facebook relies on key words associated with white supremacy, and when individuals or groups post in ways that set off those tripwires, Facebook may try to intervene in some fashion. Facebook has chosen to avoid far more effective strategies such as altering their algorithms to avoid promoting dangerous and damaging posts.[55]

What not to do?

When describing a problem, it is common to prescribe how to 'fix' it, but less common to specify what should not be done. But a problem can grow worse if the cause is misdiagnosed and the wrong solutions applied. This is the case with extremism today. As philanthropist Crystal Hayling argues,[56] too much of the current narrative frames 'the problem' of today's politics as one of 'division' rather than as the result of a concerted attack by extremist white supremacists and large segments of the Republican Party. Framing the current attack on democracy as a difference of opinion leads to remedies to address those differences. The solutions will be ineffective because the problem is not a difference of opinion but an effort to seize power and subjugate people of color and their allies to white supremacy. Making an inaccurate assessment and applying the 'wrong' solutions to attacks on democracy mean further confusion, wasted resources, and more squandered opportunities, at best. At worst, they mean broadening the extremist base, bringing more conflict and violence.

Framing the extremist problem as simply divisiveness, in part, may reflect peoples' unwillingness to face the political dystopia the nation is free-falling toward, as well as a lack of courage to sound alarm bells about it. But the framing also reflects another pattern in journalistic, scholarly, and government assessments of the current moment that we think of as racism-avoidance. Many people seem more comfortable describing the nation's political divisions in ways that avoid the central role of racism. Racism-avoidance is evident in calls for reducing polarization and bridging differences that ignore the concerted efforts of extremist white supremacists to wield practices, ideas, and emotions to dismantle the ideals inherent in multicultural democracy. One example is the Department of Homeland Security's new categories for monitoring domestic extremism, which conflate white supremacists with Black nationalists, treating them as flip sides of the same coin despite massive differences in their respective histories and extent of lethal violence. Another example is the way that the DHS distinguishes between extremist white supremacists and anti-government militias despite widespread recognition that militias consistently express core aspects of extremist white supremacy such as anti-immigrant and anti-Muslim practices, ideas, and emotions.[57] When we avoid appending a racist label to groups who embrace racist practices, ideas, and emotions, racism appears more normal and accepted or what the sociologist and Congressperson, Daniel Patrick Moynihan referred to as 'defining deviancy down.'[58]

Stereotypes about racial extremism still abound so that if anti-government extremists do not show stereotypical white supremacist 'markings,' such as white sheets and hoods or swastikas, government analysts almost automatically exclude them from the extremist white supremacist category. Researchers also fall into racism-avoidance when they discuss Trumpism and the MAGA movement without mentioning racism or when they otherwise downplay racism by reducing the cause of the movement to economic anxiety.

There are many other things we should avoid when addressing extremist white supremacy. Authorities should not fund programs aimed at countering violent extremism or preventing domestic terrorism unless there is evidence that they are effective. Developing new interventions is important, but these should be accompanied by rigorous evaluation to assess what truly works. Disturbingly, the terrorism prevention field lacks professional standards to adequately vet practitioners who claim specialized expertise but may be little more than frauds or hucksters promising cures for hate or who make overly broad claims about their programs based on superficial analysis or limited data.[59] Public safety remains at risk without improvements in terrorism prevention research and intervention, which use clear standards and evaluations to be best practices for that professional community.

Another problem to avoid is using language that extremists favor. Although written off by some opponents of extremism as an irrelevant issue of semantics, the symbolic and strategic aspects of communication are critical to the persistence and growth of extremist white supremacism. Eli Kline, one of the primary organizers of UTR, explained this point during a podcast interview in the days preceding the violent event:

> [W]e have done something in a way with the tactics we've been using and the aesthetic we've been choosing. . . . [E]verything like that has gotten the most left-leaning newspapers, magazines, and websites to quote this as a pro-white rally and movement instead of Nazi, KKK. . . . [I]t's showing we're infecting their brains which is great.'[60]

Kline's statement underscores the reality that racial extremists have always been focused on disseminating ideas, shaping narratives, and influencing public policy, both overtly and indirectly. They employ labels such as 'alt-right' and 'white nationalist' as a tactic to redirect attention from their aims, soften their rhetoric, and mainstream their ideas.[61] Scholars, journalists, and others who do not share extremist beliefs but unwittingly use their language reward extremists by helping reframe their cause and spread their ideas. We worry that terms like 'white nationalist' convey a sense of patriotism unrelated to

Nazism and violence, something we heard echoed in a recent interview with a MAGA supporter who does not openly identify with extremism. When asked about the term, 'white nationalism,' she responded, 'sounds more like patriotism . . . being patriotic, not like Nazi or anything.'[62] As far-right extremist researcher Annie Kelly observes,

> [S]uccess is primarily measured not by levels of recruitment to their ranks but in terms of their ever-increasing dissemination of extreme right-wing ideals and their ability to project an updated rhetoric of anti-left antagonism into the Overton window of acceptable political discourse.[63]

Shifting labels and language represent ongoing adaptation efforts among adherents to normalize and mainstream racial animus and polarization.

A second example of how language may unintentionally promote extremist white supremacism is how the media and pundits discuss U.S. demographic changes. They often use ominous terms to discuss the idea that White residents are becoming a minority in the United States. Sometimes commentators suggest these changes signal an end to white supremacy and domination, a prospect that, among racial extremists, generates great consternation and fuels wild dystopian scenarios of White people losing their status and rights and society devolving into ungovernable 'cesspools' controlled by 'non-whites.' This predicted demographic change plays quite differently on the left, as you might imagine, with hopes for increased progressive electoral and policy success. These characterizations of demographic change are simply inaccurate. Minority refers not only to a numerical figure but also to a group's political and economic power. Little evidence suggests that White people are becoming a minority in the United States. Wealth is concentrated in fewer and fewer hands, and those hands are overwhelmingly white. Also, since racial categories are fluid, not fixed, identifying trends in the proportion of racial groups is a suspect enterprise.[64] Substantial demographic changes in the racial populations are only evident when all 'non-white' groups are aggregated and compared to the White population – an exercise that bears little resemblance to how people of different racial and ethnic groups actually live.

In short, the conversation about U.S. demographic change has unfolded in ways that are likely to provoke fear and anxiety among White people who are not aligned with extremist white supremacism but who may be drawn toward its fears of racial replacement and white genocide. We see nothing productive in artificially inflating the extent of demographic change even if the intent is to signal an end to white supremacy. Aside from unnecessarily stoking fears, this discussion promotes an unintentional complacency: wait for the demographic change, and white supremacy will 'naturally' crumble. But, as we have shown, white supremacists are quite capable of sustaining, adapting, and reinventing their practices, ideas, and emotions. Demographic changes, to the extent these occur, will never be sufficient to address the problem.[65]

What can individuals accomplish?

We now turn to an important question about what individuals can do to counter racial extremism. A threat of this scale requires efforts at *all levels* – by government, by nongovernmental organizations and communities, and by individuals. Individuals can make a difference in traditional ways – by voting and registering voters, donating funds, signing petitions, and taking similar actions. In the 2022 mid-term elections, increased voter turnout pushed back against most of the candidates who were running on the Big Lie conspiracy and other disinformation campaigns. That was no small victory.[66] More people need to take voting seriously as a necessary but insufficient first step toward struggling for a democracy that works for all people.

Individuals can also engage this effort in deeper ways, particularly by rejecting the essentialized ways of thinking about race that allows white supremacy to persist. Individuals – and readers of this book – can work toward radical nonessentialism.[67] What does this mean?

White supremacy and similar types of authoritarian frameworks require certain *thought patterns* that understand race as a biological and cultural reality in which skin pigmentation means something more than the amount of melanin in one's biochemistry. While stereotypical white supremacist rhetoric may be the most obvious expression of racial essentialism, the country is currently awash in less overtly essentialist thinking about race.[68] The very real social consequences of racial categories can be appreciated without subscribing to the underlying logic that these categories represent. But this means abandoning a deeply entrenched shorthand that leads us to make inferences and associations – many of which may seem relatively innocuous – that perpetuate the ideas that, at the most basic level, race is real, that there are racial essences that distinguish groups from each other, and that people can be sorted by their biological and cultural characteristics in meaningful ways. Doing so is easier said than done, however, as ingrained patterns of thought and linguistic structures can be hard to redefine.[69] We found these same difficulties while writing this book. Painting with broad overly general brush strokes is hard to avoid when describing historical events or contemporary social trends.

What does rejecting essentialism look like in practice? Quite simply, it means people pushing themselves to interact and, even better, spend quality time with other people who look different, pray to different gods or don't pray to any gods, have different sexual orientations, or express their gender in a variety of possible ways. Individuals can work to extend themselves beyond the confines of what they feel most comfortable with, but the onus is on members of the historically dominant groups in the United States to understand that domination and work to shift it toward mutuality, respect, and support for others. This is no short-term quick-fix process, and some people will not accept those efforts. It is hard work to act as allies and accomplices to anti-racism. Just offering these ideas will seem like naïve idealism to some and that's fine. Moving to a better place requires that we imagine the ideal then work toward that ideal, despite the many obstacles in the way.

We find compelling recommendations in African American Studies scholar Ruha Benjamin's book, *Viral Justice*. The spirit of *Viral Justice* involves asking 'what if' questions to help see new possibilities and increase the likelihood of transforming old deeply entrenched realities. As Benjamin explains,

[E]very single one of us can weave new patterns of thinking and doing . . . drawing on our varied skills, interests and dispositions. . . . We need the loud and ferocious world-builders as much as the quiet and studious ones. The last thing we need is for everyone to do or be the same thing![70]

Another aspect of *Viral Justice* involves what Benjamin refers to as 'practicing hope' through deeply personal changes to how we think, speak, and act daily in interactions within our families and with our co-workers and communities, and in the decisions we make about how much and in what ways to engage online in what are often deeply toxic environments. These decisions are, in part, how we practice hope and radical nonessentialism.

Our final thought

We would like to end on an optimistic note, but, because the United States has waited so long, we fear a dystopian future dominated by the desire to be surrounded by only those who share our worldview. A world with no clear facts and in which conspiracy theories are the norm. A world where hate, extremism, and violence are considered perfectly justifiable and rational responses to any perceived injustice leveled against our tribal bases. Of course, none of this is inevitable. But we must end this chapter where we began. The glass is simply not half full. We need to stop telling ourselves and each other fictions about our present and future and replace false optimism with urgency and sober assessment. We need to stop confusing realism with pessimism or nihilism. Only then can we act in ways that directly confront rather than avoid the extremist realities that we face.

Notes

1 The Three-fifths Compromise refers to the agreement among delegates at the U.S. Constitutional Convention in 1787 to maintain a balance of power between

Northern and Southern states by counting individuals who were enslaved as three-fifths of a person.
2 Di Placido, 2023.
3 Bravo, 2023.
4 Burley, 2017; Burghart and Zeskind, 2020.
5 Petrosino, Petrosino, and Buehler, 2004; Rosenbaum, 2007.
6 Via and Beirich, 2022.
7 Perliger, 2020.
8 Dewey, 1922.
9 The White House, 2021; Jones, Doxsee, and Harrington, 2020.
10 Ibid, 2021.
11 Cunningham, 2005.
12 Franks, 2019. The First Amendment involves the protection of free speech as it relates to government regulations, while the Second Amendment involves the right for U.S. citizens to possess firearms.
13 Alex Jones' followers unleashed vicious attacks on families of individuals killed during a school shooting, for which he was held liable in two civil suits.
14 Karp, 2018.
15 We are not suggesting imprisonment is an effective strategy overall or that mass incarceration has been anything more than an inhumane experiment with truly tragic consequences. Yet, there may be certain types of offenders including domestic terrorists who require some form of incarceration.
16 Blazakis, 2021.
17 German, 2018.
18 Federal Bureau of Investigation, 2011.
19 Martin, 2021.
20 US Department of Justice, 2023.
21 McQuade, 2022.
22 Ibid, 2022.
23 Oversight and Reform Committee, U.S. House of Representatives, 2020.
24 Johnson, 2019.
25 Carless and Corey, 2019b.
26 *Darren Thomas et al. v. County of Los Angeles et al.*, 1992. See Johnson (2019) for additional historical and more recent examples.
27 See Sinnar (2022) for an important discussion of the limitations of hate crime and terrorism frames to respond to white supremacist violence and the need for a racial justice approach.
28 Bubolz and Simi, 2019; Simi, Blee, DeMichele, and Windisch, 2017; Windisch, Simi, Blee, and DeMichele, 2020.
29 World Health Organization, 2010.
30 Brennan Center, 2019.
31 Fox and Cunningham, 2022.
32 Our approach differs from some observers who imply that the entrenched nature of white supremacy (i.e., anti-Black racism, antisemitism, anti-gay, and misogyny) must be disentangled from initiatives to address domestic terrorism. As domestic terrorism is simply the most violent manifestation of these problems, trying to separate the issues of domestic terrorism and white supremacy more broadly only sidesteps the depth of the problem.
33 Winsor, 2018.
34 Of course, we do not suggest these factors alone will prevent a child from eventually adopting racial extremism as no one solution can do that.
35 Demopolous, 2022.

36 Pen America, 2022.

37 Tadayon, 2022.

38 Bjørgo, 1998.

39 Kelly and DeCook, 2022.

40 Simi, Windisch, Harris, and Ligon, 2019.

41 Simi, Blee, DeMichele, and Windisch, 2017.

42 Via and Beirich, 2020.

43 After the new Twitter CEO Elon Musk softened the platform's guardrails against hate speech, racist and antisemitic slurs skyrocketed (Anti-Defamation League, 2022d).

44 Ray and Anyanwu, 2022.

45 Berger and Morgan, 2015.

46 Via and Beirich, 2020.

47 Villasenor, 2021.

48 Newhouse, 2020. Telegram has served in a similar fashion for Arizona State Senator Wendy Rogers whose channel hosts posts threatening the lives of public officials. Rogers herself on multiple occasions has expressed similar sentiments as she threatened political opponents with the gallows during an American First Political Action Conference speech (Duda, 2022).

49 Pizzagate originated on a white supremacist Twitter account, then spread throughout alt-right networks, and eventually fueled early QAnon interest among extremists. The conspiracy alleged that Hillary Clinton and other 'liberal elites' abused children in a Washington D.C. pizza restaurant. This totally false claim inspired an extremist to cross state lines from North Carolina to 'investigate' and 'save' the victims. He fired shots in the restaurant, and though he found nothing, extremists continue to harass the restaurant owner. See Southern Poverty Law Center (2021) and Bleakley (2021). The Big Lie about the 2020 election 'stolen' from Donald Trump and the January 6 insurrection that followed was driven by replacement theory and white fears about threats to their social and economic status.

50 Sanchez, 2018.

51 Ibid, 2018.

52 Berger, 2016b, p. 5.

53 Stern, 2019, p. 21.

54 Miller-Idriss, 2018.

55 Although Facebook executives have repeatedly claimed they take aggressive measures to combat and extremism on their platform, whistleblower testimonials suggest otherwise (Pelley, 2021).

56 Hayling, 2022.

57 In many cases, militias may also express antisemitism and anti-Black racism along with misogyny and, in this respect, check all of the key boxes of 'traditional' white supremacists. The Oversight's Subcommittee on Civil Rights and Civil Liberties led by Representative Jamie Raskin has importantly held congressional hearings to address the overlap between anti-government militias and white supremacist extremism and, in doing so, officially acknowledged the flawed nature of the DHS categories. See Oversight and Reform Committee, U.S. House of Representatives (2021).

58 Moynihan, 1993.

59 See also Kelly and DeCook (2022).

60 Simi and Futrell, 2020.

61 Donovan, Lewis, and Friedberg, 2018.

62 See the data appendix that follows this chapter.

63 Kelly, 2017, p. 76.

64 Roediger, 1991; Warren and Winddance Twine, 1997.
65 Alba, 2020.
66 Pilkington and Levine, 2022.
67 Kendi, 2016.
68 Gilroy, 2001.
69 Foucault, 1972.
70 Benjamin, 2022, p. 284.

DATA APPENDIX

The arguments we make in this book are rooted in our analysis of a large set of wide-ranging and unique empirical data on extremist white supremacism. Indeed, our primary data source is our unparalleled corpus of first-hand, close-up studies of white supremacist extremists over the past 30 years. For these studies, we conducted many first-hand ethnographic observations of racist meetings, festivals, informal social interactions, and highly ritualized events, as well as family home life through extended home stays with white supremacist and militia families. We also have collectively conducted lengthy interviews with over 300 currently active and former members of Ku Klux Klans, neo-Nazi groups, white power skinheads, and other white supremacist groups, both men and women. These data, to our knowledge, make up the largest and most detailed scholarly body of primary information on racial extremism in the United States. They formed the basis for many of our books and articles in scholarly journals, blogs, reports, testimony, and media interviews, some of which appear in the bibliography.

We personally collected the following ethnographic and interview data:

- Simi: Fieldwork and interviews with white supremacist and anti-government networks from 1997 to 2023, with 228 interviews with 132 current or former extremists including multiple 'death row' interviews in federal and state correctional facilities; attending events, such as meetings, cross burnings, social gatherings, and music shows, including the notorious Aryan Nations former headquarters in Hayden Lake, Idaho and Elohim City, Oklahoma, reportedly linked to the 1980s domestic terror group the Covenant, the Sword and the Arm of the Lord and the Oklahoma City bomber, Timothy McVeigh; and 45 field-based, embedded house visits in Arizona, California, Nevada, Utah, Idaho, and Colorado. These studies were supported by grants from the National Science Foundation; Harry Frank Guggenheim Foundation; Department of Homeland Security; National Counterterrorism Technology, Innovation, and Education Center; National Institute of Justice; University of Nevada Las Vegas; University of Nebraska Omaha; and Chapman University.

- Blee: Formal interviews in the 1980s and 1990s with 34 women who were involved in organized racist groups and several male leaders of racist groups and numerous informal interviews and observations of racist events and racist group settings across the United States, including cross burnings, festivals, group headquarters, and the homes of currently active white supremacists. Also, formal interviews and informal conversations in the 1980s with ten elderly women who had participated in the Ku Klux Klan of the 1920s. These studies were supported by the National Endowment for the Humanities, Kentucky Foundation on Women, Southern Regional Education Board, University of Pittsburgh, and University of Kentucky.
- Simi and Futrell: A long-term ethnographic collection of data on extremist white supremacists based on direct fieldwork, interviews, documentary analysis, and digital content analysis.
- Simi and Blee (and Matthew DeMichele): Formal life history interviews in the 2010s with 47 former members of white supremacist groups in the United States and Canada. This study was supported by a grant to Matthew DeMichele (RTI) from the National Institute of Justice.

A second, and also unparalleled, source of rare primary data that we relied upon resulted from the expert testimony that Blee and Simi provided in the Federal District Court civil case in which a jury rendered a $26 million judgment against leaders of U.S. white supremacism for their actions in the violent 2017 Unite the Right (UTR) events in Charlottesville, Virginia.[1] Our role as experts in this case provided us with a particular set of data relevant to the third moment examined in this study. As experts, we had access to otherwise-unavailable postings on the Discord platform that extremist white supremacists used to plan and draw support for the UTR event. In preparing our expert report and testimony for trial, we conducted 1,502 deductive and inductive searches as well as random searches through this very large data set, read all posts in the entire discussion 'channels" and the direct messages related to UTR, and conducted a 1% random sample of all posted images (photos, memes, symbols). Overall, we personally analyzed 2,875 unique images and approximately 575,000 posts and direct messages, along with the transcripts of defendant depositions and a tranche of personal communiques compelled from defendants' cell phone calls and text messages and social media accounts. Our review of these data illuminated how the UTR events were staged and their significance for the trajectory of white supremacist extremism. But UTR cannot be fully explained by what extremists tried to make happen. It also requires knowing why hundreds of men from multiple white supremacist groups and those unaffiliated with any group responded to the UTR organizers and decided to join the assault on Charlottesville. To understand the motives of those who traveled to UTR and who were persuaded to take part in this violent melee, we were able draw on the knowledge we gained from our many earlier interviews with current and former white supremacists in which we probed why they joined racist actions, including those that were intensely violent and exposed participants to clear risk of arrest and criminal prosecution.

As a third source of primary data, we draw from a vast array of racial extremist publications, websites, platform postings, and social media messages that we have been monitoring over the past three decades.

Finally, we use secondary data, collected by government agencies, other scholars, nonprofit and watchdog organizations, and journalists. In some cases, we used the interpretations provided by those who collected these data; in other cases, we analyzed or reanalyzed these data. These sources are listed in the bibliography.

Note

1 Information on the trial is available at www.integrityfirstforamerica.org. See also Blee and Simi (2020) and Blee, Simi, and Alexander (2022).

BIBLIOGRAPHY

Aasland Ravndal, Jacob. 2021. "From Bombs to Books, and Back Again?: Mapping Strategies of Right-Wing Revolutionary Resistance." *Studies in Conflict & Terrorism*:1–29.

Abanes, Richard. 1996. *American Militias: Rebellion, Racism, and Religion*. InterVarsity Press.

Abbott, Andrew. 1997. "Of Time and Space: The Contemporary Relevance of the Chicago School." *Social Forces* 75(4):1149–1182.

Adams, Josh and Vincent J. Roscigno. 2005. "White Supremacists, Oppositional Culture and the World Wide Web." *Social Forces* 84(2):759–778.

Agiesta, Jennifer. 2016. "Most Say Race Relations Worsened under Obama, Poll Finds." CNN, October 5. (www.cnn.com/2016/10/05/politics/obama-race-relations-poll).

Aho, James Alfred. 1990. *The Politics of Righteousness: Idaho Christian Patriotism*. University of Washington Press.

Alba, Richard. 2020. *The Great Demographic Illusion: Majority, Minority, and the Expanding American Mainstream*. Princeton University Press.

Albright, Jonathan. 2018. "The Rumor Caravan: From Twitter Reply to Disaster." *Columbia Journalism Review*, October 30 (www.cjr.tow_center/the-rumor-caravan-from-twitter-reply-to-disaster.php).

American Renaissance. 2018. "2018 American Renaissance Conference." (www.amren.com/2018-american-renaissance-conference/).

Anderson, Carol. 2016. *White Rage: The Unspoken Truth of our Racial Divide*. Bloomsbury.

Andone, Dakin and Laura Dolan. 2018. "Charlottesville Suspect Shared Posts Showing Car Driving into Protestors before Attack." CNN, November 30. (www.cnn.com/2018/11/30/us/charlottesville-james-fields-trial/index.html).

Anti-Defamation League. 1998. "Explosion of Hate: The Growing Danger of the National Alliance." (www.adl.org/sites/default/files/documents/assets/pdf/combating-hate/Explosion-of-Hate.pdf).

Anti-Defamation League. 2004. "The Quiet Retooling of the Militia Movement." (www.adl.org/resources/news/quiet-retooling-militia-movement).

Anti-Defamation League. 2018. "Rise above Movement (R.A.M.)." (www.adl.org/resources/backgrounders/rise-above-movement-ram).

Anti-Defamation League. 2019a. "Free to Play? Hate, Harassment and Positive Social Experiences in Online Games." (www.adl.org/resources/report/free-play-hate-harassment-and-positive-social-experiences-online-games).

Anti-Defamation League. 2019b. "Two Years Ago, They Marched in Charlottesville. Where Are They Now?" (www.adl.org/resources/blog/two-years-ago-they-marched-charlottesville-where-are-they-now).

Anti-Defamation League. 2019c. "White Supremacists Step Up Off-Campus Propaganda Efforts in 2018." (www.adl.org/resources/reports/white-supremacists-step-campus-propaganda-efforts-2018).

Anti-Defamation League. 2019d. "Telegram: The Latest Safe Haven for White Supremacists." (www.adl.org/resources/blog/telegram-latest-safe-haven-white-supremacists).

Anti-Defamation League. 2019e. "Hardcore White Supremacists Elevate Dylann Roof to Cult Hero Status." (www.adl.org/resources/blog/hardcore-white-supremacists-elevate-dylann-roof-cult-hero-status).

Anti-Defamation League. 2020a. "Coronavirus Crisis Elevates Antisemitic, Racist Tropes." (www.adl.org/resources/blog/coronavirus-crisis-elevates-antisemitic-racist-tropes).

Anti-Defamation League. 2020b. "White Supremacists Respond to Coronavirus with Violent Plots and Online Hate." (www.adl.org/resources/blog/white-supremacists-respond-coronavirus-violent-plots-and-online-hate).

Anti-Defamation League. 2020c. "Proud Boys' Bigotry Is on Full Display." (www.adl.org/resources/blog/proud-boys-bigotry-full-display?fbclid=IwAR026x6WzNJ1NsORLoQQLdWLyOI2vE3_QNOCMwIvEz-F9FUP6OLpZXbZw6w).

Anti-Defamation League. 2021a. "For Twitter Users, Gab's Toxic Content Is Just a Click Away." (www.adl.org/resources/blog/twitter-users-gabs-toxic-content-just-click-away).

Anti-Defamation League. 2021b. "Gab CEO Andrew Torba Broadcasts His Antisemitism Across Social Media Platforms." (www.adl.org/resources/blog/gab-ceo-andrew-torba-broadcasts-his-antisemitism-across-social-media-platforms).

Anti-Defamation League. 2021c. "ADL Finds Domestic Extremist Murders in 2020 Overwhelmingly Linked to Far-Right Extremists." (www.adl.org/news/press-releases/adl-finds-domestic-extremist-murders-in-2020-overwhelmingly-linked-to-far-right).

Anti-Defamation League. 2021d. "Unite the Right: Four Years Later, Major Players Still Grappling with Fallout." (www.adl.org/resources/blog/unite-right-four-years-later-major-players-still-grappling-fallout).

Anti-Defamation League. 2022a. "Hate Beyond Borders: The Internationalization of White Supremacy." (www.adl.org/resources/report/hate-beyond-borders-internationalization-white-supremacy).

Anti-Defamation League. 2022b. "Analysis: Recent Threats to Jewish Institutions." (www.adl.org/resources/blog/analysis-recent-threats-jewish-institutions).

Anti-Defamation League. 2022c. "ADL and Princeton Bridging Divides Initiative Release New Report." (www.adl.org/resources/press-release/adl-and-princetons-bridging-divides-initiative-release-new-report-tracking/).

Anti-Defamation League. 2022d. "Twitter's Failure to Enforce Its Policy against Antisemitism." (www.adl.org/resources/blog/twitters-failure-enforce-its-policy-against-antisemitism?utm_campaign=astwit2022&utm_medium=email&utm_source= whole&utm_content=e01).

Anti-Defamation League. 2022e. "Hate Is No Game: Hate and Harassment in Online Games 2022." (www.adl.org/sites/default/files/documents/2022-12/Hate-and-Harassment-in-Online-Games-120622-v2.pdf).

Anti-Defamation League. 2022f. "White Lives Matter." (www.adl.org/resources/ backgrounder/white-lives-matter).

Anti-Defamation League. 2022g. "Exposure to Alternative & Extremist Content on YouTube." (www.adl.org/resources/report/exposure-alternative-extremist-content-youtube).

Anti-Defamation League. n.d. "Northwest American Republic." (www.adl.org/resources/ hate-symbol/northwest-american-republic).

Antisemitism Policy Trust. 2019. "Policy Briefing: Misogyny and Antisemitism." (https://antisemitism.org.uk/wp-content/uploads/2020/06/Web-Misogyny-2020.pdf).

AP and NORC at the University of Chicago. 2022. "Immigration Attitudes and Con-spiratorial Thinkers: A Study Issued on the 10th Anniversary of the Associated Press-NORC Center for Public Affairs Research." (https://apnorc.org/wp-content/ uploads/2022/05/Immigration-Report_V15.pdf).

Argentino, Marc-André. 2022. "QAnon & Hybrid Threats." Presentation at Far-right Extremism and Disinformation Workshop, American University, March 29.

Arnsdorf, Isaac. 2021. "Oath Keepers in the State House: How a Militia Movement Took Root in the Republican Mainstream." *Pro Publica.* (www.propublica.org/ article/oath-keepers-in-the-state-house-how-a-militia-movement-took-root-in-the-republican-mainstream).

Atkins, Stephen E. 2011. *Encyclopedia of Right-Wing Extremism in Modern American History.* ABC-CLIO.

Awan, Hashir Ali, Alifiya Aamir, Mufaddal Najmuddin Diwan, Irfan Ullah, Victor Pereira-Sanchez, Rodrigo Ramalho, Laura Orsolini, Renato de Filippis, Mar-garet Isioma Ojeahere and Ramdas Ransing. 2021. "Internet and Pornography Use during the Covid-19 Pandemic: Presumed Impact and What Can Be Done." *Frontiers in Psychiatry*:Article #623508. (www.frontiersin.org/articles/10.3389/ fpsyt.2021.623508/full).

Ayton, Mel. 2011. *Dark Soul of the South: The Life and Crimes of Racist Killer Joseph Paul Franklin.* Potomac Books, Inc.

Ayton, Mel. n.d. "How Hate Groups Influenced Racist Killer Joseph Paul Franklin." History News Network. (http://hnn.us/article/139368).

Back, Les, Michael Keith and John Solomos. 1998. "Racism on the Internet: Mapping the Neo-Fascist Subcultures in 'Cyberspace.'" pp. 73–101 in *Nation and Race: The Developing Euro-American Racist Subculture*, edited by J. Kaplan and T. Bjørgo. Northeastern University Press.

Bail, Christopher. 2016. *Terrified: How Anti-Muslim Fringe Organizations Became Mainstream.* Princeton University Press.

Balmer, Randall Herbert. 2021. *Bad Faith: Race and the Rise of the Religious Right.* William B. Eerdmans Publishing Company.

Barbaro, Michael. 2016. "Donald Trump Clung to 'Birther' Lie for Years, and Still Isn't Apologetic." The *New York Times*, September 16. (https://www.nytimes.com/ 2016/09/17/us/politics/donald-trump-obama-birther.html).

Barkun, Michael. 1994. *Religion and the Racist Right: The Origins of the Christian Identity Movement*. University of North Carolina Press.

Barkun, Michael. 2003. *New World Order Conspiracies II: A World of Black Helicopters*. University of California Press.

Barreto, Matt A., Cooper, Betsy L., Gonzales, Benjamin, Parker, Christopher and Towler, Christopher C. 2011. "The Tea Party in the Age of Obama: Mainstream Conservatism or Out-Group Anxiety?" pp. 105–137 in *Rethinking Obama Political Power and Social Theory* 3, edited by Go J. Emerald Group Publishing Limited.

Barrett, Devlin and Matt Zapotosky. 2021. "FBI Report Warned of 'War' at Capitol, Contradicting Claims There Was No Indication of Looming Violence." *The Washington Post*, January 12. (www.washingtonpost.com/national-security/capitol-riot-fbi-intelligence/2021/01/12/30d12748-546b-11eb-a817-e5e7f8a406d6_story.html).

Barrouquere, Brett. 2019. "White Shadow: David Duke's Lasting Influence on American White Supremacy." Southern Poverty Law Center. (www.splcenter.org/hatewatch/2019/05/17/white-shadow-david-dukes-lasting-influence-american-white-supremacy).

Barrouquere, Brett. 2020. "Once a Political Force, Richard Spencer and National Policy Institute Go Quiet." Southern Poverty Law Center. (www.splcenter.org/hatewatch/2020/01/10/once-political-force-richard-spencer-and-national-policy-institute-go-quiet).

Bates, Lydia. 2021. "Patriarchal Violence: Misogyny from the Far Right to the Mainstream." Southern Poverty Law Center. (www.splcenter.org/news/2021/02/01/patriarchal-violence-misogyny-far-right-mainstream).

Bauer, Shane. 2016. "Undercover with a Border Militia." *Mother Jones*, November/December. (www.motherjones.com/politics/2016/10/undercover-border-militia-immigration-bauer/).

Beirich, Heidi. 2022. "One Year Later: U.S. Democracy in Peril as Far-Right Extremism Spreads Globally." Global Project against Hate and Extremism. (https://globalextremism.org/post/one-year-later-u-s-democracy-in-peril-as-far-right-extremism-spreads-globally/).

Belew, Kathleen. 2018. *Bring the War Home*. Harvard University Press.

Ben-Ghiat, Ruth. 2020. *Strongmen: Mussolini to the Present*. WW Norton & Company.

Benjamin, Ruha. 2022. *Viral Justice: How We Grow the World We Want*. Princeton University Press.

Berbrier, Mitch. 1998. "'Half the Battle': Cultural Resonance, Framing Processes, and Ethnic Affectations in Contemporary White Separatist Rhetoric." *Social Problems* 45(4):431–450.

Berbrier, Mitch. 1999. "Impression Management for the Thinking Racist: A Case Study of Intellectualization as Stigma Transformation in Contemporary White Supremacist Discourse." *Sociological Quarterly* 40(3):411–433.

Berbrier, Mitch. 2000. "The Victim Ideology of White Supremacists and White Separatists in the United States." *Sociological Focus* 33(2):175–191.

Bergen, Peter and David Sterman. 2014. "US Right Wing Extremists More Deadly Than Jihadists." CNN, April 15. (http://us.cnn.com/2014/04/14/opinion/bergen-sterman-kansas-shooting/).

Bergen, Peter and David Sterman. 2021. "Terrorism in America after 9/11: A Detailed Look At Jihadist Terrorist Activity in the United States and By Americans

Overseas since 9/11." *New America*, September 10. (www.Newamerica.Org/International-Security/Reports/terrorism-in-america/).

Bergengruen, Vera and W. J. Hennigan. 2019. "'We Are Being Eaten From Within.' Why America Is Losing the Battle against White Nationalist Terrorism." *Time*, August 8. (https://time.com/5647304/white-nationalist-terrorism-united-states/).

Berger, John M. 2016a. "Nazis vs. ISIS on Twitter: A Comparative Study of White Nationalist and ISIS Online Social Media Networks." GWU Program on Extremism, September. (https://extremism.gwu.edu/sites/g/files/zaxdzs5746/files/downloads/Nazis%20v.%20ISIS.pdf).

Berger, John M. 2016b. *Making CVE Work: A Focused Approach Based on Process Disruption*. International Centre for Counter-Terrorism.

Berger, John M. 2018a. "The Alt-Right Twitter Census: Defining and Describing the Audience for Alt-Right Content on Twitter." *Vox*. (www.voxpol.eu/download/vox-pol_publication/AltRightTwitterCensus.pdf).

Berger, John M. 2018b. "Trump Is the Glue That Binds the Far Right." *The Atlantic*. (www.theatlantic.com/ideas/archive/2018/10/trump-alt-right-twitter/574219/).

Berger, John M. and Jonathon Morgan. 2015. "The ISIS Twitter Census: Defining and describing the population of ISIS supporters on Twitter." *Brookings*, March. (www.brookings.edu/wp-content/uploads/2016/06/isis_twitter_census_berger_morgan.pdf).

Berger, Peter and Thomas Luckmann. 1966. *The Social Construction of Reality: A Treatise in the Sociology of Knowledge*. Random House.

Berkowitz, Bill. 2021. "The Global Minority Initiative Aims to Support White Nationalist Prisoners." *Daily Kos*, March 20. (www.dailykos.com/stories/2021/3/20/2022003/-The-Global-Minority-Initiative-Aims-To-Support-White-Nationalist-Prisoners).

Berlet, Chip. 2001. "When Hate Went Online." Northeast Sociological Association Spring Conference.

Berlet, Chip. 2016. "What Is the Third Position?" Political Research Associates. (https://politicalresearch.org/2016/12/19/what-third-position).

Beutel, Alejandro J. and Daryl Johnson. 2021. "The Three Percenters: A Look Inside an Anti-Government Militia." New Lines Institute. (https://newlinesinstitute.org/wp-content/uploads/20210225-Three-Percenter-PR-NISAP-rev051021.pdf).

Bevensee, Emmi. 2020. "The Decentralized Web of Hate: White Supremacists Are Starting to Use Peer-to-Peer Technology. Are We Prepared?" September. (https://rebelliousdata.com/wp-content/uploads/2020/10/P2P-Hate-Report.pdf).

Bjørgo, Tore. 1998. "Entry, Bridge Burning, and Exit Options: What Happens to Young People Who Join Racist Groups." pp. 231–258 in *Nation and Race: The Developing Euro-American Racist Subculture*, edited by Jeffrey Kaplan and Tore Bjørgo. Northeastern University Press.

Blazakis, Jason M. 2021. "The Intangible Benefits of a Domestic Terrorism Statute." *Georgetown Journal of International Affairs*, June 24. (https://gjia.georgetown.edu/2021/06/24/the-intangible-benefits-of-a-domestic-terrorism-statute/).

Bleakley, Paul. 2021. "Panic, Pizza and Mainstreaming the Alt-Right: A Social Media Analysis of Pizzagate and the Rise of the QAnon Conspiracy." *Current Sociology*. (https://journals.sagepub.com/doi/epub/10.1177/00113921211034896).

Blee, Kathleen M. 1991. *Women of the Ku Klux Klan: Racism and Gender in the 1920s*. University of California Press.

Blee, Kathleen M. 1996. "Becoming a Racist: Women in Contemporary Ku Klux Klan and Neo-Nazi Groups." *Gender & Society* 10(6):680–702.

Blee, Kathleen M. 2002. *Inside Organized Racism: Women in the Hate Movement.* University of California Press.

Blee, Kathleen M. 2012. *Democracy in the Making: How Activist Groups Form.* Oxford University Press.

Blee, Kathleen M. 2020. "Where Do We Go from Here? Positioning Gender in Studies of the Far Right." *Politics, Religion & Ideology* 21(4):416–431.

Blee, Kathleen M. and Peter Simi. 2020. "Expert Report of Kathleen M. Blee and Peter Simi." Submitted on behalf of the plaintiffs in the case *Sines v Kessler.* (https://files.integrityfirstforamerica.org/14228/1614109097-832-2-expert-report-of-k-blee-and-p-simi.pdf).

Blee, Kathleen M., Peter Simi and Shayna Alexander. 2022. "Attacking White Supremacist Extremism Through the Courts." C-REX Center for Research on Extremism. (www.sv.uio.no/c-rex/english/news-and-events/right-now/2022/%E2%80%9Cattacking-white-supremacist-extremism-through-the.html).

Blee, Kathleen M. and Elizabeth A. Yates. 2017. "Women in the White Supremacist Movement." pp. 751–768 in Holly McCammon, Verta Taylor, Jo Reger, and Rachel Einwohner (eds.), *The Oxford Handbook of U.S. Women's Social Movement Activism.* Oxford University Press.

Blumenthal, Max. 2008. "How Sarah Palin Has Excluded African-Americans." *Huffington Post*, November 13. (www.huffpost.com/entry/how-sarah-palin-has-exclu_b_134403).

Bonilla-Silva, Eduardo. 2013. *Racism without Racists.* Rowman & Littlefield.

Bosi, L. 2021. "A Processual Approach to Political Violence: How History Matters." pp. 106–123 in *The Cambridge History of Terrorism.* Cambridge University Press.

Bosi, Lorenzo and Stefan Maalthaner. 2022. "Gaining Momentum: Processual Perspectives in Research on Collective Action and Political Violence." Unpublished framing statement for October 2022 workshop, Scuola Normale Superiore and Hamburg Institute for Social Research.

Bouie, Jamelle. 2014. "Eric Holder Talks about Racism the Way Obama Wishes He Could." *Slate*, May 19. (https://slate.com/news-and-politics/2014/05/eric-holder-on-racism-in-america-the-attorney-general-speaks-more-directly-than-president-obama.html).

Brathovd, B. 2017. "Richard Spencer and the Nationalist House of Pancakes." *Salting the Earth*, May 1. (www.podbean.com/media/share/dir-putb7-250dea0?utm_campaign=w_share_ep&utm_me).

Bravo, Tony. 2023. "How an 'Anti-Woke' High School Graduation Speech Would Sound in Ron DeSantis' Florida." *San Francisco Chronicle* (How an 'anti-woke' high school graduation speech would sound in Ron DeSantis' Florida | Datebook (sfchronicle.com).

Brekhus, Wayne. 1998. "A Sociology of the Unmarked: Redirecting Our Focus." *Sociological Theory* 16(1):34–51.

Brennan Center. 2019. "Countering Violent Extremism." (www.brennancenter.org/issues/protect-liberty-security/government-targeting-minority-communities/countering-violent).

Broder, John. 1997. "Ex-G.I. at Fort Bragg Is Convicted in Killing of 2 Blacks." *New York Times*, February 28.

Brownstein, Ronald. 2021. "How the GOP Surrendered to Extremism." *The Atlantic*, February 4. (www.theatlantic.com/politics/archive/2021/02/republican-extremism-and-john-birch-society/617922/).

Brunner, Jim. 2022. "Idaho Primary Pits Conservative Governor Again Trump-Backed Candidate with White Nationalist Ties." *Seattle Times*, May 16.

Bubolz, Bryan and Pete Simi. 2019. "The Problem of Overgeneralization: The Case of Mental Health Problems and US Violent White Supremacists." *American Behavioral Scientist* 1–17.

Buchanan, Patrick. 2018. "Caravan Puts Trump Legacy on the Line." *NWD Daily News*. (www.nwfdailynews.com/story/opinion/columns/2018/10/22/pat-buchanan-caravan-puts-trump-legacy-on-line/9493062007/).

Burghart, Devin. 1996. "Cyberh@Te: A Reappraisal." *Dignity Report* 3(4):12–16.

Burghart, Devin and Leonard Zeskind. 2020. *Tea Party Nationalism: A Critical Examination of the Tea Party Movement and the Size, Scope and Focus of Its National Factions*. Institute for Research & Education on Human Rights.

Burley, Shane. 2017. *Fascism Today: What It Is and How to End It*. AK Press.

Burris, Val, Emery Smith and Ann Strahm. 2000. "White Supremacist Networks on the Internet." *Sociological Focus* 33(2):215–235.

Busse, Ryan. 2021. *Gunfight: My Battle against the Industry That Radicalized America*. Hachette.

Byman, Daniel. 2022. *Spreading Hate: The Global Rise of White Supremacist Terrorism*. Oxford University Press.

Caesar, Chris. 2017. "Trump Ran against Political Correctness. Now His Team Is Begging for Politeness." *Washington Post*, May 16. (www.washingtonpost.com/posteverything/wp/2017/05/16/trump-ran-against-political-correctness-now-his-team-is-begging-for-politeness/).

Cammaerts, Bart. 2021. "The New-New Social Movements: Are Social Media Changing the Ontology of Social Movements?" *Mobilization: An International Quarterly* 26(3):343–358.

Campbell, Andy. 2022. *We Are Proud Boys: How a Right-Wing Street Gang Ushered in a New Era of American Extremism*. Hachette.

Carless, Will and Michael Corey. 2019a. "The American Militia Movement, a Breeding Ground for Hate, Is Pulling in Cops on Facebook." *Reveal News*, June 24. (https://revealnews.org/article/the-american-militia-movement-a-breeding-ground-for-hate-is-pulling-in-cops-on-facebook/).

Carless, Will and Michael Corey. 2019b. "To Protect and Slur: Inside Hate Groups on Facebook, Police Officers Trade Racist Memes, Conspiracy Theories and Islamophobia." *Reveal News*, June 14. (https://revealnews.org/article/inside-hate-groups-on-facebook-police-officers-trade-racist-memes-conspiracy-theories-and-islamophobia/).

Carney, Nikita. 2016. "All Lives Matter, But So Does Race: Black Lives Matter and the Evolving Role of Social Media." *Humanity & Society* 40(2):180–199.

Carrigan, William D. and Clive Webb. 2003. "The Lynching of Persons of Mexican Origin or Descent in the United States, 1848 to 1928." *Journal of Social History* 37(2):411–438.

Castelli Gattinara, Pietro, Caterina Froio and Andrea L. P. Pirro. 2022. "Far-Right Protest Mobilisation in Europe: Grievances, Opportunities and Resources." *European Journal of Political Research* 61(4):1019–1041.

CBS News. 2017. "Removal of Confederate Statues Raises Tensions in New Orleans." *CBS*. (www.cbsnews.com/news/removal-of-confederate-statues-raises-tensions-in-new-orleans/).

Cervini v. Cisneros. 2021. "United States District Court for the Western District of Texas." (www.documentcloud.org/documents/20971853-121-cv-00565-complaint-individuals).

Chen, Annie, Brendan Nyhan, Jason Reifler, Ronald E. Robertson and Christo Wilson. "Subscriptions and External Links Help Drive Resentful Users to Alternative and Extremist YouTube Videos." Unpublished manuscript, available: YouTube. pdf. (bpb-us-e1.wpmucdn.com).

Chermak, Steven M. and Joshua D. Freilich. 2008. "Citizen Militias." pp. 123–124 in *Encyclopedia of Social Problems*, edited by V. N. Parrillo. Sage Publications.

Chicago Tribune. 1997. "2nd Ex-Soldier Is Sentenced to Life in Slaying of 2 Blacks." May 13. (www.chicagotribune.com/news/ct-xpm-1997-05-13-9705130165-story.html).

Chinoy, Sahil. 2019. "What Happened to America's Political Center of Gravity?" *New York Times*, June 26. (www.nytimes.com/interactive/2019/06/26/opinion/sunday/republican-platform-far-right.html).

Churchill, Robert H. 2009. *To Shake Their Guns in the Tyrant's Face: Libertarian Political Violence and the Origins of the Militia Movement.* University of Michigan Press.

Clarkson, Fredrick. 1998a. "In Today's Extreme Anti-Abortion Circles, 'Patriots' and Racists Join Existing Members, With Explosive Results." Southern Poverty Law Center. (www.splcenter.org/fighting-hate/intelligence-report/1998/anti-abortion-bombings-related).

Clarkson, Frederick. 1998b. "Anti-Abortion Movement Marches on after Two Decades of Arson, Bombs and Murder." Southern Poverty Law Center. (www.splcenter.org/fighting-hate/intelligence-report/1998/anti-abortion-movement-marches-after-two-decades-arson-bombs-and-murder).

CNN. 2007. "Obama Placed under Secret Service Protection." May 3. (www.cnn.com/2007/POLITICS/05/03/obama.protection/).

CNN. 2018. "The Dangerous Consequences of Trump's All-Out Assault on Political Correctness." October 30. (www.cnn.com/2018/10/30/politics/donald-trump-hate-speech-anti-semitism-steve-king-kevin-mccarthy/index.html/).

Cobb, Jelani. 2016. "The Matter of Black Lives." *The New Yorker*, March 6. (www.newyorker.com/magazine/2016/03/14/where-is-black-lives-matter-headed).

Confessore, Nicholas. 2022a. "How Tucker Carlson Stoked White Fear to Conquer Cable: American Nationalist: Part 1." *New York Times*, April 30. (www.nytimes.com/2022/04/30/us/tucker-carlson-gop-republican-party.html).

Confessore, Nicholas. 2022b. "How Tucker Carlson Reshaped Fox News – and Became Trump's Heir." *New York Times*, April 30. (www.nytimes.com/2022/04/30/us/tucker-carlson-fox-news.html).

Confessore, Nicolas. 2022c. "What to Know about Tucker Carlson's Rise." *New York Times*, April 30. (www.nytimes.com/2022/04/30/business/media/tucker-carlson-fox-news-takeaways.html?smid=nytcore-ios-share&referringSource=articleShare).

Confessore, Nicholas and Karen Yourish. 2022. "A Fringe Conspiracy Theory, Fostered Online, Is Refashioned by the G.O.P." *New York Times*, May 15. (www.nytimes.com/2022/05/15/us/replacement-theory-shooting-tucker-carlson.html).

Conway, Lucian Gideon, Meredith A. Repke and Shannon C. Houck. 2017. "Donald Trump as a Cultural Revolt against Perceived Communication Restriction: Priming Political Correctness Norms Causes More Trump Support." *Journal of Social and Political Psychology* 5(1):244–259.

Cooter, Amy Beth. 2006. "Neo-Nazi Normalization: The Skinhead Movement and Integration into Normative Structures." *Sociological Inquiry* 76(2):145–165.

Corpus Ong, Jonathan. 2021. "Online Disinformation against AAPI Communities during the Covid-19 Pandemic." *Carnegie Endowment for International Peace.* (https://carnegieendowment.org/2021/10/19/online-disinformation-against-aapi-communities-during-covid-19-pandemic-pub-85515).

Cott, Emma. 2018. "How Our Reporter Uncovered a Lie That Propelled an Alt-Right Extremist's Rise." *The New York Times*, February 5. (www.nytimes.com/2018/02/05/insider/confronting-a-white-nationalist-eli-mosley.html).

Couto, Richard A. 1993. "Narrative, Free Space, and Political Leadership in Social Movements." *The Journal of Politics* 55(1):57–79.

Cox, Daniel A. 2021. "After the Ballots Are Counted: Conspiracies, Political Violence, and American Exceptionalism." *Survey Center on American Life*, February 11. (www.americansurveycenter.org/research/after-the-ballots-are-counted-conspiracies-political-violence-and-american-exceptionalism).

Crandall, Christian S., Jason M. Miller and Mark H. White. 2018. "Changing Norms Following the 2016 US Presidential Election: The Trump Effect on Prejudice." *Social Psychological and Personality Science* 9(2):186–192.

Crothers, Lane. 2003. *Rage on the Right: The American Militia Movement from Ruby Ridge to Homeland Security*. Rowman & Littlefield Publishers.

Cunningham, David. 2005. *There's Something Happening Here: The New Left, the Klan, and FBI Counterintelligence*. University of California Press.

Cunningham, David. 2012. *Klansville, U.S.A. the Rise and Fall of the Civil Rights-Era Ku Klux Klan*. Oxford University Press.

Cunningham, David. 2022. "Policing White Supremacy: Asymmetry and Inequality in Protest Control." *Social Problems.* (https://doi.org/10.1093/socpro/spac010).

Daily Stormer Website Post By Weev. July 31, 2017. "Operational Security for Right Wing Rallies." (https://stormer-daily.rw/operational-security-for-right-wing-rallies/).

Dallek, Matthew. 2023. *Birchers: How the John Birch Society Radicalized the American Right*. Basic Books.

Daniels, Jessie. 2009. *Cyber Racism: White Supremacy Online and the New Attack on Civil Rights*. Rowman & Littlefield Publishers.

Daniels, Jessie. 2018. "The Algorithmic Rise of the Alt-Right." *Contexts* 17(1):60–65.

Darby, Seyward. 2020. *Sisters in Hate: American Women on the Front Lines of White Nationalism*. Hachette.

Darren Thomas et al. v. County of Los Angeles et al. 1992. (https://law.justia.com/cases/federal/appellate-courts/F2/978/504/182989/).

Davis, Darren and David Wilson. 2022. *Racial Resentment in the Political Mind*. University of Chicago Press.

Dawkins, Richard. 1976. *The Selfish Gene*. Oxford University Press.

Dees, Morris and James Corcoran. 1996. *Gathering Storm: The Story of America's Militia Network*. Harper Collins.

Dees, Morris and Steve Fiffer. 1993. *Hate on Trial: The Case Against America's Most Dangerous Neo-Nazi*. Villard Books.

Delgado, Richard and Jean Stefancic. 2001. *Critical Race Theory: An Introduction.* New York University Press.

della Porta, Donatella. 2020. "Protests as Critical Junctures: Some Reflections Towards a Momentous Approach to Social Movements." *Social Movement Studies* 19(5–6):556–575.

della Porta, Donatella. 2022. *Contentious Politics in Emergency Critical Junctures.* Cambridge University Press.

della Porta, Donatella, Anna Lavizzari and Herbert Reiter. 2022. "The Spreading of the Black Lives Matter Movement Campaign: The Italian Case in Cross-National Perspective." *Sociological Forum* 37(3): 700–721.

Demopolous, Alaina. 2022. "Joe Rogan Admits Schools Don't Have Litter Boxes for Kids Who 'Identify' as Furries." *The Guardian*, November 4. (www.theguardian.com/culture/2022/nov/04/joe-rogan-school-litter-boxes-kids-furries-gender).

Department of Homeland Security. 2009. "Rightwing Extremism: Current Economic and Political Climate Fueling Resurgence in Radicalization and Recruitment." *DHS Assessment* 1:1–10.

DeVargas, Christopher. 2020. "Three Men Connected to 'Boogaloo' Movement Tried to Provoke Violence at Protests, Feds Say." *NBC*. (www.nbcnews.com/news/all/three-men-connected-boogaloo-movement-tried-provoke-violence-protests-feds-n1224231).

Devlin, F. Roger and Richard Spencer. 2016. "Race 101." National Policy Institute. (https://web.archive.org/web/20201027002650/https://nationalpolicy.institute/category/reports/).

Dewey, John. 1922. *Human Nature and Conduct: An Introduction to Social Psychology.* Modern Library.

DFRLab, Atlantic Council's. 2021. "#Stopthesteal: Timeline of Social Media and Extremist Activities Leading to 1/6 Insurrection." Just Security. (www.justsecurity.org/74622/stopthesteal-timeline-of-social-media-and-extremist-activities-leading-to-1-6-insurrection/).

Dignam, Pierce Alexander and Deanna Rohlinger. 2019. "Misogynistic Men Online: How the Red Pill Helped Elect Trump." *Signs: Journal of Women in Culture and Society* 44(3):589–612.

Discord post. July 15, 2017. (https://discordleaks.unicornriot.ninja/discord/view/248599?q=%27fascist+small+businesses%27#msg).

Discord post. July 30, 2017. (https://discordleaks.unicornriot.ninja/discord/view/246256?q=bootlicking+is+equally+as+bad#msg).

Discord post. July 7, 2017. (https://discordleaks.unicornriot.ninja/discord/view/238963?q=%E2%80%9CCops+are+soldiers+OF+ZOG%E2%80%9D#msg).

Discord post. August 13, 2017. (https://discordleaks.unicornriot.ninja/discord/view/381528?q=%271+dead+antifa%27#msg).

Discord posts (Aaron). (https://discordleaks.unicornriot.ninja/discord/view/242099?q=%27full+nazi+party%27#msg; https://discordleaks.unicornriot.ninja/discord/view/217907?q=%27Polos+during%22#msg; https://discordleaks.unicornriot.ninja/discord/view/222561?q=%27triggered+tonight%27#msg; https://discordleaks.unicornriot.ninja/discord/view/237997?q=%22Daily+reminder+that+nazis%27#msg; https://discordleaks.unicornriot.ninja/discord/view/237703?q=%27My+man+ran+over%27#msg).

Discord posts (Dr Ferguson). July 20, 2017. (https://discordleaks.unicornriot.ninja/discord/channel/47 and https://discordleaks.unicornriot.ninja/discord/user/1468).

Discord post (Gavius Corvus). August 7, 2017. https://discordleaks.unicornriot.ninja/discord/view/226489?q=%22the+very+survival%22#msg.

Discord post (卐 Heimdulf – VA 卐). June 30, 2017. (https://discordleaks.unicornriot.ninja/discord/user/1627).

Discord post (Ignis Faatus). August 7, 2017. (https://discordleaks.unicornriot.ninja/discord/view/236456).

Discord post (Stannismannis). August 11, 2017. (https://discordleaks.unicornriot.ninja/discord/view/238168?q=%27red+laces%27#msg).

Dobratz, Betty A. and Stephanie Shanks-Meile. 1994. "Ideology and the Framing Process in the White Separatist/Supremacist Movement in the United States." Paper presented at the Annual Meeting of the American Sociological Association.

Dobratz, Betty A. and Stephanie L. Shanks-Meile. 2000. *The White Separatist Movement in the United States: "White Power, White Pride!"* Johns Hopkins University Press.

Doerr, Nicole and Beth Gharrity Gardner. 2022. "After the Storm: Translating the US Capitol Storming in Germany's Right-Wing Digital Media Ecosystem." *Translation in Society* 1(1):83–104.

Donovan, Joan. 2020. "How an Overload of Riot Porn Is Driving Conflict in the Streets." *MIT Technology Review*, September 3. (www.technologyreview.com/2020/09/03/1007931/riot-porn-right-wing-vigilante-propaganda-social-media/).

Donovan, Joan, Emily Dreyfuss and Brian Friedberg. 2022. *Meme Wars: The Untold Story of the Online Battle Upending Democracy in America.* Bloomsbury Publishing.

Donovan, Joan, Becca Lewis and Brian Friedberg. 2018. "Parallel Ports: Sociotechnical Change from the Alt-Right to Alt-Tech." pp. 49–65 in *Post-Digital Cultures of the Far Right: Online Actions and Offline Consequences in Europe and the US*, edited by M. Fielitz and N. Thurston. Transcript Verlag.

Doxsee, Catrina. 2021. "Examining Extremism: The Militia Movement." Center for Strategic and International Studies. (www.csis.org/blogs/examining-extremism/examining-extremism-militia-movement).

Duda, Jeremy. 2022. "Senate Votes to Censure Wendy Rogers for Threatening Her Colleagues." *Arizona Mirror*, March 1. (www.azmirror.com/2022/03/01/senate-votes-to-censure-wendy-rogers-for-threatening-her-colleagues/).

Durkheim, Émile. 1912. *The Elementary Forms of Religious Life.* Free Press.

Dyck, Kirsten. 2016. *Reichsrock: The International Web of White-Power and Neo-Nazi Hate Music.* Rutgers University Press.

Economist Intelligence. 2018. *Democracy Index.* (www.eiu.com/n/campaigns/democracy-index-2018/).

Edison Hayden, Michael. 2021a. "'There's Nothing You Can Do': The Legacy of #PizzaGate." Southern Poverty Law Center, July 7. (www.splcenter.org/hatewatch/2021/07/07/theres-nothing-you-can-do-legacy-pizzagate).

Edison Hayden, Michael. 2021b. "'We Make Mistakes': Twitter's Embrace of the Extreme Far Right." Southern Poverty Law Center, July 7. (www.splcenter.org/hatewatch/2021/07/07/we-make-mistakes-twitters-embrace-extreme-far-right).

Edsall, Thomas. 2023. "The Republican Strategists Who Have Carefully Planned All of This." *New York Times*, April 12. (www.nytimes.com/2023/04/12/opinion/republican-party-intrusive-government.html).

Edwards, Griffin Sims and Stephen Rushin. 2018. "The Effect of President Trump's Election on Hate Crimes." (https://ssrn.com/abstract=3102652).

Elephrame. n.d. "Black Lives Matter Protest Data Set." Open source data edited by Elephrame. (https://elephrame.com/textbook/BLM/chart).

Eliasoph, Nina and Paul Lichterman. 2003. "Culture in Interaction." *American Journal of Sociology* 108(4): 735–794.

Elliott Kline. 2017. One People Project. (https://onepeoplesproject.com/2017/07/08/elliott-kline/).

Elliott, Philip. 2022. "Sarah Palin Paved the Way for Donald Trump. Could She Remake the GOP Again?" *Time*, August 17. (https://time.com/6206523/sarah-palin-primary-republicans-trump/).

Emirbayer, Mustafa. 1997. "Manifesto for a Relational Sociology." *American Journal of Sociology* 103(2):281–317.

Epstein, Kayla. 2015. "Trump Responds to Megyn Kelly's Questions on Misogyny – with More Misogyny." *The Guardian*, August 6. (www.theguardian.com/us-news/2015/aug/06/donald-trump-misogyny-republican-debate-megyn-kelly).

Essed, Philomena. 1991. *Understanding Everyday Racism: An Interdisciplinary Theory*. Sage.

Evans, Sara M. and Harry C. Boyte. 1992. *Free Spaces: The Sources of Democratic Change in America*. University of Chicago Press.

Evans, W. D. 2004. Reverse Discrimination Claims-Growing Like Kudzu. *Maryland Bar Journal* 37(1):48–51.

Eyerman, Ron and Andrew Jamison. 1991. *Social Movements: A Cognitive Approach*. Penn State Press.

Ezekiel, Raphael S. 1996. *The Racist Mind: Portraits of American Neo-Nazis and Klansmen*. Penguin.

Farivar, Cyrus. 2019. "Extremists Creep into Roblox, an Online Game Popular with Children." NBC. (www.nbcnews.com/tech/tech-news/extremists-creep-roblox-online-game-popular-children-n1045056).

Farrow, Ronan. 2021. "A Former Marine Stormed the Capitol as Part of a Far-Right Militia." *The New Yorker*, January 14. (www.newyorker.com/news/news-desk/a-former-marine-stormed-the-capitol-as-part-of-a-far-right-militia).

Feagin, Joe. 2009. *White Racial Frame: Centuries of Racial Framing and Counter-Framing*. Second Edition. Routledge.

Feagin, Joe R., Pinar Batur and Hernan Vera. 2001. *White Racism: The Basics*. Routledge.

Federal Bureau of Investigation. 2011. "Skinhead Convicted of Murder of Two Homeless Men in Tampa." FBI, October 18. (https://archives.fbi.gov/archives/tampa/press-releases/2011/skinhead-convicted-of-murder-of-two-homeless-men-in-tampa).

Federal Bureau of Investigation. 2014. "Serial Killers: Part 4: White Supremacist Joseph Franklin" FBI, January 14. (https://www.fbi.gov/news/stories/serial-killers-part-4).

Federal Bureau of Investigation. n.d. "Oklahoma City Bombing." (www.fbi.gov/history/famous-cases/oklahoma-city-bombing).

Feinberg, Ayal, Regina Branton and Valerie Martinez-Ebers. 2022. "The Trump Effect: How 2016 Campaign Rallies Explain Spikes in Hate." *PS: Political Science & Politics* 55(2):257–265.

Fetner, Tina and Brayden G. King. 2014. "Three-Layered Movements, Resources, and the Tea Party." pp. 35–54 in *Understanding the Tea Party Movement*, edited by N. Van Dyke and D. S. Meyer. Ashgate Publishing.

Fielitz, Malik and Nick Thurston. 2019. *Post-Digital Cultures of the Far Right: Online Actions and Offline Consequences in Europe and the US*. Verlag.

Fine, Gary Alan and Ugo Corte. 2021. "Dark Fun: The Cruelties of Hedonic Communities." *Sociological Forum* 37(1):70–90.

Fine, Gary Alan and Patricia A. Turner. 2001. *Whispers on the Color Line*. University of California Press.

Flesher Fominiya, Christina. 2010. "Collective Identity in Social Movements: Central Concepts and Debates." *Sociology Compass* 4(6): 393–404.

Forberg, Peter L. 2022. "'No Cult Tells You to Think for Yourself': Discursive Ideology and the Limits of Rationality in Conspiracy Theory QAnon." *American Behavioral Scientist*. 00027642221091199.

Ford, Jonathan. 2022 (Updated). "Covenant, the Sword and the Arm of the Lord." *Encyclopedia of Arkansas*. (https://encyclopediaofarkansas.net/).

Foucault, Michel. 1972. *The Archeology of Knowledge and the Discourse on Language*. Pantheon.

Fox, Lauren M. 2013. "The Hatemonger Next Door." *Salon*. (www.salon.com/2013/09/29/the_hatemonger_next_door/).

Fox, Nicole and David Cunningham. 2022. "Transitional Justice in Public and Private: Truth Commission Narratives in Greensboro." *International Journal of Transitional Justice* 16(2):235–253.

Franks, Mary Anne. 2019. *The Cult of the Constitution*. Stanford University Press.

Fritze, John. 2019. "Trump Used Words like 'Invasion' and 'Killer' to Discuss Immigrants at Rallies 500 times: USA TODAY Analysis." USA Today, August 8. (https://www.usatoday.com/story/news/politics/elections/2019/08/08/trump-immigrants-rhetoric-criticized-el-paso-dayton-shootings/1936742001/).

Fritzsche, Peter. 2020. *Hitler's First Hundred Days: When Germans Embraced the Third Reich*. Oxford University Press.

Froelich deposition in *Sines v Kessler*. March 9, 2020. (https://files.integrityfirstforamerica.org/14228/1641845854-samantha-froelich-deposition-as-played-at-trial.pdf).

Futrell, Robert and Pete Simi. 2004. "Free Spaces, Collective Identity, and the Persistence of U.S. White Power Activism." *Social Problems* 51(1):16–42.

Futrell, Robert, Pete Simi and Simon Gottschalk. 2006. "Understanding Music in Movements: The White Power Music Scene." *The Sociological Quarterly* 47(2):275–304.

Gais, Hannah and Michael Edison Hayden. 2022. "White Nationalists, Other Republicans Brace for 'Total War'." Southern Poverty Law Center. (www.splcenter.org/hatewatch/2022/12/11/white-nationalists-other-republicans-brace-total-war).

Gais, Hannah and Megan Squire. 2021. "How an Encrypted Messaging Platform Is Changing Extremist Movements." Southern Poverty Law Center. (www.splcenter.org/news/2021/02/16/how-encrypted-messaging-platform-changing-extremist-movements).

Gallup. n.d. "Race Relations." (https://news.gallup.com/poll/1687/race-relations.aspx).

Gamboa, Suzanne. 2015. "Donald Trump Announces Presidential Bid By Trashing Mexico, Mexicans." NBC, June 16. (www.nbcnews.com/news/latino/donald-trump-announces-presidential-bid-trashing-mexico-mexicans-n376521).

Gardell, Mattias. 2003. *Gods of the Blood: The Pagan Revival and White Separatism*. Duke University Press.

Garland, Merrick Brian. 2021. "Testimony: Hearing before the U.S. Senate Committee on the Judiciary." February 21. (www.documentcloud.org/documents/20489424-sjc-testimonyfinal).

German, Michael. 2018. "Why New Laws Aren't Needed to Take Domestic Terrorism More Seriously." Brennan Center for Justice. (www.brennancenter.org/our-work/analysis-opinion/why-new-laws-arent-needed-take-domestic-terrorism-more-seriously).

German, Michael. 2020. "Hidden in Plain Sight: Racism, White Supremacy, and Far-Right Militancy in Law Enforcement." Brennan Center for Justice. (www.brennancenter.org/our-work/research-reports/hidden-plain-sight-racism-white-supremacy-and-far-right-militancy-law).

German, Mike. 2019. *Disrupt, Discredit, and Divide: How the New FBI Damages Democracy*. The New Press.

Geschwender, James A. 1964. "Social Structure and the Negro Revolt: An Examination of Some Hypotheses." *Social Forces* 43(2):248–256.

Ghansah, Rachel. August 21, 2017. "A Most American Terrorist: the Making of Dylann Roof." GQ. (www.gq.com/story/dylann-roof-making-of-an-american-terrorist).

Gibson, James William. 1994. *Warrior Dreams: Violence and Manhood in Post-Vietnam America*. Hill and Wang.

Gilroy, Paul. 2001. *Against Race: Imagining Political Culture Beyond the Color Line*. Harvard University Press.

Glasstetter, Josh. 2014. "Operation American Dud: Effort to Oust Obama Fails Miserably." Southern Poverty Law Center. (www.splcenter.org/hatewatch/2014/05/16/operation-american-dud-effort-oust-obama-fails-miserably).

Goffman, Erving. 1974. *Frame Analysis*. Harvard University Press.

Goldman, Seth K. and Diana C. Mutz. 2014. *The Obama Effect: How the 2008 Campaign Changed White Racial Attitudes*. Russell Sage Foundation.

Goodwin, Liz. 2022. "Racist GOP Appeals Heat Up in Final Weeks before Midterms." *Washington Post*, October 15. (www.washingtonpost.com/politics/2022/10/15/racist-appeals-heat-up-final-weeks-before-midterms/).

Gordon, Linda. 2017. *The Second Coming of the KKK: The Ku Klux Klan of the 1920s and the American Political Landscape*. Liveright Publishing Corporation.

Gorski, Philip S. and Samuel L. Perry. 2022. *The Flag and the Cross: White Christian Nationalism and the Threat to American Democracy*. Oxford University Press.

Gough. 2021. "Caleb Cain: Former Far-Right Extremist Says No One Has a Strategy for Ongoing Threat." *SkyNews*. (https://news.sky.com/story/caleb-cain-former-far-right-extremist-says-no-one-has-a-strategy-for-ongoing-threat-12228120).

Graham, Roderick. 2016. "Inter-Ideological Mingling: White Extremist Ideology Entering the Mainstream on Twitter." *Sociological Spectrum* 36(1):24–36.

Greef, Kimon de and Palko Karasz. 2018. "Trump Cities False Claims of Widespread Attacks on White Farmers in South Africa." *New York Times*, August 28. (https://www.nytimes.com/2018/08/23/world/africa/trump-south-africa-white-farmers.html).

Greenberg, Stanley B. 2019. "The Tea Party–Trump Decade." *Prospect*, September 3. (https://prospect.org/power/tea-party-trump-decade/).

Grier, Peter. 2014. "Obama and Race: Why Eric Holder's Words Stirred Such Anger." *Christian Science Monitor*, July 15. (www.csmonitor.com/USA/Politics/Decoder/2014/0715/Obama-and-race-why-Eric-Holder-s-words-stirred-such-anger).

Griffiths, Brent D. 2018. "Trump: 'We Cannot Allow All of These People to Invade Our Country'." *Político*, June 24. (www.politico.com/story/2018/06/24/trump-invade-country-immigrants-667191).

Guilford, Gwynn. 2017. "What Steve Bannon Really Wants." *Quartz*, February 3. (https://qz.com/898134).

Hamm, Mark S. 2002. *In Bad Company: America's Terrorist Underground*. Northeastern University Press.

Hamm, Mark S. and Ramón Spaaij. 2017. *The Age of Lone Wolf Terrorism*. Columbia University Press.

Haney-Lopez, Ian. 2014. "The Racism at the Heart of the Reagan Presidency." *Salon*. (www.salon.com/2014/01/11/the_racism_at_the_heart_of_the_reagan_presidency/).

Hannah, Matthew N. 2021. "A Conspiracy of Data: QAnon, Social Media, and Information Visualization." *Social Media + Society* (July-August):1–15.

Harris, Elizabeth A. and Alexandra Alter. 2022. "With Rising Book Bans, Librarians Have Come under Attack." *New York Times*, July 6. (www.nytimes.com/2022/07/06/books/book-ban-librarians.html?action=click&module=Well&pgtype=Homepage&section=Books).

Hatewatch Staff. 2017. "The Florida League of the South Online Part 2: The Grooming of Christopher Rey Monzon." Southern Poverty Law Center. (www.splcenter.org/hatewatch/2017/09/06/florida-league-south-online-part-2-grooming-christopher-rey-monzon).

Hayling, Crystal. 2022. "Hey, Philanthropy: Division Isn't Our Biggest Problem." *Inside Philanthropy*, September 6. (www.insidephilanthropy.com/home/2022/9/6/hey-philanthropy-division-isnt-our-biggest-problem).

Heath, Allister. 2023. "Ron DeSantis in Conversation with the Telegraph on the War against Wokery." *The Sunday Telegraph*. (www.telegraph.co.uk/world-news/2023/05/25/ron-desantis-interview-disney-covid-war-on-wokery/).

Heimbach Matthew. 2017. "The Next Step of the Revolution." *Daily Stormer* website, February 9. (https://stormer-daily.rw/the-next-step-of-the-revolution-april-rally-in-pikeville-kentucky/).

Heimbach, Matthew. 2020. Deposition, in *Sines v Kessler;* See Background in Blee and Simi.

Helfstein, Scott. 2012. "Edges of Radicalization: Ideas, Individuals and Networks in Violent Extremism." Combating Terrorism Center at West Point. (https://ctc.usma.edu/edges-of-radicalization-ideas-individuals-and-networks-in-violent-extremism/).

Hill, Jane. 2008. *The Everyday Language of White Racism*. Wiley-Blackwell.

Hill, Kip. 2020. "Verne Merrell, Third of 4 Planned Parenthood Bombers to Be Re-Sentenced, Gets 58 Years." *The Spokesman-Review*, September 2. (www.spokesman.com/stories/2020/sep/02/verne-merrell-third-of-4-suspected-planned-parenth/).

Hillstrom, Laurie Collier. 2018. *Black Lives Matter: From a Moment to a Movement*. ABC-CLIO.

Hirsch, Eric L. 1990. *Urban Revolt: Ethnic Politics in the Nineteenth Century Labor Movement*. University of California Press.

Hodges, Adam. 2016. "Accusatory and Exculpatory Moves in the Hunting for 'Racists' Language Game." *Language & Communication* 47(March):1–14.

Hoffman, Bruce and Jacob Ware. 2020. "The Terrorist Threat from the Fractured Far Right." *Lawfare*. (www.lawfareblog.com/terrorist-threat-fractured-far-right).

Hoffman, David S. 1996. The Web of Hate: Extremists Exploit the Internet. Anti-Defamation League.

House January 6 Committee. 2022. *The January 6 Report*. Harper.

Hsiao, Yuan and Steven Pfaff. 2022. "Explaining the Diffusion of Radical Ideas." *Sociology Compass* 16(10):1–16.

Huang, Margaret. 2021. "Oklahoma City Bombing: 26 Years Later, the Same Extremist Threats Prevail." Southern Poverty Law Center. (www.splcenter.org/news/2021/04/22/oklahoma-city-bombing-26-years-later-same-extremist-threats-prevail).

Iandoli, Luca, Simonetta Primario and Giuseppe Zollo. 2021. "The Impact of Group Polarization on the Quality of Online Debate in Social Media: A Systematic Literature Review." *Technological Forecasting and Social Change* 170. (https://doi.org/10.1016/j.techfore.2021.120924).

Institute for Research and Education on Human Rights. 2022. "Breaching the Mainstream: A National Survey of Far-Right Membership in State Legislatures." IREHR. (www.irehr.org/reports/breaching-the-mainstream/).

International Association of Chiefs of Police. 2017. "Virginia's Response to the Unite the Right Rally: After-Action Review." (www.pshs.virginia.gov/media/governorvirginiagov/secretary-of-public-safety-and-homeland-security/pdf/iacp-after-action-review.pdf).

International Center for Non-For-Profit Law. n.d. "Us Protest Law Tracker." (www.icnl.org/usprotestlawtracker/?location=&status=enacted&issue=4&date=&type=legislative).

Jackson, Robert L. 1995. "Ruby Ridge Informant Denies Entrapping Weaver: Probe: Kenneth Fadeley Tells Senate Panel That the White Separatist Took the Initiative in Sale of Illegal Shotguns. However, He Offers No Corroboration." *Los Angeles Times*, September 9. (www.latimes.com/archives/la-xpm-1995-09-09-mn-44014-story.html).

Jackson, Sam. 2020. *Oath Keepers: Patriotism and the Edge of Violence in a Right-Wing Antigovernment Group*. Columbia University Press.

Jacobson, Matthew Frye. 1999. *Whiteness of a Different Color: European Immigrants and the Alchemy of Race*. Harvard University Press.

Jaffe, Logan, Lydia DePillis, Isaac Arnsdorf and J. David McSwane. 2021. "Capitol Rioters Planned for Weeks in Plain Sight. The Police Weren't Ready." *Pro Publica*. (www.propublica.org/article/capitol-rioters-planned-for-weeks-in-plain-sight-the-police-werent-ready).

Jardina, Ashley. 2019. *White Identity Politics*. Cambridge University Press.

Jenkins, Brian. 2016. "President Obama's Controversial Counterterrorism-in-Chief." Rand. (www.rand.org/blog/2016/08/president-obamas-controversial-legacy-as-counterterrorism.html).

Joffre, Tzvi. 2022. "Hungary's FM Reiterates Claim George Soros Fueling Migrant Crisis." *Jerusalem Post*, July 4. (www.jpost.com/diaspora/antisemitism/article-711188).

Johnson, Daryl. 2017. "I Warned of Right-Wing Violence in 2009. Republicans Objected. I Was Right." *Washington Post*, August 21. (www.washingtonpost.com/news/posteverything/wp/2017/08/21/i-warned-of-right-wing-violence-in-2009-it-caused-an-uproar-i-was-right/).

Johnson, Jennifer. 2021. *Grandmothers on Guard: Gender, Aging, and the Minutemen at the US-Mexico Border*. University of Texas Press.

Johnson, Jessica. 2022. "Christian Fascism Online and Off: The Proud Boys, the Big Lie, and the Great Replacement." *The Revealer*. (https://therevealer.org/christian-fascism-online-and-off-the-proud-boys-the-big-lie-and-the-great-replacement/).

Johnson, Vida. 2019. "KKK in the PD: White Supremacist Police and What to Do about It." *Lewis & Clark Law Review* 23(1): 205–261.

Johnston, Hank. 1991. *Tales of Nationalism: Catalonia, 1939–1979*. Rutgers University Press.

Jones, Jeffrey M. 2021. "U.S. Church Membership Falls Below Majority for First Time." Gallup. (https://news.gallup.com/poll/341963/church-membership-falls-below-majority-first-time.aspx).

Jones, Seth G., Catrina Doxsee and Nicholas Harrington. 2020. "The Escalating Terrorism Problem in the United States." Center for Strategic and International Studies. (www.csis.org/analysis/escalating-terrorism-problem-united-states).

Kaplan, Jeffrey. 1995. "Right-Wing Violence in North America." pp. 44–95 in *Terror from the Extreme Right*, edited by Tore Bjørgo. Routledge.

Kaplan, Jeffrey. 1997. "Leaderless Resistance." *Terrorism and Political Violence* 9(3):80–95.

Karell, Daniel, Andrew Linke, Edward Holland and Edward Hendrickson. 2023. "'Born for a Storm': Hard-Right Social Media and Civil Unrest." *American Sociological Review* 88(2):322–349.

Karp, Aaron. 2018. "Estimating Global Civilian-Held Firearms Numbers." Small Arms Survey, June. (www.smallarmssurvey.org/sites/default/files/resources/SAS-BP-Civilian-Firearms-Numbers.pdf).

Kavanaugh, Christopher. 2019. "Sentencing Memorandum of the United States, United States of America V. James Alex Fields, Jr., 18-Cr-11, Ecf No. 50, at 43." (www.courtlistener.com/docket/7299259/united-states-v-fields/).

Keating, Peter and Shaun Assael. 2021. "The Herald of the Far Right." GQ, June 11. (www.gq.com/story/the-herald-of-the-far-right).

Keierleber, Mark. 2021. "How White Extremists Teach Kids to Hate." The 74. (www.the74million.org/article/where-hate-is-normalized-how-white-extremists-use-online-gaming-communities-popular-among-teens-to-recruit-culture-warriors/).

Kelly, Annie. 2017. "The Alt-Right: Reactionary Rehabilitation for White Masculinity." *Soundings* 66:68–78.

Kelly, Meg and Salvador Rizzo. 2018. "A Grainy Video from Guatemala Sparks Trump Conspiracy Theory." *Washington Post*. (www.washingtonpost.com/politics/2018/10/19/grainy-video-guatemala-sparks-trump-conspiracy/).

Kelly, Megan and J. DeCook. 2022. "Not So Reformed: How 'Countering Violent Extremism' Groups Elevate 'Former' White Nationalists." Political Research Associates, April 1. (https://politicalresearch.org/2022/04/01/not-so-reformed).

Kendi, Ibram. 2016. *Stamped from the Beginning: The Definitive History of Racist Ideas in America*. Bold Type Books.

Kindy, Kimberly, Sari Horwitz and Devlin Barrett. 2017. "Federal Government Has Long Ignored White Supremacist Threats, Critics Say." *Washington Post*, September 2. (Federal government has long ignored white supremacist threats, critics say – The Washington Post).

King, Shaun. 2016. "Donald Trump Clearly Bringing Out the Worst in Our Country Including Volunteer Sporting Neo-Nazi Tattoo." *New York Daily News*, March 17. (www.nydailynews.com/news/national/king-trump-bigotry-popular-article-1.2567796).

Knops, Louise and Guillaume Petit. 2022. "Indignation as Affective Transformation: An Affect-Theoretical Approach to the Belgian Yellow Vest Movement." *Mobilization* 27(2):169–192.

Knowles, Hannah. 2021. "A Texas Bill Drew Ire for Saying It Would Preserve 'Purity of the Ballot Box'." *Washington Post*, May 9. (www.washingtonpost.com/history/2021/05/09/texas-purity-ballot-box-black/).

Koehler, Daniel. 2021. *From Traitor to Zealot: Exploring the Phenomenon of Side-Switching in Extremism and Terrorism*. Cambridge University Press.

Köttig, Michaela, Renate Bitzan and Andrea Pető. 2017. *Gender and Far Right Politics in Europe*. Palgrave Macmillan.

Kovaleski, Serge F. 1995. "One World' Conspiracies Prompt Montana Militia's Call To Arms." *Washington Post*. (https://www.washingtonpost.com/archive/politics/1995/04/29/one-world-conspiracies-prompt-montana-militias-call-to-arms/12505442-4e8f-43e9-9f52-b0f71e1fa753/).

Kováts, Eszter and Andrea Pető. 2017. "Anti-Gender Discourse in Hungary: A Discourse without a Movement." pp. 117–131 in *Anti-Gender Campaigns in Europe: Mobilizing against Equality*, edited by R. Kuhar and D. Paternotte. Rowman & Littlefield.

Kranish, Michael. 2021. "How Tucker Carlson Became the Voice of White Grievance." *Washington Post*, July 14. (www.washingtonpost.com/politics/tucker-carlson/2021/07/13/398fa720-dd9f-11eb-a501-0e69b5d012e5_story.html).

Kruse, Kevin M. 2015. *One Nation under God: How Corporate America Invented Christian America*. Basic Books.

Kuhar, Roman and David Paternotte. 2017. *Anti-Gender Campaigns in Europe: Mobilizing against Equality*. Rowman & Littlefield.

Kutner, Samantha, Bjørn Ihler and C. L. Murray. 2022. "Function over Appearance: Examining the Role of the Proud Boys in American Politics before and after January 6." The Khalifa Institute. (www.khalifaihler.org/store/function-over-appearance).

Latif, Mehr, Kathleen Blee, Matthew DeMichele and Pete Simi. 2018. "How Emotional Dynamics Maintain and Destroy White Supremacist Groups." *Humanity & Society* 42(4):480–501.

Latif, Mehr, Kathleen Blee, Matthew DeMichele and Pete Simi. 2023. "Do White Supremacist Women Adopt Movement Archetypes of Mother, Whore, and Fighter?" *Studies in Conflict & Terrorism* 46(4):415–432.

Lavin, Talia. 2020. *Culture Warlords: My Journey into the Dark Web of White Supremacy*. Legacy Lit.

Lawrence, David, Limor Simhony-Philpott and David Stone. 2021. "Antisemitism and Misogyny: Overlap and Interplay." Antisemitism Policy Trust. (https://antisemitism.org.uk/wp-content/uploads/2021/09/Antisemitism-and-Misogyny-Overlap-and-Interplay.pdf).

Lempinen, Edward. 2022. "Racial Resentment: The Insidious Force That Divides America." *Berkeley News*, February 3. (https://news.berkeley.edu/2022/02/03/racial-resentment-the-insidious-force-that-divides-america/).

Levin, Bess. 2021. "Senator Ron Johnson Insists It's Not Racist to Say He's Afraid of Black People." *Vanity Fair*, March 16.

Levitas, Daniel. 2002. "What Is Behind the Rare But Reoccurring Phenomenon of Jewish Anti-Semites?" Southern Poverty Law Center. (www.splcenter.org/fighting-hate/intelligence-report/2002/exploring-what-behind-rare-phenomenon-jewish-anti-semites).

Lewis, Michael and Jacqueline Serbu. 1999. "Kommemorating the Ku Klux Klan." *Sociological Quarterly* 40(1):139–158.

Liberman, Alida. 2020. "Summer of Protest." *The Philosophers' Magazine* (91):33–39.

Lichterman, Paul. 2020. *How Civic Action Works: Fighting for Housing in Los Angeles.* Princeton University Press.

Lieb, David A. 2010. "Tea Party Leaders Anxious About Extremists." April 15. (https://www.nbcnews.com/id/wbna36555655).

Lind, Dara. 2018. "Trump Just Tweeted out a Cryptic Video of People Getting Money in Spanish." *Vox*, October 18. (https://www.vox.com/2018/10/18/17996682/trump-tweet-video-spanish).

Lind, Dara, German Lopez, Lauren Williams and Amanda Taub. 2014. "An Uneasy Peace in Ferguson." *Vox*, August 21. (www.vox.com/2014/8/11/5988925/mike-brown-killing-shooting-case-ferguson-police-riots-st-louis).

Livingston, Lindsay. 2018. "Brandishing Guns: Performing Race and Belonging in the American West." *Journal of Visual Culture* 17(3):343–355.

Lizardo, Omar. 2004. "The Cognitive Origins of Bourdieu's Habitus." *Journal for the Theory of Social Behaviour* 34(4):375–401.

Lizardo, Omar, Robert Mowry, Brandon Sepulvado, Dustin S. Stoltz, Marshall A. Taylor, Justin Van Ness and Michael Wood. 2016. "What Are Dual Process Models? Implications for Cultural Analysis in Sociology." *Sociological Theory* 34(4):287–310.

Llanera, Tracy. 2023. "The Misogyny Paradox and the Alt-Right." *Hypatia* 38(1): 151–176.

López, Ian Haney. 2014. *Dog Whistle Politics: How Coded Racial Appeals Have Wrecked the Middle Class.* Oxford University Press.

Lotto, David. 2016. "The South Has Risen Again: Thoughts on the Tea Party and the Recent Rise of Right-Wing Racism." *The Journal of Psychohistory* 43(3):156–166.

Lowndes, Joseph. 2021a. "Far-Right Extremism Dominates the GOP. It Didn't Start – And Won't End – with Trump." *Washington Post*, November 8. (www.washingtonpost.com/outlook/2021/11/08/far-right-extremism-dominates-gop-it-didnt-start-wont-end-with-trump/).

Lowndes, Joseph. 2021b. "From Pat Buchanan to Donald Trump: The Nativist Turn in Right-Wing Populism." pp. 265–286 in *A Field Guide to White Supremacy*, edited by Kathleen Belew and Ramón Gutiérrez. University of California Press.

Lucks, Daniel S. 2020. *Reconsidering Reagan: Racism, Republicans, and the Road to Trump.* Beacon Press.

Lynch, Timothy. 2004. "Threats to Civil Liberties." (https://www.cato.org/sites/cato.org/files/serials/files/cato-handbook-policymakers/2005/9/hb109-19.pdf).

MacLean, Nancy. 2017. *Democracy in Chains: The Deep History of the Radical Right's Stealth Plan for America.* Penguin.

Mahler, Jonathan and Steve Eder. 2016. "'No Vacancies' for Blacks: How Donald Trump Got His Start, and Was First Accused of Bias." *New York Times*, August 27. (www.nytimes.com/2016/08/28/us/politics/donald-trump-housing-race.html).

Marantz, Andrew. 2018. "Inside the Daily Stormers Style Guide." *New Yorker*, January 15.

Martin, Douglas. 2005. "J. B. Stoner, 81, Fervent Racist and Benchmark for Extremism, Dies." *New York Times*, April 29. (www.nytimes.com/2005/04/29/us/j-b-stoner-81-fervent-racist-and-benchmark-for-extremism-dies.html).

Martin, Nick. 2021. "INTEL BRIEF: Atomwaffen Founder Gets Out of Prison." *The Informant.* (www.informant.news/p/intel-brief-atomwaffen-founder-gets).

Martin, Phillip. 2022. "A New England Neo-Nazi Group Is Attracting Members Using Republican Talking Points." NPR, June 13. (www.npr.org/2022/06/13/

1104683128/a-new-england-neo-nazi-group-is-attracting-members-using-republican-talking-point).

Maryland, University of and *Washington Post*. 2021. "Washington Post-University of Maryland Poll." (https://cdce.umd.edu/landingtopic/washington-post-umd-poll).

Mason, Carol. 2002. *Killing for Life: The Apocalyptic Narrative of Pro-Life Politics.* Cornell University Press.

Mathias, Christopher. 2022. "Living with the Far-Right Insurgency in Idaho." *Huffington Post.* (www.huffpost.com/entry/far-right-idaho_n_628277e2e4b0c84db7282bd6).

Maxwell, Angie. 2016. "How Southern Racism Found a Home in the Tea Party." Vox, July 7. (https://www.vox.com/2016/7/7/12118872/southern-racism-tea-party-trump).

Mazzei, Patricia and Alan Feuer. 2022. "How the Proud Boys Gripped the Miami-Dade Republican Party." *New York Times*, June 2. (www.nytimes.com/2022/06/02/us/miami-republicans-proud-boys.html).

McAdam, Doug. 1999. *Political Process and the Development of Black Insurgency*, 2nd edition. University of Chicago Press.

McAdam, Doug, Robert Sampson, Simon Weffer and Heather MacIndoe. 2005. "'There Will Be Fighting in the Streets': The Distorting Lens of Social Movement Theory." *Mobilization: An International Quarterly* 10(1):1–18.

McCausland, Phil. 2017. "White Nationalist Leads Torch-Bearing Protesters against Removal of Confederate Statue." NBC. (www.nbcnews.com/news/us-news/white-nationalist-leads-torch-bearing-protesters-against-removal-confederate-statue-n759266).

McClelland, Kent. 2014. "Cycles of Conflict: A Computational Modeling Alternative to Collins's Theory of Conflict Escalation." *Sociological Theory* 32(2):100–127.

McCord, Susan. 2010. "Augustans Let Off Steam at Tea Party." *The Augusta Chronicle*, April 15. (https://www.augustachronicle.com/story/news/2010/04/15/augusta-tea-party-under-way/14601356007/).

McGirr, Lisa. 2015. *Suburban Warriors: The Origins of the New American Right.* Princeton University Press.

McQuade, Barbara L. 2022. "Not a Suicide Pact: Urgent Strategic Recommendations for Reducing Domestic Terrorism in the United States (Spring)." *Texas National Security Review* 5(2):109–122.

McRae, Elizabeth Gillespie. 2018. *Mothers of Massive Resistance: White Women and the Politics of White Supremacy.* Oxford University Press.

McVeigh, Rory. 2009. *The Rise of the Ku Klux Klan: Right-Wing Movements and National Politics.* University of Minnesota Press.

McVeigh, Rory. 2014. "What's New about the Tea Party Movement?" pp. 15–34 in *Understanding the Tea Party Movement*, edited by N. Van Dyke and D. S. Meyer. Ashgate Publishing.

McVeigh, Rory and Kevin Estep. 2019. *The Politics of Losing: Trump, the Klan, and the Mainstreaming of Resentment.* Columbia University Press.

McWhirter, Cameron. 2018. "A Year after Charlottesville, the Alt-Right Movement Frays." *Washington Post.* (www.wsj.com/articles/a-year-after-charlottesville-the-alt-right-movement-frays-1533720660).

Melucci, Alberto. 2009. *Challenging Codes: Collective Action in the Information Age.* Cambridge University Press.

Michel, Casey. 2015. "Want to Meet America's Worst Racists?" *Politicio*, July 7. (www.politico.com/magazine/story/2015/07/northwest-front-americas-worst-racists-119803/).

Miller, Cassie. 2018. "The Biggest Lie in the White Supremacist Propaganda Playbook: Unraveling the Truth about 'Black-on-White Crime'." Southern Poverty Law Center. (www.splcenter.org/20180614/biggest-lie-white-supremacist-propaganda-playbook-unraveling-truth-about-%E2%80%98black-white-crime).

Miller, Cassie. 2022. "SPLC Poll Finds Substantial Support for 'Great Replacement' Theory and Other Hard-Right Ideas." Southern Poverty Law Center. (www.splcenter.org/news/2022/06/01/poll-finds-support-great-replacement-hard-right-ideas).

Miller, Cassie and Rachel Carroll Rivas. 2022. "The Year in Hate & Extremism Report 2021." Southern Poverty Law Center. (www.splcenter.org/20220309/year-hate-extremism-report-2021).

Miller-Idriss, Cynthia. 2018. *The Extreme Gone Mainstream: Commercialization and Far Right Youth Culture in Germany*. Princeton University Press.

Miller-Idriss, Cynthia. 2020. *Hate in the Homeland: The New Global Far Right*. Princeton University Press.

Mitchell, Amy, Mark Jurkowitz, J. Baxter Oliphant and Elisa Shearer. 2020. "Most Americans Who Have Heard of QAnon Conspiracy Theories Say They Are Bad for the Country and That Trump Seems to Support People Who Promote Them." Pew Research. (www.pewresearch.org/journalism/2020/09/16/most-americans-who-have-heard-of-qanon-conspiracy-theories-say-they-are-bad-for-the-country-and-that-trump-seems-to-support-people-who-promote-them/).

Mitchell, Jerry. 2011. "Evers' Assassin Said Still at Large." *Clarion Ledger*. (www.clarionledger.com/story/news/2011/01/23/evers-assassin-said-still-at-large/28936323/).

Mitchell, Jerry. 2020. *Race against Time: A Reporter Reopens the Unsolved Murder Cases of the Civil Rights Era*. Simon and Schuster.

Morlin, Bill. 2017. "'Summer of Hate' Challenged in Companion Civil Lawsuits." Southern Poverty Law Center. (www.splcenter.org/hatewatch/2017/10/19/summer-hate-challenged-companion-civil-lawsuits).

Morris, Aldon. 1984. *The Origins of the Civil Rights Movement*. Simone and Schuster.

Moser, Bob. 2002. "Leo Felton's Prison Plot, Aryan Unit One, Hits the Streets." Southern Poverty Law Center. (www.splcenter.org/fighting-hate/intelligence-report/2002/leo-felton%E2%80%99s-prison-plot-aryan-unit-one-hits-streets).

Mosse, George L. 2020. *Toward the Final Solution: A History of European Racism*. University of Wisconsin Press.

Moynihan, Daniel Patrick. 1993. "Defining Deviancy Down." *The American Scholar* 62(1):17–30.

Mudde, Cas. 2010. "The Populist Radical Right: A Pathological Normalcy." *West European Politics* 34(3):1167–1186.

Mudde, Cas. 2022. "Republicans Are Fueling Extremism Like the Buffalo Shooting." *Guardian*, May 16.

Mudde, Cas and Cristóbal Rovira Kaltwasser. 2017. *Populism: A Very Short Introduction*. Oxford University Press.

Murdock, Sebastian. 2014. "Neo-Nazi Rapist, Murderer Keith Luke Found Dead in Apparent Suicide." *Huffington Post*. (www.huffpost.com/entry/keith-luke-neo-nazi-suicide_n_5334411).

Mutz, Diana C. 2018. "Status Threat, Not Economic Hardship, Explains the 2016 Presidential Vote." *Proceedings of the National Academy of Sciences* 115(19): E4330–E4339.

Mylonas, Harris and Maya Tudor. 2021. "Nationalism: What We Know and What We Still Need to Know." *Annual Review of Political Science* 24:109–132.

Nagle, Angela. 2017. *Kill All Normies: Online Culture Wars from 4Chan and Tumblr to Trump and the Alt-Right.* Zero Books.

Nakamura David, John Hudson and Isaac Stanley-Becker. 2018. "'Dangerous and poisoned:' Critics blast Trump for Endorsing White-Nationalist Conspiracy Theory on South Africa." *Washington Post,* August 23. (https://www.washingtonpost.com/politics/dangerous-and-poisoned-critics-blast-trump-for-endorsing-white-nationalist-conspiracy-theory-on-south-africa/2018/08/23/6c3b160e-a6df-11e8-a656-943eefab5daf_story.html).

Nassauer, Anne. 2019. *Situational Breakdowns: Understanding Protest Violence and Other Surprising Outcomes.* Oxford University Press.

NBC News. 2014. "Domestic Terrorism Task Force 'More than Overdue,' Experts Say." NBC, June 11. (www.nbcnews.com/news/us-news/domestic-terrorism-task-force-more-overdue-experts-say-n128541).

Neumeister, Larry. 2023. "US Army Solider Gets 45 Years for Neo-Nazi Plot to Ambush His Own Paratrooper Unit." *Times of Israel,* March 4.

Newhouse, Alex. 2020. "Parler Is Bringing Together Mainstream Conservatives, Anti-Semites and White Supremacists as the Social Media Platform Attracts Millions of Trump Supporters." *The Conversation,* November 27. (https://theconversation.com/parler-is-bringing-together-mainstream-conservatives-anti-semites-and-white-supremacists-as-the-social-media-platform-attracts-millions-of-trump-supporters-150439).

Newhouse, Alex. 2021. "The Threat Is the Network: The Multi-Node Structure of Neo-Fascist Accelerationism." *CTC Sentinel* 14(5). (https://ctc.westpoint.edu/the-threat-is-the-network-the-multi-node-structure-of-neo-fascist-accelerationism/).

Newman, Benjamin, Jennifer L. Merolla, Sono Shah, Danielle Casarez Lemi, Loren Collingwood, and S. Karthick Ramakrishnan. 2021. "The Trump Effect: An Experimental Investigation of the Emboldening Effect of Racially Inflammatory Elite Communication." *British Journal of Political Science* 51(3):1138–1159.

Newport, Kenneth G. C. 2006. *The Branch Davidians of Waco: The History and Beliefs of an Apocalyptic Sect.* Oxford University Press.

New York Times. 1990. "2 Soldiers and 2 Civilians Arrested in Theft of Huge Weapons Cache." November 19. (www.nytimes.com/1990/11/19/us/2-soldiers-and-2-civilians-arrested-in-theft-of-huge-weapons-cache.html).

New York Young Republican Club. 2022. "History." (https://nyyrc.com/history/).

Nix, Naomi. 2022. "Facebook Bans Hate Speech But Still Makes Money from White Supremacists." *Washington Post,* August 10. (www.washingtonpost.com/technology/2022/08/10/facebook-white-supremacy-ads/).

Noble, Safiya Umoja. 2018. *Algorithms of Oppression.* New York University Press.

Noe-Bustamante, Luis, Ana Gonzalez-Barrera, Khadijah Edwards, Lauren Mora and Mark Hugo Lopez. 2021. "Measuring the Racial Identity of Latinos." Pew Research Center. (www.pewresearch.org/hispanic/2021/11/04/measuring-the-racial-identity-of-latinos/).

Olick, Jeffrey K. 1999. "Collective Memory: The Two Cultures." *Sociological Theory* 17(3):333–348.

Omi, Michael and Howard Winant. 1986. *Racial Formation in the United States: From the 1960s to the 1980s.* Routledge.

Orecchio-Egresitz, Haven. 2020. "The Proud Boys Chairman Says Members of the Extremist Organization are Running for Office — and You Might Not Know If You're Voting for One." *Insider,* September 30. (https://www.insider.com/proud-boys-chairman-says-members-run-for-office-election-2020-9).

O'Reilly, Kenneth. 1989. *Racial Matters: The FBI's Secret File on Black America, 1960–1972*. Free Press.

Otterson, Joe. 2017. "Cable News Ratings: Fox News Breaks Records, MSNBC Posts Significant Growth." *Variety*. (https://variety.com/2017/tv/news/cable-news-ratings-fox-news-msnbc-1202017940/).

Oversight and Reform Committee, U.S. House of Representatives. 2020. "Confronting Violent White Supremacy (Part IV): White Supremacy in Blue – The Infiltration of Local Police Departments." (www.congress.gov/event/116th-congress/house-event/LC65641/text?s=1&r=1).

Oversight and Reform Committee, U.S. House of Representatives. 2021. "Confronting Violent White Supremacy (Part V): Examining the Rise of Militia Extremism." (www.govinfo.gov/content/pkg/CHRG-117hhrg44688/html/CHRG-117hhrg44688.htm).

Pape, Robert. 2021. "21 Million Americans Say Biden Is 'Illegitimate' and Trump Should Be Restored by Violence, Survey Finds." (https://theconversation.com/21-million-americans-say-biden-is-illegitimate-and-trump-should-be-restored-by-violence-survey-finds-168359).

Pape, Robert. 2022. "The Jan 6 Insurrectionists Aren't Who You Think They Are." *Foreign Policy*, January 6. (foreignpolicy.com).

Pape, Robert and Chicago Project on Security and Threats. 2021. "Understanding American Domestic Extremism: Mobilization Potential and Risk Factors of a New Threat Trajectory." (https://d3qi0qp55mx5f5.cloudfront.net/cpost/i/docs/americas_insurrectionists_online_2021_04_06.pdf?mtime=1617807009).

Payne, Keith. 2019. "The Truth about Anti-White Discrimination." *Scientific American*, July 18. (www.scientificamerican.com/article/the-truth-about-anti-white-discrimination/).

PBS. 2010. "Tea Party Movement Fights Perception of Welcoming Right-Wing Fringe." July 14. (https://www.pbs.org/newshour/politics/tea-party-continues-to-fight-perception-that-it-welcomes-right-wing-fringe).

Pelley, Scott. 2021. "Whistleblower: Facebook is Misleading the Public on Progress against Hate Speech, Violence, and Misinformation." CBS News. (https://www.cbsnews.com/news/facebook-whistleblower-frances-haugen-misinformation-public-60-minutes-2021-10-03/).

Pen America. 2022. "Banned in the USA: Rising School Book Bans Threaten Free Expression and Student's First Amendment Rights." (https://pen.org/banned-in-the-usa/).

Pérez, Raúl. 2017. "Racism without Hatred? Racist Humor and the Myth of 'Colorblindness.'" *Sociological Perspectives* 60(5):956–974.

Perliger, Arie. 2012. *Challengers from the Sidelines: Understanding America's Violent Far-Right*. Combating Terrorism Center at West Point.

Perliger, Arie. 2020. *American Zealots*. Columbia University Press.

Perlstein, Rick. 2013. "The Grand Old Tea Party: Why Today's Wacko Birds Are Just Like Yesterday's Wingnuts." *The Nation*, November 6. (www.thenation.com/article/archive/grand-old-tea-party/).

Perry, Douglas. 2020. "White Supremacists on Trial for Inciting Murder Required Extraordinary Security in Portland; Case Reverberates 30 Years Later." (www.oregonlive.com/history/2020/01/white-supremacists-on-trial-for-inciting-murder-required-extraordinary-security-in-portland-case-reverberates-30-years-later.html).

Peters, Jeremy W. 2018. "How Trump-Fed Conspiracy Theories about Migrant Caravan Intersect with Deadly Hatred." *New York Times*, October 29. (www.nytimes.com/2018/10/29/us/politics/caravan-trump-shooting-elections.html).

Petrosino, Anthony, Carolyn Turpin Petrosino and John Buehler. 2004. "'Scared Straight' and Other Juvenile Awareness Programs for Preventing Juvenile Delinquency." *Campbell Systematic Reviews* 1(1):1–62.

Pew Research Center. 2013. "Big Racial Divide over Zimmerman Verdict." Pew, July 22. (www.pewresearch.org/politics/2013/07/22/big-racial-divide-over-zimmerman-verdict/).

Pilkington, Ed and Sam Levine. 2022. "US Midterm Voters Reject Election Deniers who Support Trump's False Claim." *The Guardian*. (https://www.theguardian.com/us-news/2022/nov/09/republican-election-deniers-trump-mastriano-karamo-finchem-marchant-midterms).

Pirro, Andrea L. P. 2021. "Far Right: The Significance of an Umbrella Concept." *Nations and Nationalism*. (https://doi.org/10.1111/nana.12860).

Pitcavage, Mark. 2001. "Camouflage and Conspiracy: The Militia Movement from Ruby Ridge to Y2k." *American Behavioral Scientist* 44(6):957–981.

Pitcavage, Mark. 2015. "Cerberus Unleashed: The Three Faces of the Lone Wolf Terrorist." *American Behavioral Scientist* 59(13):1655–1680.

Pizzorno, Alessandro. 1986. "Decision or Interactions? Microanalysis of Social Change." *Rassegna Italiana di Sociologia* 37:107–132.

Placido, Dani. 2023. "Anti-Woke Author Who Can't Define Woke Goes Viral." *Forbes*. (www.forbes.com/sites/danidiplacido/2023/03/16/anti-woke-author-who-cant-define-woke-goes-viral/?sh=29d505e15b3e).

Pluegers-Peters, Noah. 2022. "Do YouTube Recommendations Foster Political Radicalization?" (https://cs.ucdavis.edu/news/do-youtube-recommendations-foster-political-radicalization).

Pogue, James. 2018. *Chosen Country: A Rebellion in the West*. Henry Holt.

Polletta, Francesca. 1999. "'Free Spaces' in Collective Action." *Theory and Society* 28(1):1–38.

Posner, Sarah. 2016. "How Steve Bannon Created an Online Haven for White Nationalists." *Mother Jones*, August 22. (www.motherjones.com/politics/2016/08/stephen-bannon-donald-trump-alt-right-breitbart-news/).

Potok, Mark. 2015. "The Year in Hate and Extremism." Southern Poverty Law Center. (www.splcenter.org/fighting-hate/intelligence-report/2015/year-hate-and-extremism-0).

ProPublica and PBS Frontline. n.d. *Documenting Hate: Charlottesville*. (www.pbs.org/wgbh/frontline/film/documenting-hate-charlottesville/).

Protection, Institute for Constitutional Advocacy and. n.d. "State Fact Sheets." (www.law.georgetown.edu/icap/our-work/addressing-the-rise-of-unlawful-private-militias/state-fact-sheets/).

PRRI Staff. 2021. "Understanding QAnon's Connection to American Politics, Religion, and Media Consumption." Public Religion Research Institute. (www.prri.org/research/qanon-conspiracy-american-politics-report/).

Quinnipiac University. 2017. "Trump Is Dividing the Country, U.S. Voters Say 2-1, Quinnipiac University National Poll Finds; Most Trust Media More Than President." (https://poll.qu.edu/images/polling/us/us08232017_Usgdv94.pdf).

Quraishi, J. 2010. "More Signs of Tea Party Racism?" *Mother Jones*, September 28.

Radosh, Ronald. 2016. "Steve Bannon, Trump's Top Guy, Told Me He Was a Leninist." *Daily Beast*, April 13. (thedailybeast.com).

Rajghatta, Chidanand. 2021. "Trump Loyalists Float Anglo-Saxon Based 'America First Caucus.'" *The Times of India*, April 17. (indiatimes.com).

Ralston, Robert, Matthew Motta and Jennifer Spindel. 2022. "When OK Is Not OK: Public Concern about White Nationalism in the US Military." *Armed Forces & Society* 48(1):228–239.

Ramirez, Nikki. 2022. "Trump-Endorsed Candidate Appears to Be Paying for Followers on Extremist Platform." *Rolling Stone*, July 15. (www.rollingstone.com/politics/politics-news/doug-mastriano-paying-followers-gab-1383734/).

Rand, Kristen. 1996. "Gun Shows in America: Tupperware® Parties for Criminals." Violence Policy Center. (https://www.vpc.org/studies/tupfive.htm).

Ray, Rashawn and Joy Anyanwu. 2022. "Why Is Elon Musk's Twitter Takeover Increasing Hate Speech?" Brookings Institute. (www.brookings.edu/blog/how-we-rise/2022/11/23/why-is-elon-musks-twitter-takeover-increasing-hate-speech/).

Ray, Victor. 2019. "A Theory of Racialized Organizations." *American Sociological Review* 84(1):26–53.

Reagan, Ronald. 1981. Presidential Inauguration Speech. (www.reaganfoundation.org/ronald-reagan/reagan-quotes-speeches/inaugural-address-2/).

Reform, House Committee on Oversight and. 2020. "Confronting Violent White Supremacy (Part IV): White Supremacy in Blue – The Infiltration of Local Police Departments." (https://oversight.house.gov/legislation/hearings/confronting-violent-white-supremacy-part-iv-white-supremacy-in-blue-the).

Reid, Jonathan and Miltonette O. Craig. 2021. "Is It a Rally or a Riot? Racialized Media Framing of 2020 Protests in the United States." *Journal of Ethnicity in Criminal Justice* 19(3):1–20.

Reid, Shannon and Matthew Valasik. 2020. *Alt-Right Gangs: A Hazy Shade of White*. University of California Press.

Reitman, Janet. 2018. "U.S. Law Enforcement Failed to See the Threat of White Nationalism: Now They Don't Know What to Do about It." *New York Times Magazine*, November 3. (www.nytimes.com/2018/11/03/magazine/FBI-charlottesville-white-nationalism-far-right.html).

Reny, Tyler T. and Benjamin J. Newman. 2021. "The Opinion-Mobilizing Effect of Social Protest against Police Violence: Evidence from the 2020 George Floyd Protests." *American Political Science Review* 115(4): 1499–1507.

Reuters. 2022a. "Oath Keepers Founder Spoke of 'Bloody' War ahead of US Capitol Attack." VOA, October 7. (www.voanews.com/a/oath-keepers-founder-spoke-of-bloody-war-ahead-of-us-capitol-attack/6780819.html).

Reuters. 2022b. "Campaign of Fear: The Trump World's Assault on U.S. Election Workers." Reuters. (www.reuters.com/investigates/section/campaign-of-fear/).

Reuters. 2023. "Fact Check – No Evidence for Alleged George Soros 'Life Mission' Quote in Newsweek Interview." February 16. (www.reuters.com/article/factcheck-soros-newsweek/fact-check-no-evidence-for-alleged-george-soros-life-mission-quote-in-newsweek-interview-idUSL1N34W1P4?gclid=CjwKCAjwm4ukBhAuEi wA0zQxkzO5axU_mJ7I0Qc9i6kSLqfcjlv59BR3nbwp8ZUm8GA8tbLZ6g_Zsho Cy3sQAvD_BwE).

Reuters and Ipsos. 2021. "Trump's Coattails: It's Been Almost Three Months since Trump Left the White House, Most Republicans Still Believe His Election Loss Was the Result of a Rigged Election or Illegal Voting." (www.ipsos.com/sites/default/files/ct/news/documents/2021-04/topline_write_up_reuters_ipsos_trump_coattails_poll_-_april_02_2021.pdf).

Rhodes, Christopher. 2023. "Why 'White' Supremacists are Not Always White." *Aljazeera*, June 2. (https://www.aljazeera.com/opinions/2023/6/2/why-white-supremacists-are-not-always-white).

Rhone, Kailyn. 2021. "Social Media Companies Can't Ban Texans over Political Viewpoints under New Law." *The Texas Tribune*, September 2. (www.texastribune.org/2021/09/02/texas-social-media-censorship-legislature/).

Ribeiro, Manoel Horta, Jeremy Blackburn, Barry Bradlyn, Emiliano De Cristofaro, Gianluca Stringhini, Summer Long, Stephanie Greenberg and Savvas Zannettou. 2021. "The Evolution of the Manosphere across the Web." *Proceedings of the International AAAI Conference on Web and Social Media* 15(1):196–207.

Rimer, Sara and Sam Howe Verhovek. 1993. "Growing Up under Koresh: Cult Children Tell of Abuses." *New York Times*, May 4. (www.nytimes.com/1993/05/04/us/growing-up-under-koresh-cult-children-tell-of-abuses.html).

Roberts, Steven O. and Michael T. Rizzo. 2021. "The Psychology of American Racism." *American Psychologist* 76(3):475–487.

Robertson, Campbell, Christopher Mele and Sabrina Tavernise. 2018. "11 Killed in Synagogue Massacre; Suspect Charged with 29 Counts." *New York Times*, October 27. (www.nytimes.com/2018/10/27/us/active-shooter-pittsburgh-synagogue-shooting.html).

Roediger, David. 1991. *The Wages of Whiteness: Race and the Making of the American Working Class*. Verso.

Romero, M. 2018. "Trump's Immigration Attacks, in Brief." *Contexts* 17(1): 34–41.

Roose, Kevin. 2017. "This Was the Alt-Right's Favorite Chat App. Then Came Charlottesville." *New York Times*, August 15. (www.nytimes.com/2017/08/15/technology/discord-chat-app-alt-right.html).

Rosenbaum, Dennis. 2007. "Just Say No to D.A.R.E." *Criminology & Public Policy* 6(4):815–824.

Rosenthal, Lawrence and Christine Trost. 2012. *Steep: The Precipitous Rise of the Tea Party*. University of California Press.

Ruffin II, Herbert G. 2015. "Black Lives Matter: The Growth of a New Social Justice Movement." Black Past. (www.blackpast.org/african-american-history/black-lives-matter-growth-new-social-justice-movement/).

Ryan, MacKenzie. 2022a. "A White Nationalist Pyramid Scheme: How Patriot Front Recruits Young Members." *The Guardian*, September 2.

Ryan, MacKenzie. 2022b. "'We Must Defeat Them': New Evidence Details Oath Keepers's 'Civil War' Timeline." *The Guardian*, October 9.

Sanchez, James Chase. 2018. "Trump, the KKK, and the Versatility of White Supremacy Rhetoric." *Journal of Contemporary Rhetoric* 8(1–2):44–56.

Saric, Ivana. 2022. "The Times Trump has Advocated for Violence." *Axios*, May 2. (https://www.axios.com/2022/05/02/trump-call-violence-presidency).

Sarteschi, Christine. 2021. "Sovereign Citizens: More Than Paper Terrorists." Just Security. (www.justsecurity.org/77328/sovereign-citizens-more-than-paper-terrorists/).

Schaffner, Brian F. 2018. "Follow the Racist?: The Consequence of Trump's Expressions of Prejudice for Mass Rhetoric." Ashford. (www.ashford.zone/images/2018/09/followtheracist_v2.pdf).

Scheuerman, William. 2021. "Politically Motivated Property Damage." *The Harvard Review of Philosophy* (28):1–58.

Schiano, Chris. 2017a. "Data Release: Discord Chats Planned Armed Neo-Nazi Militia Operations in Charlottesville." (https://unicornriot.ninja/2017/data-release-discord-chats-planned-armed-neo-nazi-militia-operations-charlottesville/).

Schiano, Chris. 2017b. "Data Release: 'Unite the Right' Planning Chats Demonstrate Violent Intent." (https://unicornriot.ninja/2017/data-release-unite-right-planning-chats-demonstrate-violent-intent/).

Schroer, Todd J. 2001. "Issue and Identity Framing Within the White Racialist Movement: Internet Dynamics." *The Politics of Social Inequality, Research in Political Sociology* 9:207–231.

Schuster, Henry and Charles Stone. 2005. *Hunting Eric Rudolph: An Insider's Account of the Five-Year Search for the Olympic Bombing Suspect.* Berkley Books.

Seegmiller, Beau. 2007. "Radicalized Margins: Eric Rudolph and Religious Violence." *Terrorism and Political Violence* 19(4):511–528.

Setter, Davyd. 2021. "Changes in Support for U.S. Black Movements 1966–2016: From Civil Rights to Black Lives Matter." *Mobilization: An International Quarterly* 26(4):475–488.

Setter, Davyd and Sharon Erickson Nepstad. 2023. "How Social Movements Influence Public Opinion on Political Violence: Attitude Shifts in the Wake of the George Floyd Protests." *Mobilization: An International Journal* 28(1):429–444.

Sewell, William H. 1996. "Historical Events as Transformations of Structures: Inventing Revolution at the Bastille." *Theory and Society* 25(6):841–881.

Shapira, Harel. 2013. *Waiting for Jose: The Minutemen's Pursuit of America.* Princeton University Press.

Shapira, Harel and Samantha J. Simon. 2018. "Learning to Need a Gun." *Qualitative Sociology* 41(March):1–20.

Shapira, Ian. 2019. "The Parking Garage Beating Lasted 10 Seconds: Deandre Harris Still Lives With the Damage." *Washington Post*, September 16. (www.washingtonpost.com/local/the-parking-garage-beating-lasted-10-seconds-deandre-harris-still-lives-with-the-damage/2019/09/16/ca6daa48-cfbf-11e9-87fa-8501a456c003_story.html).

Sharpe, Mike. 2010. "Tea Party Politics." *Challenge (White Plains)* 53(3):128–131.

Sheffield, Matthew. 2017. "'This Is Just the Beginning': Alt-Right Rejoices as Violent Protests Rock Berkeley." *Salon.* (www.salon.com/2017/04/17/this-is-just-the-beginning-alt-right-rejoices-as-violent-protests-rock-berkeley/).

Signer, Michael. 2020. *Cry Havoc: Charlottesville and American Democracy under Siege.* Hachette.

Silva, Eric O. 2019. "Accounting for Trump: The Neutralization of Claims of Racism in the Early Stages of the 2016 Presidential Campaign." pp. 197–216 in *The Interaction Order*, edited by Norman Denzin. Emerald Publishing.

Simi, Pete. 2010. "Why Study White Supremacist Terror?: A Research Note." *Deviant Behavior* 31(3):251–273.

Simi, Pete, Kathleen Blee, Matthew DeMichele and Steven Windisch. 2017. "Addicted to Hate: Identity Residual Among Former White Supremacists." *American Sociological Review* 82(6):1167–1187.

Simi, Pete and Bryan F. Bubolz. 2017. "Far Right Terrorism in the United States." pp. 297–309 in *The Handbook of the Criminology of Terrorism.* Wiley.

Simi, Pete, Bryan F. Bubolz and Ann Hardman. 2013. "Military Experience, Identity Discrepancies, and Far Right Terrorism: An Exploratory Analysis." *Studies in Conflict & Terrorism* 36(8):654–671.

Simi, Pete and Robert Futrell. 2006. "Cyberculture and the Endurance of White Power Activism." *The Journal of Political and Military Sociology* 34(1):115–142.

Simi, Pete and Robert Futrell. 2009. "Negotiating White Power Activist Stigma." *Social Problems* 56(1):89–110.

Simi, Pete and Robert Futrell. 2015. *American Swastika: Inside the White Power Movement's Hidden Spaces of Hate*, 2nd edition. Rowman & Littlefield.

Simi, Pete and Robert Futrell. 2020. "Active Abeyance, Political Opportunity, and the 'New' White Supremacy." pp. 112–139 in *Racialized Protest and the State: Resistance and Repression in a Divided America*, edited by Hank Johnston and Pam Oliver. Routledge.

Simi, Pete, Robert Futrell and Bryan F. Bubolz. 2016. "Parenting as Activism: Identity Alignment and Activist Persistence in the White Power Movement." *The Sociological Quarterly* 57(3):491–519.

Simi, Pete and Seamus Hughes. 2023. "Understanding Threats to Public Officials." National Counterterrorism Innovation, Technology, and Education Center. (www.unomaha.edu/ncite/research/index.php).

Simi, Pete, Karyn Sporer and Bryan F. Bubolz. 2016. "Narratives of Childhood Adversity and Adolescent Misconduct as Precursors to Violent Extremism: A Life-Course Criminological Approach." *Journal of Research in Crime and Delinquency* 53(4):536–563.

Simi, Peter, Steven Windisch, Daniel Harris and Gina Ligon. 2019. "Anger From Within: The Role of Emotions in Disengagement From Violent Extremism." *Journal of Qualitative Criminal Justice & Criminology* 6:3–28.

Simko, Christina, David Cunningham and Nicole Fox. 2022. "Contesting Commemorative Landscapes: Confederate Monuments and Trajectories of Change." *Social Problems* 69(3):591–611.

Simonelli, Frederick. 1999. *American Fuehrer: George Lincoln Rockwell and the American Nazi Party*. University of Illinois Press.

Sines v. Kessler plaintiff exhibit 0219A. (www.integrityfirstforamerica.org/exhibits?q=fields+enemy&v=1).

Sines v. Kessler plaintiff exhibit 0502. (www.integrityfirstforamerica.org/exhibits?q=%22race-specific+bioweapons%22&v=0).

Sines v Kessler plaintiff exhibit 1060. "Chesney Post." (www.integrityfirstforamerica.org/exhibits?q=chesny+ax&v=0).

Sines v. Kessler plaintiff exhibit 1399. "Kessler-Spencer Text Exchange." (www.integrityfirstforamerica.org/exhibits?q=Battle&v=32).

Sines v. Kessler plaintiff exhibit 1448. (www.integrityfirstforamerica.org/exhibits?q=payback&v=0).

Sines v. Kessler plaintiff exhibit 1554. (www.integrityfirstforamerica.org/exhibits?q=sublime+civilization&v=0).

Sines v. Kessler plaintiff exhibit 1827. (https://files.integrityfirstforamerica.org/14228/1641845854-samantha-froelich-deposition-as-played-at-trial.pdf).

Sines v. Kessler plaintiff exhibit 1827. (www.integrityfirstforamerica.org/exhibits?q="join+us+in+Charlottesville).

Sines v. Kessler plaintiff exhibit 1827. (www.integrityfirstforamerica.org/exhibits?q=symbol+of+resistance&v=0).

Sines v. Kessler plaintiff exhibit 2082. (www.integrityfirstforamerica.org/exhibits?q=incredible+moment&v=0).

Sines v. Kessler plaintiff exhibit 2101. (www.integrityfirstforamerica.org/exhibits?q=dark&v=0).

Sines v. Kessler plaintiff exhibit 348. (www.integrityfirstforamerica.org/exhibits?q=0348&v=0).

Sines v Kessler plaintiff exhibit 8652. "Post on the Discord platform by MadDimension (Jason Kessler)." (www.integrityfirstforamerica.org/exhibits?q=%22fight+this+shit%22&v=0.)

Sines v. Kessler plaintiff exhibit. SCnazi post, July 24, 2017. (https://discordleaks.unicornriot.ninja/discord/view/249562?q=%22Hate+van%2#msg).

Sinnar, Shirin. 2022. "Hate Crimes, Terrorism, and the Framing of White Supremacist Violence." *California Law Review* 110(2). (https://californialawreview.org/print/hate-crimes-terrorism-and-the-framing-of-white-supremacist-violence/).

Skocpol, Theda and Vanessa Williamson. 2016. *The Tea Party and the Remaking of Republican Conservativism*. Oxford University Press.

Smith, Barbara. 2020. "The Problem Is White Supremacy." *Boston Globe*, June 30. (www.bostonglobe.com/2020/06/29/opinion/problem-is-white-supremacy/).

Smith, Erica. 2021. "Hate Crime Recorded by Law Enforcement, 2010–2019." Bureau of Justice Statistics. (https://bjs.ojp.gov/sites/g/files/xyckuh236/files/media/document/hcrle1019.pdf).

Smith, Gregory A. 2021. "About Three-in-Ten U.S. Adults Are Now Religiously Unaffiliated." Pew. (www.pewresearch.org/religion/2021/12/14/about-three-in-ten-u-s-adults-are-now-religiously-unaffiliated/).

Smith, R. Jeffrey. 2011. "Homeland Security Department Curtails Home-Grown Terror Analysis." *Washington Post*. (www.washingtonpost.com/politics/homeland-security-department-curtails-home-grown-terror-analysis/2011/06/02/AGQEaDLH_story.html).

Smolla, Rodney A. 2020. *Confessions of a Free Speech Lawyer: Charlottesville and the Politics of Hate*. Cornell University Press.

Snow, David A., Peter B. Owens and Anna E. Tan. 2014. "Libraries, Social Movements, and Cultural Change: Toward an Alternative Conceptualization of Culture." *Social Currents* 1(1):35–43.

Snow, Shawn. 2018. "EOD Marine Separated for Ties to White Supremacist Groups." *Marine Corps Times*. (www.marinecorpstimes.com/news/your-marine-corps/2018/04/19/eod-marine-separated-for-ties-to-white-supremacist-groups/).

So, Linda and Jason Szep. 2021. "Two Election Workers Break Silence after Enduring Trump Backers' Threats." Reuters. (www.reuters.com/world/us/exclusive-two-election-workers-break-silence-after-enduring-trump-backers-2021-12-10/).

Solender, Andrew. 2022. "Capitol Police Data Indicates Threats to Lawmakers Have Surged Since 2017." *Axios*. (www.axios.com/2022/06/22/capitol-police-threats-congress).

Soufan Center. 2020. "The Atomwaffen Division: The Evolution of the White Supremacy Threat." Soufan Center. (https://thesoufancenter.org/research/the-atomwaffen-division-the-evolution-of-the-white-supremacy-threat/).

Southern Poverty Law Center. 2002. "White Power Bands." (www.tolerance.org/news/article_hate.jsp?id=403).

Southern Poverty Law Center. 2008. "FBI Reports on Extremists in Military." (www.splcenter.org/fighting-hate/intelligence-report/2008/fbi-reports-extremists-military).

Southern Poverty Law Center. 2012. "As Election Season Heats Up, Extremist Groups At Record Levels." (www.splcenter.org/news/2012/03/08/southern-poverty-law-center-report-election-season-heats-extremist-groups-record-levels).

Southern Poverty Law Center. 2014a. "Active Patriot Groups in the United States in 2013." Intelligence Report. (www.splcenter.org/fighting-hate/intelligence-report/2014/active-patriot-groups-united-states-2013).

Southern Poverty Law Center. 2014b. "SPLC Report: Bundy Ranch Standoff Was Highly Coordinated, Reflecting Threat of Larger Far-Right Militia Movement." (www.Splcenter.Org/News/2014/07/10/Splc-Report-Bundy-Ranch-Standoff-Was-Highly-Coordinated-Reflecting-Threat-Larger-Far-Right).

Southern Poverty Law Center. 2014c. "War in the West: The Bundy Ranch Standoff and the American Radical Right." (www.splcenter.org/20140709/war-west-bundy-ranch-standoff-and-american-radical-right).

Southern Poverty Law Center. 2017. "White Nationalists Work to Make Inroads at U.S. Colleges." (www.splcenter.org/fighting-hate/intelligence-report/2017/white-nationalists-work-make-inroads-us-colleges).

Southern Poverty Law Center. 2019. "Whose Heritage?: Public Symbols of the Confederacy." (www.splcenter.org/20190201/whose-heritage-public-symbols-confederacy).

Southern Poverty Law Center. 2021. "Oklahoma City Bombing: 26 Years Later, the Same Extremist Threats Prevail." (www.splcenter.org/news/2021/04/22/oklahoma-city-bombing-26-years-later-same-extremist-threats-prevail).

Southern Poverty Law Center. n.d. a. "Alex Jones." (www.splcenter.org/fighting-hate/extremist-files/individual/alex-jones).

Southern Poverty Law Center. n.d. b. "Andrew Anglin." (www.splcenter.org/fighting-hate/extremist-files/individual/andrew-anglin).

Southern Poverty Law Center. n.d. c. "Atomwaffen Division." (https://www.splcenter.org/fighting-hate/extremist-files/group/atomwaffen-division).

Southern Poverty Law Center. n.d. d. "Christopher Cantwell." (www.splcenter.org/fighting-hate/extremist-files/individual/christopher-cantwell).

Southern Poverty Law Center. n.d. e. "David Lane." (www.splcenter.org/fighting-hate/extremist-files/individual/david-lane).

Southern Poverty Law Center. n.d. f. "Donald V. United Klans of America." (www.splcenter.org/seeking-justice/case-docket/donald-v-united-klans-america).

Southern Poverty Law Center. n.d. g. "Frazier Glenn Miller." (www.splcenter.org/fighting-hate/extremist-files/individual/frazier-glenn-miller).

Southern Poverty Law Center. n.d. h. "Identity Evropa/American Identity Movement." (www.splcenter.org/fighting-hate/extremist-files/group/identity-evropaamerican-identity-movement).

Southern Poverty Law Center. n.d. i. "Michael 'Enoch' Peinovich." (www.splcenter.org/fighting-hate/extremist-files/individual/michael-eno(ch-peinovich).

Southern Poverty Hall Center, n.d. j. "Michael Hill." (www.splcenter.org/fighting-hate/extremist-files/individual/michael-hill).

Southern Poverty Law Center. n.d. k. "Michael Tubbs." (www.splcenter.org/fighting-hate/extremist-files/individual/michael-ralph-tubbs).

Southern Poverty Law Center. n.d. l. "National Alliance." (www.splcenter.org/fighting-hate/extremist-files/group/national-alliance).

Southern Poverty Law Center. n.d. m. "Oath Keepers." (www.splcenter.org/fighting-hate/extremist-files/group/oath-keepers).

Southern Poverty Law Center. n.d. n. "Occidental Quarterly." (www.splcenter.org/fighting-hate/extremist-files/group/occidental-quarterly).

Southern Poverty Law Center. n.d. o. "Patriot Front." (www.splcenter.org/fighting-hate/extremist-files/group/patriot-front).

Southern Poverty Law Center. n.d. p. "Person V. Carolina Knights of the Ku Klux Klan." (www.splcenter.org/seeking-justice/case-docket/person-v-carolina-knights-ku-klux-klan).

Southern Poverty Law Center. n.d. q. "Richard 'Bertrand' Spencer." (www.splcenter.org/fighting-hate/extremist-files/individual/richard-bertrand-spencer-0?gclid=CjwKCAjwkYGVBhArEiwA4sZLuCnOUq0CquNCHwX_e6azJHwRh2Jg Yp73n0YsxPkBGDLwcWp6rkl8BRoCh44QAvD_BwE).

Southern Poverty Law Center. n.d. r. "Sovereign Citizens Movement." (www.splcenter.org/fighting-hate/extremist-files/ideology/sovereign-citizens-movement).

Spellman, Jim. 2009. "Tea Party Movement has Anger, No Dominant Leaders." CNN, September 12. (https://www.cnn.com/2009/POLITICS/09/12/tea.party.express/index.html).

Spencer, Hawes. 2018. *Summer of Hate: Charlottesville, USA*. University of Virginia Press.

Spillar, Kathy. 2022. "The Anti-Abortion Movement Has a Long History of Terrorism: A Roe Repeal Will Make It Worse." *Ms. Magazine*, May 6.

Sports Business Daily. 2016. "Number of Fox News Viewers in Primetime in the United States From 2014 to 2016, by Month." (www.statista.com/statistics/648087/fox-news-primetime-viewership-usa/).

Squire, Megan. 2018. "Social Network Analysis of the 2017 'Summer of Hate." (https://ocean.sagepub.com/blog/2018/8/6/social-network-analysis-of-the-2017-summer-of-hate).

Squire, Megan. 2019. "Which Way to the Wheat Field? Women of the Radical Right on Facebook." Proceedings of the 52nd Hawaii International Conference on System Sciences. (https://scholarspace.manoa.hawaii.edu/server/api/core/bitstreams/5f22ffcf-177f-4aeb-9dc5-fca7cb799dfe/content).

Squire, Megan. 2020. "Alt-Tech & the Radical Right, Part 3: Why Do Hate Groups and Terrorists Love Telegram?" (www.radicalrightanalysis.com/2020/02/23/alt-tech-the-radical-right-part-3-why-do-hate-groups-and-terrorists-love-telegram/).

Squire, Megan and Hannah Gais. 2021. "Inside the Far-Right Podcast Ecosystem, Part 3: The Rise and Fall of 'the Daily Shoah'." Southern Poverty Law Center. (www.splcenter.org/hatewatch/2021/09/29/inside-far-right-podcast-ecosystem-part-3-rise-and-fall-daily-shoah/).

Staff, Politico. 2017. "Full Text: Trump's Comments on White Supremacists, 'Alt-Left' in Charlottesville." *Político*. (www.politico.com/story/2017/08/15/full-text-trump-comments-white-supremacists-alt-left-transcript-241662).

Statista. 2016. "Number of Fox News Viewers in Primetime in the United States from 2014 to 2016, by Month." (www.statista.com/statistics/648087/fox-news-primetime-viewership-usa/).

Stern, Alexandra Minna. 2019. *Proud Boys and the White Ethnostate: How the Alt-Right Is Warping the American Imagination*. Beacon Press.

Stern, Kenneth S. 1997. *A Force Upon the Plain: The American Militia Movement and the Politics of Hate*. University of Oklahoma Press.

Swidler, Ann. 1986. "Culture in Action: Symbols and Strategies." *American Sociological Review* 41(2):273–286.

Tadayon, Ali. 2022. "Anti-Mask Protesters Gather Outside Principal's Home in Sacramento Area." *EdSource*, January 25. (https://edsource.org/updates/anti-mask-protesters-gather-outside-principals-home-in-sacramento-area).

Taddonio, Patrice. 2020. "'A Serial Liar:" How Sarah Palin Ushered in the "Post-Truth" Political Era in Which Trump Has Thrived." *Frontline*, January 10. (https://www.pbs.org/wgbh/frontline/article/a-serial-liar-how-sarah-palin-ushered-in-the-post-truth-political-era-in-which-trump-has-thrived/).

Takaki, Ronald. 1998. *Strangers from a Different Shore: A History of Asian Americans (Rev. ed.)*. Little, Brown and Company.

Taleb, Nassim Nicholas. 2010. *The Black Swan: The Impact of the Highly Improbable.* New York. Random House.

Tarrow, Sidney. 2021. *Movements and Parties: Critical Connections in American Political Development.* Cambridge University Press.

Tavenner, Emily. 2022. "5 Questions about CPAC in Hungary and Far-Right Extremism." (www.american.edu/sis/news/20220520-5-questions-about-cpac-in-hungary-and-far-right-extremism.cfm).

Taylor, Malaena and Mary Bernstein. 2019. "Denial, Deflection, and Distraction: Neutralizing Charges of Racism by the Tea Party Movement." *Mobilization: An International Quarterly* 24(2):137–156.

Taylor, Verta. 1989. "Social Movement Continuity." *American Sociological Review* 54(October):761–775.

Taylor, Verta and Alison Crossley. 2013. "Abeyance." in *The Wiley-Blackwell Encyclopedia of Social and Political Movements*, edited by David. A. Snow, Donatella. della Porta, Bert Klandermans and Doug McAdam. Wiley-Blackwell.

Taylor, Verta, Katrina Kimport, Nella Van Dyke and Ellen Ann Anderson. 2009. "Culture and Mobilization: Tactical Repertoires, Same-Sex Weddings, and the Impact on Gay Activism." *American Sociological Review* 74(6):865–890.

Taylor, Verta and Leila Rupp. 1987. *Survival in the Doldrums: The American Women's Rights Movement, 1945 to the 1960s.* Oxford University Press.

Terry, Don. 2014. "Murder's Price." Southern Poverty Law Center. (www.splcenter.org/fighting-hate/intelligence-report/2014/murders-price).

Tesler, Michael. 2016. *Post-Racial or Most-Racial: Race and Politics in the Obama Era.* Chicago University Press.

Thiel, David and Miles McCain. 2022. "Gabufacturing Dissent: An In-Depth Analysis of Gab." Stanford Digital Repository. (https://purl.stanford.edu/ns280ry2029).

Thomas, Emma F. and Danny Osborne. 2022. "Protesting for Stability or Change? Definitional and Conceptual Issues in the Study of Reactionary, Conservative, and Progressive Collective Actions." *European Journal of Psychology* 52(7):1–9.

Thompson, Jared. 2021. "Examining Extremism: The Boogaloo Movement." Center for Strategic and International Studies. (www.csis.org/blogs/examining-extremism/examining-extremism-boogaloo-movement).

Törnberg, Anton and Petter Törnberg. 2021. "'Wake-Up Call for the White Race': How Stormfront Framed the Elections of Obama and Trump." *Mobilization: An International Quarterly* 26(3):285–302.

Tope, Daniel, Justin T. Pickett and Ted Chiricos. 2015. "Anti-Minority Attitudes and Tea Party Movement Membership." *Social Science Research* 51:322–337.

Trelease, Allen W. 1971. *White Terror: The Ku Klux Klan Conspiracy and Southern Reconstruction.* Harper & Row.

Ture, Kwame, Stokely Carmichael and Charles V. Hamilton. 1967. *Black Power: The Politics of Liberation in America.* Vintage.

US Department of Justice. 2022a. "Recent Cases on Violence against Reproductive Healthcare Providers." (www.justice.gov/crt/recent-cases-violence-against-reproductive-health-care-providers).

US Department of Justice. 2022b. "U.S. Army Soldier Pleads Guilty to Attempting to Murder Fellow Service Members in Deadly Ambush." (www.justice.gov/usao-sdny/pr/us-army-soldier-pleads-guilty-attempting-murder-fellow-service-members-deadly-ambush).

US Department of Justice. 2023. "Maryland Woman and Florida Man Charged Federally for Conspiring to Destroy Energy Facilities." (www.justice.gov/opa/pr/maryland-woman-and-florida-man-charged-federally-conspiring-destroy-energy-facilities).

US House of Representatives. 1996. "Investigation into the Activities of Federal Law Enforcement Agencies Toward the Branch Davidians." House Report 104-749. (www.govinfo.gov/content/pkg/CRPT-104hrpt749/html/CRPT-104hrpt749.htm).

University of Chicago. 2022a. "National Online Survey." (https://uchicagopolitics.opalstacked.com/uploads/homepage/IOP-Poll-Topline.pdf).

University of Chicago. 2022b. "Our Precarious Democracy." (https://uchicagopolitics.opalstacked.com/uploads/homepage/Polarization-Poll.pdf).

Vaisey, Stephen. 2009. "Motivation and Justification: A Dual-Process Model of Culture in Action." *American Journal of Sociology* 114(6):1675–1715.

Valentino, Lauren and D. Adam Nicholson. 2021. "Message Received?: The Roles of Emotion, Race, and Politics in Social Movement Perceptions and Support." *Mobilization* 26(1):41–64.

Van Dijk, Teun A. 1992. "Discourse and the Denial of Racism." *Discourse & Society* 3(1):87–118.

Van Dyke, Nella and David Meyer (eds.). 2014. *Understanding the Tea Party Movement*. Routledge.

Vest, Jason. 1995. "The Spooky World of Linda Thompson." *Washington Post*, May 11. (www.washingtonpost.com/archive/lifestyle/1995/05/11/the-spooky-world-of-linda-thompson/d09e85b3-a789-47b0-bb66-fb21d95bc712/).

Via, Wendy and Heidi Beirich. 2020. "A New Transnational Agenda to Combat Rising White Supremacist Violence and Terrorism." Global Project against Hate and Extremism, November 12. (https://globalextremism.org/post/transnationalagenda/).

Via, Wendy and Heidi Beirich. 2022. "The Road to January 6 and How Metastasizing Far-Right Extremism Leaves Democracy in Peril." Global Project against Hate and Extremism, June 1. (https://globalextremism.org/post/the-road-to-january-6-and-how-metastasizing-far-right-extremism-leaves-democracy-in-peril/).

Via, Wendy and Heidi Beirich. 2023. "Neo-Nazis Spreading Hate to Millions Through TikTok Hashtags." Global Project against Hate and Extremism, April 21. (https://globalextremism.org/post/neo-nazis-tiktok-hashtags/).

Villasenor, John. 2021. "Texas' New Social Media Law Is Blocked for Now, But That's Not the End of the Story." Brookings, December 14. (www.brookings.edu/blog/techtank/2021/12/14/texas-new-social-media-law-is-blocked-for-now-but-thats-not-the-end-of-the-story/).

Villiers, P.G. 2018. "The Spirituality of Apocalyptic and Millenarian Groups: The Case of the Branch Davidians in Waco." *Hts Teologiese Studies-theological Studies* 74 (www.scielo.org.za/scielo.php?script=sci_arttext&pid=S0259-942220 18000300065).

Vysotsky, Stanislav and Eric Madfis. 2014. "Uniting the Right: Anti-Immigration, Organizing, and the Legitimation of Extreme Racist Organizations." *Journal of Hate Studies* 12:129–151.

Vysotsky, Stanislav and Adrienne L. McCarthy. 2017. "Normalizing Cyberracism: A Neutralization Theory Analysis." *Journal of Crime and Justice* 40(4):446–461.

Walker, Mason and Naomi Forman-Katz. 2021. "Cable News Fact Sheet." Pew. (www.pewresearch.org/journalism/fact-sheet/cable-news/).

Wallace, Hunter. 2017a. "The Alt-Right Defends Southern Heritage in Charlottesville." *The Occidental Dissent*, May 14. (http://occidentaldissent.com/2017/05/14/the-alt-right-defends-southern-heritage-in-charlottesville/).

Wallace, Hunter. 2017b. "Unite the Right: Towards Alt-Right Activism." *The Occidental Dissent*, July 10. (http://occidentaldissent.com/2017/07/10/unite-the-right-towards-alt-right-activism/).

Wang, Hansi Lo. 2017. "Trump Lost More of the Asian-American Vote than the National Exit Polls Showed." National Public Radio. (www.npr.org/2017/04/18/524371847/trump-lost-more-of-the-asian-american-vote-than-the-national-exit-polls-showed).

Ward, Geoff. 2018. "Living Histories of White Supremacist Policing: Towards Transformative Justice." *Du Bois Review* 15:167–184.

Ware, Jacob. 2020. "Testament to Murder: The Violent Far-Right's Increasing Use of Terrorist Manifestos." ICCT Policy Brief. DOI: 10.97812345/2020.4.2. (www.icct.nl/publication/testament-murder-violent-far-rights-increasing-use-terrorist-manifestos).

Warren, Donald I. 1976. *The Radical Center: Middle Americans and the Politics of Alienation*. University of Notre Dame Press.

Warren, Jonathan W. and France Winddance Twine. 1997. "White Americans, the New Minority?: Non-Blacks and the Ever-Expanding Boundaries of Whiteness." *Journal of Black Studies* 28(2):200–218.

Washington Post. 2011. "Homeland Security Curtails Home-Grown Terror Analysis." June 7. (www.washingtonpost.com/politics/homeland-security-department-curtails-home-grown-terror-analysis/2011/06/02/AGQEaDLH_story.html).

Weigel, Moira. 2016. "Political Correctness: How the Right Invented a Phantom Enemy." *The Guardian*, November 30. (www.theguardian.com/us-news/2016/nov/30/political-correctness-how-the-right-invented-phantom-enemy-donald-trump).

Wendling, Mike. 2018. *Alt-Right: From 4Chan to the White House*. Pluto Press.

Westwood, Sean J., Justin Grimmer, Matthew Tyler and Clayton Nall. 2022. "Current Research Overstates American Support for Political Violence." *Proceedings of the National Academy of Sciences* 119(12):e2116870119.

"What Berkeley Means". 2017. (https://altcensored.com/watch?v=VCvZZIroDQ4).

Whitehead, Andrew and Samuel Perry. 2020. *Taking America Back for God: Christian Nationalism in the United States*. Oxford University Press.

White House. 2021. "Fact Sheet: National Strategy for Countering Domestic Terrorism." (FACT SHEET: National Strategy for Countering Domestic Terrorism | The White House).

Williams, Joanna L., Haley E. Johnson, Lauren C. Mims, Kimalee C. Dickerson, Andrea Negrete and Miray Seward. 2021. "From Apathy to Vigilance: Young Adolescents' Reactions to the Unite the Right Rally in Charlottesville." *Journal of Research on Adolescence* 31(1):218–239.

Williams, Paige. 2021. "Kyle Rittenhouse, American Vigilante." *The New Yorker*, July 5. (www.newyorker.com/magazine/2021/07/05/kyle-rittenhouse-american-vigilante).

Williams, Pete. 2020. "Missouri Man Planned to Bomb Hospital during Pandemic to Get Attention for White Supremacist Views." NBC News. (www.nbcnews.com/news/us-news/missouri-man-planned-bomb-hospital-during-pandemic-get-attention-white-n1172346).

Williamson, Vanessa, Theda Skocpol and John Coggin. 2011. "The Tea Party and the Remaking of Republican Conservatism." *Perspectives on Politics* 9(1):25–43.

Williamson, Vanessa, Kris-Stella Trump and Katherine Levine Einstein. 2018. "Black Lives Matter: Evidence That Police-Caused Deaths Predict Protest Activity." *Perspectives on Politics* 16(2):400–415.

Windisch, Steven, Pete Simi, Kathleen Blee and Matthew DeMichele. 2020. "Measuring the Extent and Nature of Adverse Childhood Experiences (ACE) Among Former White Supremacists." *Terrorism and Political Violence* 34(6):1207–1228.

Winsor, Morgan. 2018. "Steve Bannon: 'Let Them Call You Racist . . . Wear It as a Badge of Honor'." ABC, March 10. (https://abcnews.go.com/Politics/steve-bannon-call-racist-wear-badge-honor/story?id=53656814).

Wood, Lesley. 2020. (https://compass.onlinelibrary.wiley.com/doi/full/10.1111/soc4.12833).

Woodrow Cox, John. 2016. "'Let's Party Like It's 1933': Inside the Alt-Right World of Richard Spencer." *Washington Post*, November 22. (www.washingtonpost.com/local/lets-party-like-its-1933-inside-the-disturbing-alt-right-world-of-richard-spencer/2016/11/22/cf81dc74-aff7-11e6-840f-e3ebab6bcdd3_story.html).

World Health Organization. 2010. "Violence Prevention: The Evidence." (https://apps.who.int/iris/bitstream/handle/10665/77936/9789241500845_eng.pdf).

Wright, Stuart A. 2007. *Patriots, Politics, and the Oklahoma City Bombing.* Cambridge University Press.

Wu, Lin and Nhu Nguyen. 2022. "From Yellow Peril to Model Minority and Back to Yellow Peril." *AERA Open* 8:1–10.

Yancey, George. 2022. "Robin Kelley: White Indifference Is Normalizing Spectacular Acts of Violence." *Truthout*, May 5. (https://truthout.org/articles/robin-kelley-white-indifference-is-normalizing-spectacular-acts-of-violence).

Yost, Pete. 1987. "Federal Arms Indictments against Men in Klan and Successor Group." *AP News*, January 8. (https://apnews.com/article/3c03ca0295231b96607f7b1f0ce2c8a0).

Zaitchik, Alexander. 2019. "The Brawler." Southern Poverty Law Center. (www.splcenter.org/fighting-hate/intelligence-report/2018/brawler/).

Zeller, Michael C. 2021. "Patterns of Demobilization: A Qualitative Comparative Analysis (QCA) of Far-Right Demonstration Campaigns." *Mobilization* 26(3):267–284.

Zerubavel, Eviatar. 1999. *Social Mindscapes: An Invitation to Cognitive Sociology.* Harvard University Press.

Zeskind, Leonard. 2009. *Blood and Politics: The History of the White Nationalist Movement from the Margins to the Mainstream.* Farrar, Straus and Giroux.

Zuboff, Shoshana. 2021. "The Coup We Are Not Talking about." *The New York Times* (www.nytimes.com/2021/01/29/opinion/sunday/facebook-surveillance-society-technology.html).

Zweigenhaft, Richie. 2020. "Fortune 500 CEOs, 2000–2020: Still Male, Still White." *The Society Pages.* (https://thesocietypages.org/specials/fortune-500-ceos-2000-2020-still-male-still-white/).

INDEX

For Product Safety Concerns and Information please contact our EU
representative GPSR@taylorandfrancis.com Taylor & Francis Verlag GmbH,
Kaufingerstraße 24, 80331 München, Germany

Printed and bound by CPI Group (UK) Ltd, Croydon, CR0 4YY
08/06/2025
01897002-0009